GET A HORSE!

M. M. MUSSELMAN

GET A HORSE!

The Story of the Automobile in America

J. B. LIPPINCOTT COMPANY
Philadelphia   New York

COPYRIGHT, 1950, BY
M. M. MUSSELMAN

PRINTED IN
THE UNITED STATES OF AMERICA

FIRST EDITION

To my mother and father in memory of those days when a Marmon touring car was their pride and joy

CONTENTS

	FOREWORD	11
1	I REMEMBER, I REMEMBER	15
2	THE VILLAIN OF GASOLINE ALLEY	24
3	LOOK, MA, NO HORSE!	33
4	LONG AND LOW AND RACY	50
5	FIFTEEN CARS A DAY	66
6	THE MOTOR MEN AND THE GIRLS	76
7	FASTEST THING ON WHEELS	86
8	HOLD ONTO YOUR HATS!	100
9	MAN WITH A MAD ON	119
10	TURN RIGHT AT BLACKSMITH SHOP	134
11	DON'T USE A LIGHTED MATCH!	148
12	FIVE CYLINDERS AND EIGHT WHEELS	162
13	THE SUPER-SELLERS	176
14	DOUBLE OR NOTHING!	188
15	THE SPEED DEMONS	199
16	A ROAD FOR HONEST ABE	212

CONTENTS

17	MR. FORD'S PARTNERS	225
18	MILADY AT THE WHEEL	237
19	BEAUTY VS. THE BEAST	250
20	THE BOY FROM POTTAWATOMIE	260
21	FOUR WHEELS—NO BRAKES	268
22	JOHNNY-COME-LATELY	278
23	THOSE DREAM BOATS	286
	INDEX	299

ILLUSTRATIONS

Grouped in this order following page 64

George Selden in a car built to his patent drawings
A typical early horseless carriage
The first auto race in America
Pope Manufacturing Company officials in a Columbia electric
Hiram Percy Maxim at the wheel of a Mark VIII Columbia
Henry B. Joy in one of the first Packard cars
The Stanley brothers
1901 Oldsmobile
An electric rubberneck bus of 1900
A Stanley Steamer squad car
The first official New York Automobile Show
The little Mobile steam car caused something of a sensation
In 1896 automobiles were circus freaks
Brake tests on Riverside Drive
Gentlemen racers of 1900
A one-cylinder Buffalo car
An automobile outing of the New York Athletic Club, 1902
James Ward Packard in a 1902 custom model
Mark XLII Columbia, 1904
"Old Pacific" driven by Tom Fetch in 1903
"Old Pacific" crossing desert
"999," first car in America to travel over a mile a minute
"Grey Wolf," second car to achieve that speed
Entries in a five-hundred mile endurance run in 1901
1902 Peerless
Mayor Thomas Johnson of Cleveland, proud owner of a Winton
Society belle of 1903 in her Franklin
Electric carriage of about 1901-05

ILLUSTRATIONS

A Clement car, 1905
Eddie "Cannon" Bald, at the wheel of a Columbia racer, 1904
A completed test run from Detroit to Chicago and return

Grouped in this order following page 192

Mother and mule seem to have taken charge
The owner of a 1906 Reo beset by tire trouble
One-thousand mile race at Grosse Pointe, Michigan
A Pope-Toledo with Prest-O-Lite tank, 1906
Proper garb for Miss Automobilist of 1905
Best automobile advertising always included a pretty girl
Cadillac, about 1908
William Howard Taft and family in a White Steamer, 1909
First family ever to motor across the United States
Touring Europe by auto in 1905
Steering wheel and dashboard of 1909 Fiat racer
A daring lady at the wheel of a Columbia
One day's production at the Indianapolis Overland plant, 1909
Four female motorists driving a brand-new 1909 Maxwell
Publicity pose of 1911
Member of Los Angeles Horseless Carriage Club
Billy Durant's dream baby Buick
No wolf of 1916 was complete without a Stutz Bearcat
The author, with his mother and father, in a Marmon, 1909
Pretty chauffeuse at wheel of an Anhut
In 1910 New England had numerous toll roads and bridges
A Thomas Flyer and a Packard in a match race
Two Newport society matrons in a Maxwell runabout
Electric hansom cab of 1905 in Newport
Model T Ford
British Napier driven by Charles J. Glidden
In 1912 the Lincoln Highway was a red line on the map
A brave gentleman from Maine at the wheel of a Lozier
Millionaire's sleek electric cab which caused a stir in 1912
Electric cabs were a common New York sight
Petite Anna Held in the door of her milk-white limousine
Hot Rod drivers joining the National Safety Council

FOREWORD

THE COMPLETE STORY of motor cars and motoring in America would take a good many volumes to tell. This book hits only the high spots, but I hope it hits the most interesting ones.

My chapters are often rather sprawling in respect to time. They overlap and some of them cover a span of several years. To try to give the story a direct chronological line, on which I could hang each chapter in its *approximate* place, I have headed my chapters, beginning with Chapter 2, with a date, the production and registration figures for that date and also one of the year's innovations. These italicized chapter headings are merely an attempt to show the year-by-year progress of the industry both economically and esthetically, without any intention of keeping strictly to this chronological period in the chapter itself.

Also, showing an invention or innovation like the windshield under the date 1905 does not mean that it was invented or first appeared on that date. It merely means that about that time the windshield came into use.

A bibliography is likely to be a device on which a writer can blame his errors. I am not going to list the various books about automobiles that I have read nor to blame them for any errors of fact that may be in this book. No man's memory or research is infallible. I have tried to be accurate but if my errors of fact are as much as two percent this book will be at least as accurate as any book about automobiles that I have yet examined. I read every one that I have been able to find as well as a great many old magazine articles. Where these various sources disagreed I have tried to pin down the truth or at least evaluate the contradictions in order to arrive at what seemed to be reasonable and probable. Unfortunately, too many press agents and non-professional historians have exploited too many untruths, half-truths and complete myths about the industry for any one ever to be one hundred percent right or accurate in a story about the automobile business.

I wish to acknowledge the help I have had from the various public relations departments of all the automobile companies, the American Automobile Association, the Automobile Manufacturers Association, the antique automobile clubs and the personnel of the Santa Barbara Public Library, as well as a number of old-car enthusiasts.

M. M. MUSSELMAN

Santa Barbara,
California

GET A HORSE!

1

I REMEMBER, I REMEMBER

PERHAPS THE MOST wonderful and exciting period of America's past is that span of years when the automobile industry was born and grew into the fabulous, ever-expanding giant that it is today. Some of us were fortunate enough to have been contemporaries of the automobile, to have arrived here in time to witness its advancement from a noisy one-cylinder infant, to a rambunctious four-cylinder brat, to a muscular six-cylinder youth and finally to affluent eight-cylinder maturity.

But the smooth power of today, the sleek, well-fed lines, the two-tone color combinations, the automatic gearshift, fluid drive and all the other slick refinements of the automotive art are apt to seem unimportant to those of us who have known the birth pangs and the growing pains of what was once called the horseless carriage. For no matter what wondrous shapes the automobiles of the future may assume, or what atomic gadgets may be added to their present machinery, I am sure that none will ever stir the blood of future adolescents as the youth of the past was stirred by the sight of a Thomas Flyer, its white, baked-enamel finish gleaming, its red leather upholstery glowing, its brasswork polished to mirror brightness, and its engine growling under its long hood, ready to prove that it was truly the "World's Champion."

Nor will any motor car of the future ever create such covetous admiration as the Stutz "Bearcat," a sensational two-seater that looked as though it was intended only for the race track; it was a car that college boys dreamed about with the same devotion that they dreamed of Bebe Daniels and Norma Talmadge.

And there was the Hudson Super-Six, with what used to be called a "torpedo body." This car came only in bright colors, usually red; it was designed for the young country-club set and was called the "Speedster."

I also recall, just after World War I, a car at which we ex-doughboys used to cast many a yearning glance. It was the Jordan "Playboy," a significant name, and usually came in robin's-egg blue or buttercup yellow.

After that I think the next automotive desire among my rapidly maturing friends was the Chrysler with balloon tires, indicating that despite past indiscretions we had finally become conservative family men.

Anyone who lived through that period of motor car growth treasures special memories that today's kids will never experience. I recall vividly, for instance, the first time I ever rode in a horseless carriage. It was in 1904 and my father was at the tiller. The machine, which had no name, had been built in Chicago at the factory of the American Bicycle Company and was a frank imitation of a Merry Oldsmobile, at that time the most popular car in America.

The car resembled a buggy, but seated four people *dos-à-dos*. On that first ride I sat on the rear seat behind mother and father and directly above the engine. It was the most thrilling thing that had ever happened to me. As we rolled down the Midway in Jackson Park we overtook prancing horses that sometimes veered off in terror; we passed the Del Prado Hotel where broughams and hansom cabs stood waiting for fares and where an old gentleman shouted imprecations and shook his cane at us as we chugged too close to his coattails; and finally we passed a bicycle cop who gave us a severe warning to slow down to ten miles per hour.

My day was complete. We had been scorching on the boulevard! When we got back home I rounded up all my small friends and described our exciting adventure in detail.

I remember, about 1907, that according to a naive myth of that day, the Stanley Steamer Company would GIVE you a Stanley car if you would drive it for one minute with the throttle wide open. Almost every one of my youthful acquaintances believed there was absolutely no limit to the speed of a Stanley Steamer; but it was also generally conceded that no driver had the ability or courage to stay with it; for in one minute, with the throttle wide open, it was thought that the car might easily take off into the sky!

Back of this myth was the attempt of the Stanley Steamer Company, in 1907, to break its own speed record on the sands of Daytona Beach. While traveling over three miles a minute, the car hit a bump and, because of the air-pressure against its flat underbelly, literally did take off, flying through the air for a distance of almost a hundred feet and very nearly killing its driver.

The boys in my gang were torn between a desire to own a Stanley Steamer and the wish to continue living. We all hinted that we intended to try for that prize once we had reached a proper age but no one would absolutely commit himself, cross-my-heart-and-hope-to-die.

On May 29, 1911, I accompanied mother and dad to Indianapolis to see the first 500-mile speed classic. By that time father owned a Marmon touring car, one of the fastest automobiles of those days. We joined a cavalcade of Wintons, Oldsmobiles with 42-inch wheels, Royals with underslung chassis, Stevens-Duryeas, Apperson Jackrabbits, Reos, Maxwells, Hupmobiles and even lowly Fords, all heading south over Indiana's limestone roads, famous in their day as some of the best in the country.

Dressed in linen dusters and goggles we braved the dense clouds of white dust that hung over the main highways and drifted slowly across the green fields, leaving a gray coating over everything. I remember that somewhere in the vicinity of LaFayette we came upon a stalled Winton Six. We stopped, of course, to help a fellow motorist in distress. The gentleman who was in trouble had his wife and two boys along with him, so mother and Mrs. Stalled Winton got together for female talk while we kids watched our male parents huddle over the Winton's ailment.

It seemed that the copper gas line had developed a leak. The owner had shut off the gas at the tank and was preparing to repair the pinhole with a piece of friction tape. But father protested. The friction tape, he declared, would soon be leaking like a sieve. So he got down under the car, beside the owner, took a wad of chewing gum from his mouth and applied it to the gas line. Then the friction tape was wrapped around that.

The Winton owner was generous in his praise of this strategy and father assured him that he always carried a package of gum on motor trips for just such an emergency. The two men then exchanged business cards and, as a result, became lifelong friends. Not more than two years ago they met and reminisced. Father's friend claimed that he drove the Winton for another year and finally sold it with the chewing-gum patch still in place on the gas line.

I remember also, on that trip to Indianapolis, that somewhere near Lebanon we were very chagrined when a sporty crowd in a Lozier passed us on the highway and made us eat their dust.

We reached Indianapolis after dark and stayed all night at the Claypool Hotel. Early next morning we were at the race track ready for the starting flag. Ray Harroun, driving a Marmon, avenged our disgrace of the day before by winning the race from Ralph Mulford who piloted a Lozier. The Marmon's average speed was a hair-raising 74.61 miles per hour. You may be sure that on the way home nobody passed our Marmon. Father had his dander up. He knew he had the best car and nobody could make him eat dust!

I remember that in those days our filling station was a big, red, sixty-gallon tank in the backyard. This was supplied to automobile owners by the Standard Oil Company and after you had purchased a certain number of gallons from the tank wagon the big red container was yours.

One of my jobs on Saturday morning was to ready the car for any jaunt that mother and dad might be contemplating for the weekend. I would fill up a five-gallon can from the sixty-gallon tank, then carry it to the car and insert a chamois-covered funnel into the car's gas tank. The gasoline was thus filtered as it was poured. And invariably there would be a thimbleful of water and some rusty sediment caught by the chamois. But at nine cents a gallon (no tax) we never complained.

As I recall, the first filling station in our town was the Standard Oil depot on the south side. It wasn't a real filling station, just the place where the tank wagons loaded up. As an accommodation the man in charge would also fill up your car, but he liked you to have the exact change and if you had suggested that he wipe off your windshield he would have told you to go jump in the lake.

I was twelve years old when father decided that it was high time I learned to drive. He still owned the Marmon, a stolid, bulky car with a steering wheel approximately the size of a barrel hoop. When I sat in the driver's seat I had to look through the wheel to see where I was heading. This car had a right-hand drive and the brakes were so hard to apply that in order to stop the car I always had to grasp the steering column with both hands and hold on as I pushed down on the brake pedal.

There were no such things as drivers' examinations or licenses in those days. Father gave me two lessons, announced that I knew how to drive and from that day on I drove the Marmon. There was a standing joke in the neighborhood that Old Man Wheeler took the pledge the first time he saw the Marmon go down the street with me at the wheel. I was so short they claimed he couldn't see me and thought the car was running itself. Twenty years later, in New York, I was pretty incensed when I had to take a driver's test.

Late that summer the local motoring club, which father belonged to, decided to hold a reliability contest for members. The course was from Oak Park, Illinois, to Milwaukee. Probably because there was free beer to be had in the town that made Schlitz famous.

Father and his Marmon were chosen as the pathfinders and pacemakers for the affair. Father said that I could go along and be the official road marker for the competing cars that followed us. That meant that I sat in the tonneau of the Marmon and every time we made a turn I blazed the trail by throwing out handfuls of flour, taken from an open fifty-pound sack.

I remember that somewhere near Fox Lake on a narrow dirt road, we encountered a skittish horse attached to a rather elegant-looking surrey. The horse reared up on its hind legs and backed the surrey sidewise across the road. In a twinkling father swung the Marmon off the road and through a barbed-wire fence. Then, instead of slowing down, he plowed through a cornfield for a hundred feet, then finally swung back through the fence and regained the road. It's no wonder that farmers had an intense dislike of motorists in those days.

We were about halfway to Milwaukee when it started to rain. It was a moderately light rain so father didn't consider it worth stopping for. We continued on, at the same pell-mell pace, without putting up the top. By the time we reached Milwaukee we had only ten pounds of flour left in the flour sack, but there must have been twenty pounds of dough spread over the tonneau.

About 1914 or 1915 my father bought the first in a long series of Ford cars that we were to own. It was a roadster with a rumble seat. It cost, as I recall, $395 and was a sort of utility car. Mother drove it most of the time and it used to take quite a beating. For mother thought nothing of scraping a fender on the barn door or, for that matter, of smashing halfway through the rear wall.

But little accidents like that didn't bother a Ford nor even its owner, for there never was and never will be anything to compare with a Model T Ford when it came to economy. You could buy the car part-by-part for less than today's Ford. A front fender cost $2.50, a carburetor was $6, a muffler was priced at $1.25, and you could purchase a new radiator for $15!

Father used to come home at night, settle down in his easy chair and instead of inquiring what had happened during the day, he'd say, "Well, mother, what did you run into today?"

Mother didn't think he was very funny.

I remember that a year or two later was the first time I ever took a girl riding in the family car. By this time it was an air-cooled Franklin touring car with doors both fore and aft and an electric starter. I was sixteen. I drove out to the Country Club with my girl and parked in a secluded spot. It was broad daylight but no one was around so I wondered if she'd get mad if I kissed her. Pretty revolutionary idea, I figured, bussing a girl in an automobile; but I threw caution to the winds and kissed her anyway. She slapped me for it. After all, a girl had to think of her reputation. Imagine, kissing in an automobile!

The days are gone when almost every city in the land had its automobile factory, when a company could start with one hand-made car and take orders on the strength of that pilot model; and when a week never passed without two or three new companies announcing rosy production plans. Today, of the more than two thousand makes of American cars that have come and gone, some twenty are left to choose from. They all look pretty much alike; they all have about the same gadgets and the same improvements; a great many of the parts are so standard that they may be found in any filling station. They have reached such a state of perfection that the buyers' choice is apt to rest on the curve of a car's fender, or the length of its snout. More often the deciding factor is the size of the monthly instalments which he cannot afford but does.

Today one seldom questions the style of the clutch, the mechanism of the brakes, the type of engine. There is no longer a choice to be made between right and left drive, three or four cylinders, gear or friction transmission, chain or shaft drive, underslung or overhung chassis, rear or side doors, two or four cycles, self-generating acetylene or Prest-o-Lite illumination.

Cold, practical stability has come to the industry; the transition period is gone and with it the exciting, playtime, holiday spirit that used to belong to motor cars and motoring.

Today automobiles are a necessity: our entire lives are molded around various types of gasoline conveyances. They have become as utilitarian as a can opener and just about as thrilling. The damn things are no longer our toys; they are our masters. That is why it will be difficult for any future product of Detroit to excite the blasé motorists of the future as the cars of the past excited the artless *automobiliers* of the past.

This book is for those unfortunate people who have been born into an era which takes the motor car for granted. And also for anybody who may be curious as to how and why, in fifty years, the American automobile industry has advanced from the Merry Oldsmobile, with the curved dash, one cylinder, and a total weight of seven hundred pounds, to the Cadillac V-8, with a Fisher body, weighing two tons. And how, along with the automobile industry, America acquired four-lane highways, motor parkways, motels, buses, soft shoulders, trailer camps, super-markets, parking lots, stop lights, free road maps, parking meters, drive-in theaters, school buses, motorcycle cops, squad cars, the white line, no parking, safety zones, right turn, left turn, U-turn, diagonal parking, collective bargaining, C.I.O., Taft-Hartley, used-car lots, monthly payments and the jitters.

2

THE VILLAIN OF GASOLINE ALLEY

1879
Production o
Registration o

ACCORDING TO THE United States Patent Office, the gasoline road locomotive, later called the automobile, was invented by George Baldwin Selden.

If you accept the opinion of the Patent Office, you might easily assume that a statue approximately a mile high should have been erected to Mr. Selden in Detroit; and at least a dozen biographies should have been written extolling his virtues and proclaiming for posterity the multiple benefits he has brought to the world and especially to the United States.

But strangely enough it is difficult to find a single kindly word spoken of Mr. Selden in any literature dealing with the automobile.

To put it mildly he was much despised by his contemporary motorists; practically every early automobile owner in America had only hisses and jeers for Mr. Selden. This was when motor madness was first sweeping the country; the citizens were slightly daffy over all cars, from Lizzies to Pierce-Arrows, and they felt sure that every time Selden added his legal royalty to the purchase price, they were being flimflammed, cheated and robbed.

But that is a story we will go into later. For the moment, let us think of Mr. Selden as a bright, young patent attorney living in Rochester, New York. It is 1876 and he is thirty years old and has a more inventive mind than most of his not-too-numerous clients. In fact, Selden has always been more interested in mechanics than in law. In 1874 he invented and built a combustion engine that operated on a combination of nitrous gas and kerosene. But it was not a compression type of engine nor was it of much use. Since then, with time on his hands, he has been thinking about the possibilities of operating an internal combustion engine with gasoline for fuel.

Back in 1867 a German inventor named Otto had patented a four-cycle engine which operated with illuminating gas, but as yet nobody had discovered a way to combine gasoline and air to run an Otto engine. In those days gasoline was a mere by-product of the coal oil refineries in Pennsylvania. Not only was the stuff almost useless, it was also dangerous; so it was often dumped into rivers or burned. A smart young patent attorney might well dream of finding a use for this waste product. It could be a short cut to riches.

But however long and well Selden may have thought about a gasoline motor, nothing came of it, apparently, but his thinking. Then, in the important year of 1876 Selden went to the Philadelphia Centennial Exposition. There, he saw the first two-cycle gasoline motor. It was being shown by its inventor, George B. Brayton, in the mechanical arts exhibit at the Exposition.

Selden, with the analytical eye of a patent lawyer, examined the engine; he also had a talk with its inventor. Brayton enthusiastically explained the workings of his motor and why it was superior to the Otto, four-cycle, gas engine. After all, why should an engine revolve through four cycles to produce one explosion, when it could do the same job in two? Those German engineers! Always choosing the most complex way to do things.

On his way back to Rochester Selden sat in the train and pondered how he could cash in on what he had just seen. As a patent lawyer he knew that if he could find a new application for the Brayton engine it would be possible to get a combination patent.

Why not a self-propelled road vehicle? Steam engines had not proved very successful for this purpose; they were too bulky and required a heavy load of water. Nor was electric power practical, as yet, for a road wagon. But a lightweight Brayton type of engine attached to a wagon might conceivably be a very useful invention. It might even be more practical than a horse and buggy.

When Selden reached home he hired a machinist to build for him an improved three-cylinder Brayton type motor, which he designed. The three cylinders were cast in one block, but to save time and money, only one cylinder was bored and fitted with a piston. This one cylinder was finally made to run, but by this time Selden was short of cash and the engine was abandoned.

But it was a definite improvement on the engine Brayton had shown Selden. It weighed some six hundred pounds less per horsepower and turned over at the rate of 500 r.p.m. as against 250 r.p.m. for Brayton's engine. Selden decided to make this improved two-cycle engine the basis for a patent application covering a gasoline-powered "road locomotive."

Selden was not the only bright young man in the world who was thinking along the lines of a gasoline road wagon. In Germany Gottlieb Daimler had an idea that he could make an Otto gas engine run with gasoline to operate a road vehicle, but it took him several years to do it.

Others doubtless tinkered with the idea, too. But none of them accomplished anything. None of them built a gasoline-powered vehicle. Neither did Selden, for that matter, but he knew he didn't have to build anything to apply for a patent. That was where he had the jump on the others. He was a patent attorney; he knew the law. His mind at once began to evolve a way to tie up his idea in a monopoly that would eventually make him an honest buck or two.

We must give him credit; for a lawyer Selden was a damned good mechanical engineer. In 1877 he sat down and drew a sketch from which, in later years, an automobile was constructed that actually ran. Today most any lad with a mechanical bent might do that, but Selden had no precedents or examples to aid him. The only self-propelled vehicles then in existence were driven by steam.

But a steam engine could be attached directly to the wheels of a carriage. A gasoline engine, on the other hand, had to run at a high speed and could not be connected directly to the wheels of a vehicle. Its power had to be applied gradually.

To accomplish this, Selden designed a crude friction clutch and a method of changing gears. Not that he did anything very original. Neither his engine, his clutch, nor his gear-change device were new in themselves, but when they were combined and attached to the wheels of a road vehicle, the total result was a new and useful machine. The Patent Office said so and no court of law has ever denied it.

Selden, however, was not a man who liked to work with his hands. He was, for the most part, an abstract thinker in the field of mechanics. After he had conceived his combination of engine, clutch, transmission and running gear, he drew a sketch of his idea, then wrote up an application for a patent on this little monster he had pictured and sent it off to Washington.

In the world of science an Albert Einstein can write down the formula $E = MC^2$ and announce to the world that he has just come up with a new idea which he thinks might be the basis for something called an atomic bomb.

But in the industrial world an Einstein is called a "paper inventor" and it is a mild term of opprobrium. Selden was not entirely a paper inventor for he did build an engine, but he never actually created a three-dimensional automobile. All he did was have an idea and apply for a patent on it.

However, a patent as revolutionary as the one Selden applied for can be issued too soon, and often is. As a result it runs its life of seventeen years before the public is ready to accept it.

Selden applied for his patent in 1879. If it had been issued that same year it would have expired in 1896, the same year that Charles and Frank Duryea claimed the first commercial sale of a gasoline car.

Selden was nobody's fool. There were ways to delay patents from being issued in those days. He figured he had a good thing if he could stall it along for a few years. He thought of it as a sort of old age pension. It might take ten or twenty years for the world to catch up to his "paper invention," but when it did he intended to punch the cash register.

To that end he employed every device he knew to impede and hinder the issuance of his patent. It was possible to do this by various devices. An inventor could, for instance, add new and impossible claims to his original application. When these claims were disallowed by the patent examiner, the inventor was permitted two years to alter his application and add more wild claims. A smart patent lawyer could keep this up for many years and often did. As long as no patent was issued, the invention remained a secret between the inventor and the Patent Office. Thus, Selden kept his patent in the secret files of the Patent Office for some sixteen years.

Meanwhile, the world was catching up with Selden's paper invention. Not only catching up but passing it by. In America at least five automobiles had been built by different inventors. And in Europe the gasoline motor car was already a commercial reality. In 1894 the world's first automobile race was run from Paris to Rouen and the news was carried in most every newspaper in America that a horseless carriage had dashed eighty miles at the astonishing speed of ten miles per hour.

Selden now decided he had hidden his light under a bushel just about long enough. So he quit annoying the patent examiner with outlandish claims and, on November 5, 1895, the Patent Commissioner mailed him an impressive and beribboned document which granted George Baldwin Selden a patent and a monopoly on the manufacture and sale of gasoline motor vehicles for seventeen years!

At that moment the leading maker of bicycles was the Pope Manufacturing Company of Hartford, Connecticut. The bossman of that concern was Colonel Albert A. Pope, a self-made millionaire, who had built his company into the largest in the world and who always had a sharp weather eye on the horizon in search of any new way to pick up another million or two.

When the gasoline motor car hove into view Colonel Pope viewed it with a jaundiced eye; he had little faith in the contraption, for the internal combustion engine was noisy and greasy and chock-full of bugs. In politics, machinery and economics the Colonel's tenets were simple. He believed in the Republican party, the bicycle and good roads.

Incidentally, with the development of storage batteries the electric automobile had recently proved practical and the Colonel looked on it with a degree of approbation. For it, at least, was quiet, smooth running and clean.

As for gasoline motor cars, the Colonel thought they were a damned nuisance, but he could scarcely afford not to be prepared, in case the gas buggy turned out to be a winner. So he arranged to have a talk with Charles and Frank Duryea, who had built a horseless carriage in 1893. Colonel Pope suggested to them that his company might consider manufacturing the Duryea car and would pay a royalty of five dollars per car. The Duryeas are said to have countered with a demand for fifty dollars a car.

This, the Colonel felt, was highway robbery. Some years later, when the Colonel got control of the Selden patent, he changed his tune. Then he was all in favor of high royalties. But at this time he turned the Duryeas down and hired as the company's automotive engineer, Hiram Percy Maxim, who had already built a successful motor tricycle. Colonel Pope instructed his new engineer to create a line of gasoline and electric cars worthy to bear the company's name, "Columbia," which was already famous on bicycles.

Maxim worked day and night to design and build the first Columbia Motor Carriages. In 1897 he put ten gasoline machines into production. Just about that time, a young man from the company's legal department discovered that a patent on an automobile had been issued to a man named Selden.

When Colonel Pope learned about this patent he was somewhat annoyed, for by this time it was obvious that gasoline motor cars were going places. There were a lot of patents around on engines and transmissions and what-not. But here was a man with an honest-to-God patent on an automobile! A hell of a note!

The Colonel rushed young Hiram Maxim off to Rochester to see just what kind of an automobile this unknown inventor from the sticks had put together.

It turned out, of course, that all he had was his patent. But there was no doubt it was a bona fide, valid, ribbon-spangled patent. When Colonel Pope heard how good it looked to Maxim and to his lawyers he knew that Selden had a potential gold mine. So he sent for the inventor and talked to him like a Dutch Uncle. There might be years of expensive litigation over his patent if Selden tried to play a lone hand, Colonel Pope warned, but if he were to make a deal with the Colonel and a few of his influential friends, all would be beer and skittles. For he and his friends were in a position to kick the automobile industry into line; after that they could all sit back and let the royalties roll in.

Selden agreed to play ball. Then the Colonel sent for a few special pals, such as P. A. B. Widener, of Philadelphia, and Thomas Fortune Ryan, of New York, both known as electric traction magnates; William C. Whitney, prominent capitalist and former Secretary of the Navy; and Anthony M. Brady, a New York banker. These men were stockholders in a closely held corporation, the Electric Vehicle Company, which had been organized to manufacture and operate electric taxicabs in the large cities of the United States. But the company's charter permitted it to do almost anything except raise an army or sponsor free-love cults. Selden assigned his automobile patent to the Electric Vehicle Company on a royalty contract.

At this point there are conflicting statements about the maneuvers that were made by Colonel Pope and his friends as they prepared to put the bite on the automobile industry. C. R. Glasscock in *The Gasoline Age* states that "the Electric Vehicle Company, which had acquired the rights to the Selden patent, started suit against the Pope-Hartford Company which was building Columbia cars."

This is not quite accurate. The Columbia automobile was first manufactured by the Pope Manufacturing Company. Later, the Columbia was taken over by the Electric Vehicle Company. So it may be that Mr. Glasscock meant the Pope Manufacturing Company, when he said Pope-Hartford Company. Assuming that to be true, and that the rest of Glasscock's statement is correct, then Colonel Pope's Electric Vehicle Company sued Colonel Pope's Pope Manufacturing Company.

If there was such a suit it could only have been for one purpose. Doubtless Colonel Pope, the defendant, must have admitted that Colonel Pope, the plaintiff, had a cause of action and accepted a consent decree. Thus the validity of the Selden patent was recognized by Colonel Pope for the benefit of Colonel Pope.

However, federal court records neither in New York nor in Hartford show any such suit. But they do show that suit was brought by the Electric Vehicle Company against the Buffalo Gasoline Motor Company and the Automobile Fore Carriage Company. The Buffalo company accepted a consent decree. Then the Winton Motor Carriage Company was sued and also took a consent decree.

After that it was like shooting fish in a barrel. Most of the other motor car manufacturers came running to beg a license before they were sued. To keep things chummy and well policed, Colonel Pope and his friends formed the Association of Licensed Automobile Manufacturers, of which the Electric Vehicle Company was the boss. Every manufacturer was taxed a royalty of five per cent of the retail price of his cars. Part of this was to go to Selden, part was retained by the A.L.A.M. to pay for accountants, lawyers, etc., and the rest went to the Electric Vehicle Company.

Mr. Selden went back to Rochester to spend his royalties. Mr. Widener, Mr. Ryan, Mr. Whitney, Mr. Brady and Colonel Pope doubtless shook hands with each other and told themselves that they had the automobile industry tied up in a very neat package.

3

LOOK, MA, NO HORSE!

1895
Production 1
Registration 4
Two cylinders . . . water cooled

CITIZENS OF THE United States have never been noted for their modesty. We like to boast about the length of our rivers, the depth of our oil wells, the height of our office buildings, the breadth of Texas and the beauty of our women.

Any schoolboy will tell you that we also have the fastest, biggest and most motor cars in the world. And there is no doubt we have the loudest advertising agencies, which have been guilty of shouting, through every possible medium, that all things automotive originated in the vicinity of Detroit, South Bend or Toledo.

This is a myth that Americans will never allow to die, but the truth of the matter is that the first real gasoline vehicle was a motor tricycle designed by Carl Benz and powered by Gottlieb Daimler's engine. This happened, without fanfare, in Mannheim, Germany, in 1885. Selden was still drawing pictures and submitting them to the Patent Office; Henry Ford was trying to decide whether to be a farmer or a machinist; Charles and Frank Duryea, Elwood Haynes, Alexander Winton and R. E. Olds were still satisfied with flesh and blood horsepower.

Daimler took his four-cycle gasoline engine to France. There, sometime before 1890, M. Levassor of the great carriage-building firm of Panhard and Levassor built the first horseless carriage ever driven by a gasoline engine.

In later years Duryea, Haynes, Ford, Winton and Olds, through their advertising agents or publicity departments, laid fantastic claim to various kinds of unofficial, dubious and pseudo "firsts." But, excepting Selden's theoretical patent sketches of 1879, Levassor's Panhard car was the original, authentic, real-McCoy, nonpareil first.

No hotter spot than Paris could have been found to introduce this new toy for the rich. Parisian *boulevardiers* and *bon vivants* found the automobile almost as delightful a plaything as a new coryphee at the *Folies Bergère*. The machine of the future also charmed their wives; they were as excited over the horseless carriage as they might have been over a new style by Worth. Although every lady had her chauffeur—a handsome one, preferably—every man who was not a cripple or a septuagenarian learned to drive. First they motored along the boulevards of Paris, then they ventured out over the fine roads of France. Soon the younger crowd were going far afield for basket parties and all-day tours. And, no doubt, there were a good many who discovered the biological possibilities of the automobile. That may, in fact, have helped it to become the rage.

By 1895 the basic design of the Panhard car had advanced until it was not much different from today's automobile. The engine had been placed in front of the passengers and the power was transmitted beneath them to the rear wheels, while the clutch, the gearshift and the differential were all recognized parts of the car.

But in the United States people were, as yet, unprepared for anything as revolutionary as the automobile. Probably no more than a few thousand Americans were aware that in France men were driving carriages without horses attached. In the early 1890's not more than a handful of very young and imaginative men even bothered to try to learn the principles of the gasoline road locomotive, as it was called.

Among those who did were America's pioneers in the automobile industry. They must be commended for their determination and perseverance; they had little to guide them except hearsay and they solved their problems with no encouragement from the world around them. They made their crude engines from their own pencil sketches; they designed their own clutches, their own transmissions, their own change-gear devices. They were, in fact, inventors of their own automobiles, despite the activity that had preceded them in Paris.

But any speculation as to which of them first perfected and drove a horseless carriage in the United States has no more significance than what brave man first ate an oyster. They were all of an inquiring and daring disposition; they all performed their tasks without seeing the work of their fellow experimenters; they were all about equally competent. Unfortunately they did not profit equally from their labors. One died in relative poverty; most fared quite well; but one of them became the richest man in the world. And the difference between them seemed to be nothing more than a matter of luck.

Charles and Frank Duryea were a couple of farmer boys born and raised near Peoria, Illinois. They were both mechanically inclined but, in addition, Charles was bookish and erudite—the sort of fellow that schoolmates sought out to help them solve their algebra problems. When he was seventeen, with only a picture to go by, he built his own bicycle. When he graduated from high school he wrote an essay in which he prophesied that airplanes would be the transportation of the future and that Europe would be only half a day's journey from the United States.

Frank, who was six years younger than Charles, had a hard time living up to the reputation of his brilliant older brother. But even though he was not as imaginative he was more practical and in some studies he got higher grades.

When he had finished school Charles left the farm and tried a number of jobs, finally landing in Chicopee Falls, Massachusetts, with a bicycle company. Frank followed Charles to the little manufacturing town where he became a toolmaker.

In 1891 Charles found a book that described and pictured an Otto gas engine. He and Frank both studied the book, and Charles, who had read about the horseless carriages that were being manufactured in Paris, used his spare time to design his idea of a gasoline road wagon.

But Charles had no money to build a horseless carriage so he went out to find some. Always a fairly good promoter though never a successful businessman, Charles located someone with one thousand dollars who was crazy enough to want to gamble it on a buggy that would go without a horse.

Not being as capable a mechanic as his toolmaker brother, Charles hired Frank to help him build this first American automobile. Just who did what, from that point on, has been long and furiously disputed. For although Charles was inquisitive and intelligent beyond his times he was also erratic and impractical. For example, after 1896 he clung doggedly to the belief that three wheels were superior to four, and he refused to admit that his brother ever played an important part in building their first automobile. On the other hand Frank's claims to a share in the credit for the building and designing of the first car have recently been recognized by the Smithsonian Institution.

Apparently the brothers went to work on their car in 1892 at Springfield, Massachusetts. But Charles lost interest in the project and when he was offered a business opportunity back in Peoria he left the completion of the half-finished car to Frank.

In later years Frank declared that it was necessary for him to design a new engine for the machine, which was then completed and given a road test on September 22, 1893. At that time Charles Duryea was still in Peoria, and had helped very little in building the first Duryea car, except to promote the money and make the first designs.

This original model was simply a buggy with an engine hung beneath it, a clutch and a chain drive. Frank was not satisfied with its appearance, so he designed a new model, in which the engine was concealed beneath a bustle-like protrusion in the rear. The usual, flat dashboard was replaced with a rounded one, which gave the carriage much better lines than its predecessor.

Charles came back from Peoria about this time and had his first ride in a horseless carriage. Somehow he cut himself back into the deal he had once walked out on and the brothers were again partners.

Today that famous Model 2 Duryea gas buggy is in the Smithsonian Institution at Washington. The tablet displayed with the machine reads as follows:

> Duryea Automobile, 1893-1894. Built by the Duryea brothers, Charles E. and J. Frank, at Springfield, Massachusetts. It was operated on the streets there in 1893 with a friction drive and in 1894 with the present transmission.
>
> It has a one-cylinder, four-stroke, four-horsepower, water-cooled, gasoline engine with make-and-break, electric ignition. Up-and-down movement of the steering tiller shifts the gears to give two forward speeds and reverse. Weight about 750 pounds.

In 1895 Frank won the first automobile race in America driving this machine. With the two thousand dollar first prize the brothers went back to Springfield, organized the Duryea Motor Wagon Company and prepared to manufacture twelve duplicates of the prize-winning car to sell to the public.

The first of these cars was sent on tour with Barnum and Bailey Circus as an advertising stunt. The car was a feature of the daily street parade, as well as the opening grand march in the tent. Circus posters gave the machine star billing along with the elephants and the trapeze performers. Beneath the colored lithograph of the little Duryea were these words:

> The Famous Duryea Motor-Wagon, or Motocycle, the Identical Horseless Carriage that won the great race in Chicago last November.
> To Be Seen Every Day In The New Street Parade.

By April the Duryeas had completed four more cars and on Memorial Day, 1896, a Duryea, with Frank again at the tiller, won the *Cosmopolitan* magazine contest and a prize of three thousand dollars.

The reputation of the Duryea brothers was now nationwide. They placed an advertisement in *The Horseless Age,* which boasted that the Duryea Motor Carriage was "adapted for general use on all kinds of roads in all weather" and traveled over one hundred miles on five gallons of gasoline.

"Our new models," the ad went on, "are the finest specimens of carriage makers' art ever produced for motor vehicles, embodying the handsome lines of a high-grade carriage, yet having a 'complete' appearance—not a 'carriage-without-a-horse' look—and yet not a machine in appearance. Particulars upon request."

The Duryeas now sent two cars to England and Frank went along to drive in the first automobile race to be run in England—a fifty-mile event from the Hotel Metropole in London to Brighton, celebrating the repeal of the "red flag" law, which for many years had retarded motoring in England by making it unlawful to operate an automobile unless preceded by a man on horseback waving a red flag. Most of the entries in this first English racing event were German or French cars and one of them was a phaeton made by Panhard and Levassor, which had recently won the Paris to Marseilles race.

As the race started, according to the New York *Times* of November 15, 1896, "the spectators were very enthusiastic and indulged in uproarious cheers . . . the steering was admirable, and when the carriages became blocked by ordinary traffic of the streets their pace was checked instantly."

Frank Duryea won the race by almost an hour, covering the fifty miles in approximately four hours. The New York *Times* was not too impressed, however, for the event was printed on page 17.

The triumph of the Duryea car could have meant a great deal to the two brothers, for at that moment the Duryea was certainly supreme in American automobile circles. But for some reason the Duryea brothers were unable to work together; they split up that same year and the Duryea Wagon Company went out of business.

Frank went to the Stevens Arms Company, where he designed and was in charge of the manufacture of the Stevens-Duryea car. It became one of America's leading quality cars.

Charles went back to Peoria, where he established the Duryea Manufacturing Company and turned out the first of his three-wheeled motor vehicles. In 1900 he moved to Reading, Pennsylvania, and started the Duryea Power Company. Again he built a three-wheeled car, until pressure from his stockholders forced him to add a fourth wheel to his product.

When the company in Reading went bankrupt Duryea was still able to get backers. He moved to Saginaw, Michigan, incorporated the C. S. Duryea Company, and manufactured there a machine called the Duryea Electra Motor Carriage.

It was while Charles was in Saginaw that he also named one of his machines a "Buggyaut." This name has since then been juggled out of historical context and applied to the early cars that the brothers manufactured. Automotive history is full of errors and inaccuracies which will never be fully corrected. One of the most persistent of all is the name "Buggyaut" as applied to the first Duryea car. It was called a "Motor Wagon," a "Motorcycle," and a "Motocycle," but never a "Buggyaut."

The company at Saginaw was Charles Duryea's last appearance as a manufacturer. Soon he was lost in the rush of the automobile's advance. He drifted down and out of the automobile world until he was reduced to running a question-and-answer column on a trade paper and writing pamphlets protesting that it was not Haynes or Winton or Ford or Olds who deserved credit for fathering the American automobile, but he, Charles Duryea.

If Elwood Haynes had had his way his name would have led the Duryeas' in the history of the American automobile. He always contended that he was the first to design a true motor car and not merely attach an engine to a buggy. The legend on the Haynes machine in the Smithsonian Institution reads as follows:

> Haynes Automobile, 1893-94: Built by Elwood Haynes in Kokomo, Indiana. This vehicle, equipped with a one-horsepower motor, made a successful trip on July 4, 1894, at a speed of six or seven miles an hour. About two years after the trial, certain changes were embodied in the machine as it now stands. The original steering mechanism which consisted of a worm gear attached to the center of the axle, was discarded; and the original 28-inch cushion tired wheels were replaced by the present 36-inch pneumatic tired wheels.

Haynes was a rarity among the monkey-wrench engineers of the early days, for he had actually gone to college. He had graduated from Worcester Polytechnic Institute in 1881 and had then taken postgraduate work at Johns Hopkins

University. For a year after that he taught science courses at Eastern Indiana Normal School.

But Haynes was a man with a gourmet's appetite and he soon saw that schoolteachers were eating very far back on the steer, and no tenderloin even on Sunday. So the practical Mr. Haynes took a job with the gas company in his home town of Portland, Indiana, and in a few years became field superintendent for the Indiana Natural Gas and Oil Company, of Kokomo.

It is likely that Haynes visited the Columbian Exposition held at Chicago in 1893, saw the imported Benz that was on exhibit there, came back to Kokomo and drew up sketches for a car of his own. He had had a technical education and was much interested in chemistry, metallurgy and things mechanical. There is every reason to believe that as the field superintendent of a gas and oil company he might have been looking for a likely way to use up some of the gasoline that the company was plagued with and, at the same time, to get into a likely new business which was already flourishing in France and Germany.

In any case he gave his sketches and plans for an automobile to Edgar and Elmer Apperson, who owned the Riverside Machine Shop, and hired them to build the first Haynes automobile, to which they contributed several ideas of their own. This machine was given a public demonstration in 1894 down the main street of Kokomo, as part of the Fourth of July parade and celebration. To the amazement of the citizens, and possibly Haynes and the Apperson brothers, it ran without breaking down, catching fire or exploding.

A year or so later Haynes and the Apperson brothers formed the Haynes-Apperson Company and, after the Duryea Motor Wagon Company folded up, their advertisements boasted that they were "The Oldest Makers of Motor Cars in America."

With typical disregard for the truth, a fault of automobile advertising even in those days, an early Haynes-Apperson ad says: "It is the only machine that has won *every* endurance contest held in America and every contest or race ever entered."

At this time the Haynes-Apperson 12-horsepower surrey was priced at $1,800—"front head-light extra."

Sometime later Haynes and the Apperson brothers had a falling out. They formed separate companies, both of which were successful until the early twenties when so many automobile companies collapsed.

After the Duryeas were out of the picture the man that Elwood Haynes considered his most serious rival was Alexander Winton. They wrangled for many years over who manufactured the first production car, who made the first commercial sale, who had won the most prizes and who held the most records.

The two men were as different as two Americans could be. Winton had been born in Scotland, and had received only a rudimentary education; he came to this country after he was twenty years old and he never lost the Scotch burr in his speech. He landed a job in New York with a marine engine works and later went to sea as an assistant engineer on a steamship. When he married the first of four wives, in 1884, he went to Cleveland and opened a bicycle shop.

Nine years later he began experimenting with a gasoline engine, in 1895 built a motorcycle, and in 1896 put his engine into a four-wheeled vehicle. This machine was a two-cylinder job with a friction clutch and pneumatic bicycle tires.

So far Winton had spent a lot of money on experiments without any return on his investment. Being a Scotsman and a good businessman he was determined to get out of the red as soon as possible. Although it was obviously a foolhardy gamble, he formed the Winton Motor Carriage Company and jumped into production—two Winton phaetons. He is supposed to have sold one of these, but his customer was dissatisfied. Even though it wounded his Scot's soul to return the money, Winton took the car back.

This was the first and surely the last time any such thing ever occurred in the automobile industry. In those days most manufacturers never worried about the customer, once they had sold him a car. Even Winton, in a year or two, grew hard-boiled about the kicks of his customers. One of them was said to have had his car hauled through the streets by a team of horses, while a placard on the car announced: "This is the only way you can drive a Winton."

The man threatened to continue to drive the car with the aid of horses until he got his money back. So Winton retaliated by having a Winton car follow him wherever he went. The Winton hauled a farm wagon in which rode a tired old jackass. Upon the wagon was a placard which read: "This is the only animal unable to drive a Winton." Needless to say, the disgruntled Winton owner soon gave up his campaign to get his money back.

But in 1897 when his *only* customer was dissatisfied and nobody was clamoring to buy automobiles, as they soon would be, all Winton could do was take the car back. Then he was worse off than before. He had the entire output of his automobile factory on his hands and a nasty rumor going around town that the Winton car was a frost and a bust.

Winton decided on a heroic measure to kill, once and for all, any suggestion that his product was not efficient. His idea was to make a spectacular trip to advertise the qualities of his machine. So he drove a Winton car from Cleveland to New York, a distance of eight hundred miles, in approximately ten days.

At first it seemed that Winton's sensational trip was to bring him nothing but fame. However, in a few months, on the strength of his car's performance he was able to get backing to manufacture four more cars. The sale of one of these on March 24, 1898, for one thousand dollars was claimed as the first sale of a gasoline automobile manufactured on a regular production schedule. Along with the second Duryea and the first Haynes car it is enshrined at the Smithsonian.

Winton was a smart publicity-getter as well as mechanic. He went in extensively for track and road racing, reliability runs, hill-climbing contests and any other event that would keep his and his car's name before the public. He became one of the most expert race drivers in America and was proclaimed the National Track Champion.

By 1901 he was one of the leading manufacturers in the country as well as an outstanding race driver. But there was a builder of automobiles in Detroit who aspired to Winton's racing crown. His name was Henry Ford.

Ford had built a two-cylinder racing machine which he hoped would bring him fame. He was so confident of its ability that he challenged Track Champion Alexander Winton to a ten-mile contest at a fall race meeting held at the Grosse Pointe race track.

Ford's confidence in himself as a race driver was completely misplaced. The Detroit *Free Press,* of October 11, 1901, described the race as follows:

"For the first seven miles Mr. Winton led and gradually increased his lead to nearly half a mile. Mr. Ford had not had experience in driving his machine, and did not dare keep on the pole as did Mr. Winton. E. S. Huff, Ford's mechanician, hung far out in his effort to balance the car, but she swung wide at every turn, and Mr. Ford had to shut off the power. Suddenly the Winton machine began to slow down.

"Then a thin wreath of blue smoke appeared at the rear of the machine and it gradually increased to a cloud. Mr. Shanks, who was riding, poured oil on it, but it did no good, and Mr. Ford swept by them as though they were standing still. Down the stretch he came like a demon and the crowd yelled itself hoarse. In the next three miles Ford increased his lead to fully three-fourths of a mile and won amid great cheering, his time being 13:23 4/5 for ten miles. Mr. Winton made the best mile in 1:14 2/5."

The Ford news bureau used to give the spring of 1893 as the official date on which Ford drove his original motor car through the streets of Detroit. Ford, in his autobiography, written in collaboration with Samuel Crowther, claimed that in 1885, while working for the Eagle Iron Works in Detroit, he repaired an Otto four-cycle engine, the first he had ever seen. And that he then built one himself which he completed in 1887. In 1890, his autobiography relates, he began work on a two-cylinder gasoline engine and in 1892 he completed his first motor car, but this one did not run to his satisfaction "until the spring of the following year."

This latter statement was complete and utter fiction. But since neither Mr. Ford nor his press bureau were ever noted for their Diogenean accuracy, it is difficult to know which one was to blame for the juggling of dates and facts. However, it is altogether likely that the 1892-93 date for the first Ford was something cooked up by an eager press agent in an effort to ease Henry into the Hall of Fame ahead of, or at least in a dead heat with, Charles and Frank Duryea. This was in the nature of smothering a steak with pork chops, since Mr. Ford was to accomplish many more important feats than any brought off by the Duryeas.

But Ford doubtless encouraged the phony date. He loved publicity and would go to almost any lengths to get it. If he could sell the public on the idea that he had built the first automobile, that was okay with him. And then, of course, during the period from 1903 to 1909 there was a continuous war over dates in connection with the Selden patent. Ford, at that time, made exaggerated statements to the press about his early experiments, in an effort to back up his legal stand in the Selden suit.

However, there was one early historian of the automobile industry who discovered that something was wrong with the

1893 date and tried to nail down the facts. Peter Clark Macfarlane went to Detroit in 1915 to write a series of articles for *Collier's*. There he came in contact with the 1892-93 myth. However, his interviews with people in the industry who were not employed by Ford led him to skeptics who told him the real date of Henry's first Lizzie.

For by this time Charles B. King, builder of the first gasoline carriage ever seen in Detroit, had begun to fret a bit over the tireless efforts of Ford's press bureau to make Henry the great Jehovah of automobile transportation. King had designed the King and the Northern cars, and in the early days had helped Ford with his first car. So he often pointed out to friends and business associates that it was not in 1893 that the Grand Gaekwar of mass production made his first car; it was in 1896 and King knew because he was there—in person.

Whatever information or misinformation Macfarlane may have run into, he tried to straighten the facts out by saying that the machine Ford drove in 1893 was a steam car, and that Ford later followed this one up with his gasoline automobile in 1896.

The Ford steam car seems to have been some sort of a compromise. The only other person who backs up this story is Eugene W. Lewis, president of the Industrial National Bank of Detroit, who states in his *Motor Memories*: "In 1893 Henry Ford succeeded in inducing his first steam-powered contraption to propel itself. This is not generally known and is disputed by some, and it may as well be admitted Mr. Ford's first car was no howling success."

Despite Macfarlane's discovery of the press agent's exaggeration, the Ford press bureau continued to give out the fictitious 1893 date. It became such a fixture in Ford's biography, as well as in recognized encyclopedias and automotive histories, that Ford's own men began to accept it for fact. In 1932 his advertising department was preparing an exhibit for the Chicago Century of Progress at which the first Ford automobile was to be part of the display. The ad men had written a well-worded legend to go with the car giving the 1893 date.

Both the advertising and publicity departments were dumbfounded when Ford announced that they had the date wrong; it was 1896—not 1893.

The placard for the exhibit at Chicago was changed, but that seems to be the last time the publicity department has frankly admitted the 1896 date.

In 1937 C. B. Glasscock's *The Gasoline Age* insisted on the 1893 date and called Macfarlane's 1896 date a palpable error.

In 1939 William Cameron, on the Ford Sunday Evening Hour, told how Henry ran his first gasoline engine in 1893 in the kitchen of his home.

But in 1940 Arthur Pound, in *Detroit, Dynamic City,* published a letter from Mr. King, giving an eyewitness account of the scene in the Ford kitchen when that first engine was finally made to run. King gave 1895 as the true date for that historic event.

In 1944 the old 1893 myth popped up again in David L. Cohn's *Combustion on Wheels.*

However, Keith Sward in *The Legend of Henry Ford* and William C. Richards in *The Last Billionaire,* both published in 1948, finally beat the 1893 myth to earth and agreed on the spring of 1896 as the date of Czar Henry's first car. And in "The Chronicle of the Automotive Industry" published in 1949 by the Automobile Manufacturers Association, June 4, 1896, is given as the exact date on which Ford successfully operated Lizzie No. 1.

Even though Ford did not actually build a gasoline motor car that ran, until 1896, and though some people say that many of the parts of that car were given to him by Charles King, there is no doubt that in the next few years he earned a reputation as an expert engineer and soon had no trouble getting backers.

In 1899 he quit his job with the Detroit Electric Company to become manager and chief engineer of the Detroit Automobile Company, a corporation that was formed specifically to manufacture Ford's idea of a horseless carriage. But it was four years and two companies later before Ford manufactured a car for sale.

The trouble was that he seemed determined not to turn out a car until he felt that it was worthy of him. Another difficulty was that Ford was not a good production man. He always left production to others. And he was bull-headed and scornful of critics and stockholders.

After two years as chief engineer of the Detroit Automobile Company, the stockholders had lost faith in Ford and by mutual agreement he stepped out of the company.

Ford was undaunted. He formed the Henry Ford Automobile Company and built the car with which he beat Winton. But he knew that he had won that race by luck, so he decided to build the biggest, fastest racer ever constructed. By breaking speed records he would make the world sit up and notice Ford and then he would make cars for sale.

An ex-bicycle racer named Tom Cooper helped Ford construct two cars designed exclusively for speed. They named one the "999" and the other was called the "Arrow."

But when they took their mammoth racers out on the track neither man had guts enough to open them up. So Cooper sent for a daredevil bicycle racer he had known and who, he assured Ford, would do anything for money. This man's name was Barney Oldfield.

Oldfield had never driven an automobile in his life. But he circled the 999, puffing on a black cigar, and finally decided to have a go at it. After a week of lessons and thrills he was ready for his debut in an auto race. The machine was entered in a meet at the Grosse Pointe track where Ford had beaten Winton.

At the starting line for his first race Barney is said to have remarked to Ford, "This damn thing may kill me but the records will show I was going like hell when it got me."

Barney won the three-mile race by half a mile. It was the making of Ford as well as Barney Oldfield. A week later the Ford Motor Company was organized. It was June, 1903. Thomas Flyer, Pierce-Arrow, Rambler, Pope-Hartford, Columbia, Winton, White Steamer, Stanley Steamer, Packard, Apperson Jackrabbit, Locomobile, Haynes, Peerless, Franklin, Stevens-Duryea, Cadillac, Oldsmobile, Studebaker and Buick were some of the big names in the automobile business.

Already the field was crowded but, despite that fact, eleven optimistic people put up $28,000 to back Ford, who had already failed twice as a manufacturer of automobiles. They weren't smart; they were foolhardy. They should have listened to the advice of the bankers and the smart money men. They were the ones in the know and they were saying that the boat had sailed, that the market was saturated, that the automobile fad had just about run its course!

4

LONG AND LOW AND RACY

1896
Production 8
Registration 16
Chambered spark plug

THE HUMAN RACE is well named. One of its primary emotions seems to be a powerful interest in contests having to do with going from here to yonder in the shortest space of time.

The Greeks made heroes of their fastest runners; the Romans made a spectacle of the chariot race; and when the motor carriage appeared in France it was no time at all until some promoter had cooked up an auto race.

This first motor car contest, sponsored by *Le Petit Journal,* was from Paris to Rouen, a distance of about eighty miles; the winner was a Panhard-Levassor with a 3.5 horsepower Daimler motor. It covered the distance at an average speed of thirteen miles an hour, defeating various makes of steam and electric automobiles.

The 1894 race was so successful that a second was announced for 1895 with prizes totaling about sixty thousand francs. That kind of money would buy a lot of bouillabaisse and red wine in 1895, so every self-propelled machine within a radius of a thousand kilometers showed up for the party, an assortment of sixty-five go-buggies of all shapes and sizes.

Even millionaires were not averse to pocketing sixty thousand francs (about $12,000 in those halcyon days, with no income taxes) so the Comte de Dion was on hand with his self-designed steam carriage, also M. Serpollet, builder of France's most popular steamer, and holder of several speed records. Among the electric cars was the famous Jeantaud, which was later to hold the world's record for one kilometer.

The 1895 race was a severe test of endurance, since the course was from Paris to Bordeaux and return, a distance of 732 miles. The *Cosmopolitan* magazine reported:

"On June 10th the automobiles assembled at the Arc de Triomphe, in the presence of an enormous crowd. From there they went, at a moderate pace, to Versailles, where the real start was begun. A few kilometers farther on, the steam-automobiles came to grief. Twelve hours passed when news arrived that M. Levassor, on his petroleum auto-car, was an hour and a half ahead of his rivals. Twenty-four hours later and he had reached Bordeaux and was back on the return journey to Paris, crossing his rivals on the road with an advantage of four hours. No sign of fatigue in either man or machine could be seen. Porte Maillot was reached at last, the whole distance of one thousand two hundred kilometers having been run in forty-eight hours and forty-seven minutes."

This was an average speed of fifteen miles an hour and caused a flurry of excitement in the United States where only a few people had ever seen an automobile. The total United States registration in 1895 was said to have been four cars. But the law was lax and some states did not require registration; there were actually a few more cars than that jouncing about the country.

In Springfield, Massachusetts, the residents had grown used to the Duryea brothers chugging around town. Out in Kokomo, Indiana, the natives had stopped gawking at Elwood Haynes when he rode by in his motor buggy. In Detroit, Michigan, Charles King had tried out his first car, and in Lansing, Ransom E. Olds was bumping over muddy roads in his first Oldsmobile. In New York there were a couple of electric carriages and a few foreign cars.

But in Chicago, even though few people had ever seen a real horseless carriage, the residents were preparing for the first automobile race ever to be staged in the United States. It was to be a road race from Jackson Park to Waukegan, Illinois, and return, a distance advertised as ninety-two miles.

Frederick Upham Adams, an engineer-journalist who worked for the Chicago *Times-Herald,* had conceived this cockeyed project in 1894, immediately after the Paris-Rouen race. His boss, H. H. Kohlsaat, owner of the paper, had fallen for his scheme. Adams had an idea that with a year to prepare for the event, a lot of American inventors would build their own motor carriages to enter the race and that for a large enough prize many French manufacturers would be attracted. Kohlsaat put up prizes totaling five thousand dollars and told Adams to go ahead and promote his horseless carriage race, but it better be good, by God!

Adams got busy and began writing articles about the future of the automobile and what it would do for America. He also toured the country hunting up men like Duryea and Haynes, who already had built cars, as well as dozens of screwball inventors who thought they could build an automobile even though they had never tried.

Among others, he visited the Pope Manufacturing Company, in Hartford, Connecticut, in hopes that that company would build and enter a car in the race. But although Colonel Pope had young Hiram Maxim working on an experimental model, he was not yet ready to produce automobiles. He was wisely waiting until the public was a little more anxious to buy them.

In his swing around the country Adams aroused only a bare flicker of interest. The Chicago *Tribune* had already started throwing rocks at the *Times-Herald* race. Now Adams and Kohlsaat began to worry. The race was postponed from July 4 to November 2 in hopes that more inventors would send in their entries.

It looked as though the whole thing would be a fiasco until reports of the Paris-Bordeaux race came over the cables. The imagination of the American public was immediately captured. Between July 1 and November 1, monkey-wrench inventors began building over three hundred different types of horseless carriages. Some proposed to use gasoline as a motive power, others steam, still others electricity. But a good many preferred more radical types of fuel, such as carbonic acid, acetylene gas, compressed air and liquid air, while at least six long-haired geniuses of the screwdriver undertook to use steel springs for their motive power.

Of the three hundred very few progressed beyond the blueprint stage, but during the summer and fall of 1895 Adams was delighted to receive eighty-eight entries for his big race. When the chips were down, however, and the starting date drew close only a bare dozen machines showed up in Chicago.

Meanwhile, Adams found that in writing about the coming event he was severely handicapped by the lack of a generic name for the machine-age chariots that would compete in his race. "Horseless carriage" was as unwieldly as a boat without oars and "motor vehicle" had a thoroughly utilitarian sound, not proper for the snorting racers that Adams hoped would come to his party.

So he conducted a name contest in the *Times-Herald* and offered a prize of five hundred dollars for the most suitable name for the new contraptions. Some of the names submitted were "quadricycle," "autocycle," "automotor," "petrocar," "motocar," and several hundred others.

After careful consideration, the judges divided the prize money among three persons, each of whom had suggested the name "motocycle." With the exception of the writers for the *Times-Herald,* who tried vainly to put over "motocycle," no journalist would deign to use the horrible word. They struggled along with "horseless carriage," "motor carriage," "motor vehicle" and "gasoline machine" until the French Academy finally relieved the strain by inventing the word "automobile."

By October Adams had great hopes that his "motocycle" race would be a big success. Things looked so promising that he rented a vacant storeroom at Wabash Avenue and Fourteenth Street, where he installed the dozen entries that had showed up for his affair. The machines were assembled at this early date in order to be tested by some elaborate devices that had been brought up from Purdue University along with a couple of mechanical engineering professors.

With his twelve "motocycles" gathered under one roof, Adams enticed his boss into a cab and drove down to the building on Wabash Avenue. Without any preparation for the sight he was to behold, the publisher was ushered into the presence of the most automobiles ever before collected together in America. It was, in effect, America's first automobile show, held primarily for Kohlsaat's benefit. The newspaper owner was delighted with the sight of these twelve powerful "motocycles," ready to roar away in pursuit of the five thousand dollars he was offering.

Not that he expected them to startle the world by their performance. All he hoped for was something that could reasonably be termed a race, so that his hated rival, the Chicago *Tribune,* would be confounded. For the *Tribune* had been scoffing at his "motocycles" and implying that the

Times-Herald race would be the biggest bust of the century. And that was a day of large busts.

But a couple of weeks later, on the eve of the big race, it looked as though the *Tribune* would have a triumphant last laugh at Mr. Kohlsaat. For only three of the dozen machines could leave the Wabash Avenue building under their own power. The owners of the other "motocycles" were still working furiously to get them in running order.

It was too late to postpone the race again, but Adams perused the rules he had concocted for the contest and discovered an "out." There had to be more contestants than prizes. So a preliminary or "consolation" race was held for a purse of five hundred dollars while the real contest was moved up to Thanksgiving Day, November 28, giving the inventors another twenty-six days to get their temperamental machines in shape.

Five machines actually turned up at the Midway Plaisance in Jackson Park on the morning of November 2. But two of these had been hauled there before daylight. They had four-inch pneumatic tires, engines brightly polished, a nice paint job, but they could not have been made to run ten feet on their own power. The inventor was selling stock in his new company and he had his two machines there for advertising purposes. Later, he hauled them away again. Still later, he left the country with most of the company's cash in his pocket and a sheriff on his trail.

Of the machines that would run, only two meant business —the Duryea and an imported Benz. But despite the international nature of the "consolation" race it turned out to be a pretty dismal affair. The Duryea, which was the favorite, of course, suffered a broken driving-chain and was delayed for almost an hour making repairs. Later, to escape a collision with a fractious horse, the Duryea smashed up in a ditch. The Benz finished alone in nine and a half hours.

The Chicago *Tribune* chortled over Kohlsaat's "race" and gloom descended on the *Times-Herald*. Adams spent the next three weeks wheedling his protégés into redoubling their efforts to make their machines behave. He also managed to get a new entry. R. H. Macy & Company, of New York, had decided to become agents for the Rogers car, made in Paris. They sent one of these machines to Chicago in hopes of winning the race and getting free advertising for their new line of merchandise.

Meanwhile, the Duryea brothers had repaired their motor carriage and were once more ready to compete.

A Philadelphia firm was represented by an electric machine called an "Electrobat." Its motor was connected to the front wheels while the rear wheels steered the vehicle. When moving it seemed to be progressing backward. The company was well-heeled and had established a number of supply depots along the route to furnish fresh batteries as needed.

One queer entry, which never started, was a tricycle with a gasoline motor connected directly to the rear axle, an arrangement about as practical as roller skates on a horse.

The imported Benz, owned by Oscar Mueller, of Decatur, Illinois, was once more on hand. It was driven by a hefty leather belt. This belt was slackened to allow the engine to idle; when it was pulled taut by a hand lever, the belt acted as a friction clutch and the machine took off. To give the belt better traction it was impregnated with rosin and sand.

Elwood Haynes had entered his machine, but an accident prevented it from participating in the race. He had already been awarded a prize, however, for the "best designed" car.

Another entry was an affair called a Motor-Drag. This was a motor on two wheels, which could be attached to your old buggy or Victoria in place of a horse.

The pre-race favorite was a heavy electric car, considerably faster than any of the gasoline carriages, called a Sturges. Its inventor had also placed extra supplies of batteries along the route to Waukegan.

According to Hiram Maxim, designer of the future

Columbia automobile, who had come to Chicago as an observer for the Pope Manufacturing Company, the Duryea brothers had the most efficient motor carriage in the race. But because it had failed to finish in the previous race with the Benz, the crowd had switched its affection to the Sturges and the Electrobat. After all, storage batteries and an electric motor were simple and reliable.

Three days before Thanksgiving an unseasonable blizzard swept down on Chicago. The ground was covered with eight inches of snow; streetcars and even railroad trains were halted. Mr. Kohlsaat held his head; the *Tribune* gloated.

Adams had a hunch that his job was in jeopardy if the race once more failed to come off. He called on all of his prospective contestants and gave them pep talks. Eleven promised faithfully that they would be present on Thursday morning, come hell or high water.

The final blow fell on Wednesday night; it started to snow again. Next morning the owners of the eleven racing behemoths dashed about trying to buy, borrow or steal a few lengths of hemp rope or clothesline to wrap the wheels of their cars. Tire chains were unknown at the time.

Adams tore his hair and announced that the race would be shortened. It would be run only to Evanston and back, but the prize money would positively be paid.

After considerable delay, six cars managed to reach the starting line, either under their own power or in drays. Besides the Duryea, there were two Benz cars, the Electrobat, the Sturges and R. H. Macy's Rogers.

The *Tribune* sent a reporter noted for his barbed sense of humor. He was to follow the race with a horse and carriage so as not to miss any part of the ridiculous performance.

Adams was on hand for the start of the race, but as soon as the six contestants were on their way, he caught a train to downtown Chicago, hailed a cab and dashed to Kohlsaat's home on Lake Shore Drive to report to his boss that the intrepid race drivers were speeding northward.

The Duryea machine led off at 8:55 with Frank Duryea at the tiller and Arthur W. White as his passenger-umpire. Next came one of the Benz cars, then the Rogers. The ponderous Sturges electric was driven by its inventor, Harold Sturges. The Electrobat was operated by Mr. Morris, one of its designers, and beside him sat his umpire, Hiram Maxim. The last car away was the defending champ, Mr. Oscar Mueller's Benz. He was accompanied by Charles B. King, who had already built his own automobile and would some day design two well-known American automobiles, the Northern and the King.

The lightweight Duryea with its pneumatic buggy wheels was the only starter that was not soon caught in a snowdrift somewhere along the Midway. The spectators, who followed after the cars on foot, keeping pace with them in most cases, came to their rescue. They pushed and boosted one discouraged "motocyclist" after another out of the snow, despite the protests of the umpires that this was against the rules.

The first Benz gave up the fight before reaching downtown Chicago; the Electrobat wisely quit at Rush Street Bridge rather than risk the humiliation of stalling before its first relay of batteries could be reached.

The second Benz stalled a dozen times in the snow, but its determined driver shoveled it out and continued on his way until he came triumphantly to the Duryea at the Rush Street Bridge, undergoing repairs for a broken steering gear.

The first machine to pass Kohlsaat's home on Lake Shore Drive was the Rogers. Next came the Sturges, battling gamely against the odds of its weight in the heavy snow. Then the Benz thrashed by making enough noise to waken the dead. Finally, thirty-five minutes after the leader, came the Duryea, its wheels wobbling and its engine throbbing defiantly as it made up for lost time.

Adams and Kohlsaat turned from the window with a sigh of relief and shook hands. Whatever happened now four contestants were on their way to Evanston. With any luck one of them ought to make it back.

The Sturges gave up at Lincoln Park, its batteries exhausted, its motor overheated. The Rogers looked like a sure winner when it reached Evanston, made the turn and started back, but shortly after that it tried to beat a streetcar through an intersection and then there were only two little Indians—the Duryea and the Benz.

Mr. White, umpire with the Duryea, reported that after leaving Evanston the loss of a tire and the adjusting of a new tire caused a twenty-minute delay, losing the route caused a four-minute delay and a troublesome sparking machine caused numerous delays totaling six minutes. Overheating necessitated several stops to take on water and during one emergency stop a pail of slush from the street was used to cool the engine.

But despite these troubles the Benz suffered more serious difficulties and once it had been overtaken was left farther and farther behind. Frank Duryea finally crossed the finish line in Jackson Park at 7:18 P.M. His elapsed time was ten hours and twenty-three minutes; his average speed was slightly better than five miles per hour. The Benz did not finish until shortly after midnight. And Mr. King was at the tiller, since Oscar Mueller, the owner of the car, had been overcome by exhaustion!

Next day the *Times-Herald* declared the race a tremendous success and the future of the "motocycle" assured. The Chicago *Tribune* chuckled derisively and announced that the horseless carriage was a complete failure.

Despite the ludicrous aspects of the *Times-Herald* race the East was not to be outdone by Chicago. In the following May, the *Cosmopolitan* magazine offered a prize of three thousand dollars for the best all-around horseless carriage. The contest was conducted in Westchester County with none of the crude rough-and-tumble tactics that had characterized the Chicago melee. That sort of thing might be allowed in Cook County but not in Westchester. The *Cosmopolitan* contest ran off as slick as melted butter. No one was inconvenienced and apparently all entries behaved beautifully. The cars were judged on the following basis:

Speed, 35%
Simplicity of construction and durability, 30%
Ease in operating and safety, 25%
Cost, 10%

The board of judges included Chauncey M. Depew, president of the New York Central Railroad; General Nelson A. Miles, Commanding the United States Army; John Jacob Astor, and several other socially prominent gentlemen.

The Ardsley Country Club "placed its clubhouse and grounds at the disposal of the judges for the conduct of examinations and tests." It was strictly a white flannels and blue coat affair. Gentlemen only allowed.

There were nine automobiles in the contest. The *Cosmopolitan* had requested permission from the New York Park Commissioners for the motor cars to pass through Central Park, but this request was refused so they drove in single file from City Hall up Broadway to Kings Bridge, the starting point of the race.

The race course ran north on Broadway to the Cosmopolitan Building in Irvington-on-Hudson, then back to the Ardsley Country Club, a distance of 16.5 miles.

The moment the last of the nine racers had been sent on his way, the judges stepped aboard a special train supplied by Chauncey Depew and sped north to Ardsley in a matter of fourteen minutes.

The *Cosmopolitan* account pointed out that, notwithstanding the fact that the road through Yonkers contained many steep hills, the contestants began arriving shortly after the judges reached the country club. The Duryea machine was the winner.

After that the judges sat on the club veranda and watched the cars being put through driving tests by their various chauffeurs. The Duryeas' car, with Frank at the tiller, won the contest on every count.

The *Cosmopolitan*'s editor stated, after watching the Duryea's "amazing performance," that "horseless carriages will soon be on the market at qualities and prices suitable for general use, we must believe."

If the *Cosmopolitan*'s solemn statement was read in France it must have caused chuckles, for the Paris-Marseilles race that year was over a course of 1,700 kilometers or slightly more than 1,000 miles. The race was conducted by the newly formed Automobile Club of France. There were twenty-two starters, nine of which finished, despite heavy rainstorms. The winner was a four-cylinder Panhard-Levassor car, which averaged better than 16 miles per hour.

It was impossible, because of the atrocious roads in the United States, to hold long road races of the kind that were being held in France, so we tried to make up for this with track racing.

On September 7, 1896, America's first track races for motor vehicles were run at Narragansett Park, Rhode Island. Five heats of one mile each were run and A. L. Riker in a Riker Electric Stanhope won all five. His best speed was 26.8 miles per hour.

But by 1900 Mr. Riker was having trouble beating gasoline cars. At the Tri-State Fair in Guttenberg, New Jersey, he competed with A. C. Bostwick, driving his own imported 70-horsepower Panhard, and with D. Wolfe Bishop in his 50-horsepower Panhard. Mr. Bostwick won the ten-mile championship at an average speed of 39.2 miles per hour.

In Newport, Rhode Island, that same year, several gentlemen race drivers formed the National Automobile Racing Association of Newport. They held their first race in 1901 with more than sixty cars and drivers entered. William K. Vanderbilt, Jr., in his Mercedes, won the ten-mile championship with an average speed of close to 39 miles per hour.

But in that same year the Paris to Berlin automobile race attracted 110 starters, 30 of whom finished. M. Fournier won the race, averaging 47 miles per hour for a distance of 1,198 kilometers (744 miles).

Two spectators were killed and several injured during the race. The *Scientific American* was worried by the speeds attained and by the increasing hazards of automobile racing; it commented editorially, "It may well be asked if the limit of speed in racing vehicles has been reached."

Unable to race over our miserable roads, the automobile clubs introduced another type of contest in which racing was strictly forbidden. This was the reliability or endurance test. The contestants were given specified routes to travel in certain specified times according to the power and weight of their machines. Mishaps and delays were penalized and a perfect score on a reliability run was highly regarded.

One of the earliest recorded reliability tests was a run from New York to Boston and return, conducted by the American Automobile Club in October, 1902. The cars in this race included a Packard, a White Steamer, a Winton, a Haynes, an Apperson and an Oldsmobile. Some of the newer cars, it was noted in one of the newspapers, were a Rambler, a Stevens-Duryea, a Fredonia, an Elmore and an Autocar tonneau. Mr. A. L. Riker, president of the Locomobile Company, drove a large gasoline Locomobile designed by himself.

The contest began on Thursday morning, and occupied three days from New York to Boston. There the drivers rested over Sunday. The return to New York was begun on Monday and also took three days. The distance traveled was 488 miles.

The craze for road racing in France reached a climax in 1903 with the Paris-Madrid race. The course was 784 miles in length. Handsome prizes were offered and some 228 automobiles started the race. Among the entrants were William K. Vanderbilt, Jr., driving a 90-horsepower Mors car, painted white. Another gentleman racer, Foxhall Keene, drove a Mercedes. Much excitement was caused by the entry of Madame du Gast, the first female race driver.

The start of the race took place from Versailles shortly after three o'clock in the morning on May twenty-fourth and no less than 200,000 Parisians were reported to have gone out along the road during the night to watch the early morning start. There was said to have been a continuous procession of cyclists, each carrying lighted Chinese lanterns, together with hundreds of automobiles heading toward Versailles, which gave a festive air to the road the whole night through.

The number of inexperienced contestants and the crowds along the race course, as well as the increased speed of the cars, many of which were capable of seventy miles per hour, turned the race into a slaughter. Three contestants and four spectators were killed and several more were critically injured on the first lap of the race into Bordeaux. The race was peremptorily stopped by the French authorities, and the first man into Bordeaux was declared the winner.

But the fascination of the public for races and racing cars did not seem to be in the least dampened by the fatalities of the Paris-Madrid race. Mr. Kenneth A. Skinner, a Boston socialite and amateur race enthusiast, whose name was often prominent in racing events of that day, came back from Europe with one of the cars which had participated in the fatal race. It rather resembled some of the cruder entries in today's soap box derbies, with its square-cut hood and "bucket" seats as upright as kitchen chairs. The magazine *Automobile* took chop-licking delight in this car. It printed a picture of the racer with its new owner at the wheel, along with the following dispatch:

"Boston, Mass., October 26—Since its arrival on this side of the Atlantic some weeks ago, much interest has been created in local automobile circles by Kenneth A. Skinner's sporty De Dion-Bouton Paris-Madrid racer. Boston is fairly used to seeing big machines of both domestic and foreign manufacture, but when this long, low car comes snorting along the street like a blooded horse restrained, the crowd stops and looks.

"To those who know the history of the car, its participation in that fatal race of last summer, gives it an added attraction. It is the first real foreign racing machine that Boston has seen and Mr. Skinner has had many callers who wish to examine the car at close range. . . .

"The car has been called by some the 'White Streak,' and this name fits it as well as any other. The car, which in reality is swung well off the ground, has the appearance of being very long and low and racy. It is painted white with brass trimmings. The hood over the engine adds to the lengthy appearance of the car for it is fully four feet long and finely tapered. The car weighs 1,600 pounds and the 2-cylinder engine develops 16 horsepower."

But when Mr. Skinner's De Dion-Bouton, with its two cylinders and sixteen mechanical horses went snorting down the streets of Boston, the older generation found little to admire in its long, low and racy lines. As the *Review of Reviews* pointed out, editorially, "The French have built special machines for traveling at high rates of speed, but it seems certain that high speed will not obtain in this country, for it is dangerous and unnecessary. There has been considerable legislation against the speed of automobiles, and this will continue if the tendency toward racing on the public highways continues."

In Chicago there was talk of giving examinations to automobile drivers. Good eyesight, sound hearing and a stable nervous system were considered important.

George Selden, who was granted a patent on the gasoline automobile in 1895, seated in a car built to his patent drawings by Engineer Henry Cave almost twenty years after Selden conceived his idea of a gasoline road locomotive. This gas wagon is labeled 1877, the date on which Selden's original ideas were put on paper.

Brown Brothers

This is typical of the early horseless carriage. It looked more like a buggy than an automobile. Most distinctive feature is the modern-type radiator in place of the dashboard.

The first auto race in America. The Chicago *Times-Herald* race from Chicago to Evanston and return, held on Thanksgiving Day, 1895. J. Frank Duryea, who designed this car and is shown in the driver's seat, not only won this race but also received a cash award of $2,000.

Henry Cave

Four officials of the Pope Manufacturing Company seated in a Columbia electric, about 1897. At that time this company was world leader of the bicycle industry and the most important maker of automobiles in the United States.

Henry Cave

Hiram Percy Maxim at the wheel of one of the Mark VIII Columbia cars which he designed for the Pope Manufacturing Company, Hartford, Connecticut.

This is Henry B. Joy, who made the Packard car one of the finest early cars in America. He is here seen in one of the first Packards built at Warren, Ohio.

Brown Brothers

The Stanley brothers were identical twins. For twenty years they made the famous Stanley Steamer and refused to spend a penny for advertising.

1901 Oldsmobile with the famous curved dash.

Brown Brothers

These grim ladies are about to enjoy a tour of Manhattan in an electric rubberneck bus of 1900.

Brown Brothers

Boston cops were first with the latest. This Stanley Steamer squad car, about 1900, was the pride of the force.

Brown Brothers

The first official New York Automobile Show was held in 1900 at old Madison Square Garden, Madison Avenue between 26th and 27th Streets. The sign in the right foreground shows that one of the important displays at the show was owned by the American Bicycle Company, a sort of General Motors of its day.

During the first New York Automobile Show, this little Mobile steam car caused something of a sensation by performing hill-climbing chores on a specially constructed ramp built on the roof of the old Madison Square Garden.

Brown Brothers

In 1896 automobiles were circus freaks. This poster shows a Duryea car which was loaned to Barnum and Bailey for advertising purposes.

Brown Brothers

In 1902, brake tests on Riverside Drive. A curved-dash Oldsmobile going 14 miles per hour stopped dead at 21 feet, 7 inches; a Victoria and pair doing 13.8 miles per hour required 36 feet, 10 inches; and a four-horse coach, 77 feet, 6 inches.

Brown Brothers

These gentleman racers of 1900 all appear to be driving steam cars. At the tiller of the car on the extreme left is John Jacob Astor. The race was held at Newport, Rhode Island.

Brown Brothers

This appears to be a one-cylinder Buffalo car, about 1902, which used an engine manufactured by the E. R. Thomas Company, Buffalo, New York.

Brown Brothers

An automobile outing of the New York Athletic Club at Travers Island, 1902. At this early date few American cars are in evidence.

James Ward Packard, the inventive engineer who founded the Packard Motor Car Company, is shown here in one of the company's first custom models, 1902. It was still a one-cylinder car. The crank can be seen at the side.

Henry Cave

These two test drivers for the Electric Vehicle Company, manufacturers of this Mark XLII Columbia four-cylinder touring car, are justly proud of having established a new record from Chicago to New York. 1904.

A one-cylinder Packard, "Old Pacific," driven by Tom Fetch, Packard test driver and plant foreman, made the fastest time of three automobiles that, within a few days of each other, crossed the continent for the first time in the summer of 1903.

Old Pacific's driver crossed this stretch of sand by laying down canvas strips and driving over them.

Brown Brothers

Famous "999," the first car in America to travel over a mile a minute. On the right stands the designer, Henry Ford. At the steering lever is Barney Oldfield. In 1904, Ford drove over a mile straightaway for a new record of 93 miles per hour.

The second car to go faster than a mile a minute in the United States was this Packard, "Grey Wolf." At the wheel is Charles Schmidt, of the Mors plant in France, designer of the first multi-cylinder Packards.

Brown Brothers

These three identical cars are entries in a five-hundred mile endurance run in 1901. The drivers' white uniforms will not be nearly so immaculate by the end of the contest.

Moe Leiter

The rear door on this 1902 Peerless, 18 inches in width, is here shown open and ready for milady to squeeze in. Once the door was closed, the lower half could be raised to form a jump seat and thus accommodate an extra passenger.

Brown Brothers
Mayor Thomas Johnson of Cleveland was the proud owner of a Winton—"Made in Cleveland," of course.

Brown Brothers
This society belle of 1903 is said to have driven her Franklin runabout with great skill and daring.

Keystone View

This stylish equipage was an electric carriage of about 1901-05. It could be rented, complete with chauffeur, for $180 a month.

Keystone View

This is apparently a Clement car, about 1905.

Henry Cave

Eddie "Cannon" Bald, at the wheel of a Columbia racer, about 1904. He has just completed a trial spin on the horse track at Charter Oak Park in Hartford.

These three knights of the road have just completed a test run from Detroit to Chicago and return.

The *Scientific American* found the suggested regulations thoroughly common sense, and pointed out that it was high time for some such action, for "nothing will hurt the automobile industry more than a series of accidents."

5

FIFTEEN CARS A DAY

1899
Production 2,500
Registration 3,200
The detachable tonneau

THE ONLY MAN who ever had two successful American cars named after him was Ransom E. Olds. The two companies he organized are still in business; the Oldsmobile is a product of General Motors and Reo is a famous name on trucks. And it is very likely that Ranny Olds' interest in the automobile may have preceded any of the other big five among the early pioneers. It was in 1887, while working in his father's engine works at Lansing, Michigan, that he completed his first steam-driven road vehicle.

In Lansing, Olds' steamer created more excitement than a two-headed calf, but was considered much less useful. A substitute for the horse was something few men thought practical. Some even argued that any attempt to replace Dobbin might wreck the economic structure of the civilized world. In the United States alone there were twenty million horses—one to every three human beings. Eliminate the horse and what would we do—eat them? Don't be silly! The automobile can *never* replace the horse!

In England the fox-hunting crowd was appalled at the thought of permitting roads to be used for anything but horse-drawn vehicles. Beastly idea! Tallyho!

With pompous dignity British M.P.'s rose to protest this nonsense and to prevent it, if possible. Steam coaches, operating on the public highways, were forthwith taxed two pounds per year, whereas a horse-drawn coach paid only five shillings. Righto! Keep the beggars off the bloomin' 'ighways!

To be certain that no mechanical contraption would ever endanger a horse, Parliament also passed a law requiring self-propelled vehicles to carry three drivers and be preceded by a man carrying a red flag!

But in the United States we were more liberal and far-seeing. Editorial writers asked what good could possibly come from those noisy, stinking machines? Ministers called them contraptions of the devil! Our federal, state and city law-makers passed laws prohibiting automobiles from (1) operating between the hours of 9 A.M. and 9 P.M., (2) boarding a ferry boat, (3) operating over streets commonly used by horses, (4) traveling over eight miles per hour, and (5) entering public parks—to name but a few. In Mitchell, South Dakota, one sweeping ordnance took care of the auto menace: automobiles were forbidden within the city limits!

But men like Duryea, Haynes, Ford, Winton and Olds were untroubled by legal hazards and prejudice. They may even have been unaware of them. Men who create with their hearts, as well as their hands and brains, have no time to worry over the antics of fools who make laws.

In 1893, at the age of thirty, Ranny Olds completed his second steam carriage. It was described so vividly in the *Scientific American* that a patent medicine firm in Bombay, India, made inquiry about purchasing the machine, and eventually Olds sold it to them. This is believed to have been the first sale of an American car, and was undoubtedly the first to be sold for export.

Olds next tried his hand on a gasoline car and was working on it when the *Times-Herald* in Chicago announced its road race to be held in July, 1895. He tried to get his car ready for that event, but failed to do so. It is interesting to speculate on whether Olds would have been able to give Duryea a contest. Probably not, for he was dissatisfied with his first gas buggy and built a second one in 1897. This was apparently a more successful vehicle and is now in the famous collection at the Smithsonian Institution.

The success of this second gasoline carriage inspired the formation of the Olds Motor Vehicle Company. But capital was hard to raise in Lansing, especially for horseless carriage companies. So Olds went east to Newark, New Jersey, hoping to interest that industrial city in an automobile plant. Newark was looking for new businesses and was encouraging them with factory sites and finances. But none of the city's financiers was foolish enough to put money into a horseless carriage venture.

On his way back to Lansing, Olds stopped in Detroit. It was a bustling city of slightly more than two hundred thousand people, sixty-five thousand horses, three or four motor carriages, and not a single automobile factory.

There Olds met S. L. Smith, a retired copper millionaire, with two sons who wanted to go into business. They were just young enough not to know any better, so they were enthusiastic about the future of the automobile. Their father happened to be a man who was either crazy or had absolutely no idea of the value of a buck. For Old Man Smith put up $199,600 to start the Olds Motor Works, with the understanding that the new corporation would set up business in Detroit and that his two sons would have jobs.

Detroit's first automobile company started off with a very fancy model priced at $1,250, which was a lot of spending money in 1899. You could buy a gallon of whiskey for $1.00 and a steak dinner for 35 cents. Sears, Roebuck & Co. sold a complete bicycle for $8.95 and an imported, one-cylinder Renault automobile was only $715.

At the J. L. Hudson Company, a Detroit department store, men's quality white shirts were selling for 50 cents each; nightshirts, full length, with Cash's trimming, 75 cents; gentlemen's four-ply linen collars 15 cents each; cuffs 20 cents per pair; Derby hats $1.75. Ladies' night robes, with insertions of Platt Valenciennes lace cost $1.10, ladies' fine walking hats of Milan straw, trimmed with ribbon and birds' wings were priced at $4.00, complexion powder was 45 cents a box, Milady's foundation garment was called a corset and cost $1.00 in young ladies models, while something called Tampico pads, covered with fine cambric, were worn beneath the corset and sold for 50 cents a pair.

The first Oldsmobile had numerous high-toned features to warrant its high price, such as a pneumatic clutch and an electric push-button starter (which seldom worked), but it was still just a surrey with an engine under the rear seat. The public found it too expensive and much too complicated to operate or repair. The company lost $80,000 on its first Oldsmobile.

Olds now decided to add a medium-priced car and a low priced runabout to his line—to cover all the bases, as it were. The runabout he designed was very simple in construction. It had a one-cylinder engine, weighed about seven hundred pounds and was supposed to sell for $600, but the price was eventually raised to $650. It was the famous curved-dash Oldsmobile that would be famous in song as the Merry Oldsmobile.

At this point it may be well to examine history as it actually happened, compared to history arranged by Oldsmobile's press agents. The press representatives of the industry like to make the little curved-dash Oldsmobile one of those great inspirations of genius by a master mind. The truth is that no matter how capable Olds may have been as an engineer, mechanic and businessman, the Olds Motor Works became the first great American automobile manufacturer through a stroke of luck.

On March 9, 1901, a fire broke out in the Olds plant. When the blaze started the one and only model of the new runabout happened to be standing near an open doorway. One of the employees tried to start the engine but couldn't, so he pushed the little car out into an open yard and rushed back to help fight the fire. But efforts to save the plant were futile; when it was all over the little runabout was the company's sole tangible asset.

Everything else was gone. Even the blueprints of the larger and more expensive cars had been destroyed. Only the little runabout was left and only the little runabout could be made ready for the New York show in November. Olds and his board of directors decided it was better to be represented at the show by their orphan than not at all, so all hands went to work on the Oldsmobile with the curved dash, because that was the one car the company could produce by November.

Besides being a smart engineer Olds was a good salesman and promoter. Having determined that his new car had stamina and roadability as well as the sort of simplicity that made it easy to repair, he decided to give New York something to talk about.

Suppose, he supposed to himself, the new Oldsmobile were to make a cross-country run from Detroit to New York and arrived on Fifth Avenue on or about the opening day of the show. What a whopping front-page story that would be! The Oldsmobile would steal all the thunder from the big cars.

But what if something went wrong and the car broke down and never reached New York? The hell with pessimistic thoughts! He had to shoot the works and hope for the best. Another year like the first one and the Olds Motor Works would be flat busted.

Olds looked over his factory full of youthful assistants and chose Roy D. Chapin, just turned twenty-one, as the man to whom he would entrust the future of the Oldsmobile.

Roy Chapin was an impatient young man who wanted to make a million dollars and make it fast. He had started in pursuit of his pot of gold in the winter of 1900-01. Leaving the University of Michigan during mid-year exams he struck out for Detroit and Destiny. He had heard about the Oldsmobile factory and he soon located it and put the bee on Olds for a job.

Olds was a man of little education, himself, and was suspicious of most college boys, but Chapin was so intense, insistent and self-assured that he offered to put him to work for $35 per month. The salary didn't matter; Chapin wanted to be in the automobile business. He went to work in the shop filing down rough gear castings to make them fit.

There Chapin met a mechanic named John Maxwell who had helped the Appersons build the first Haynes car, and another young man named Charles B. King who had built a car of his own in 1894. Both of these men would one day have cars named after them. The Olds plant was, in fact, full of men who would one day be leaders in the industry.

Maxwell and Chapin became pals. Probably because they were both so nuts about automobiles that they used to come back to the factory at night and do overtime without extra pay, just to tinker with the wonderful toys that would some day be the heart and guts of the whole city of Detroit.

After the Olds plant had been destroyed by fire, Chapin became the company's official advertising manager, which meant that he wandered about the new factory snapping pictures for a direct-by-mail catalogue that was to describe the virtues of the new Oldsmobile runabout.

But by the fall of 1901 Chapin was working with Maxwell again, testing cars as they came off the production line (one per day). And that was when Olds asked him if he thought he could drive one of the runabouts to New York City.

A silly question! Chapin would have answered in the affirmative though the destination had been Tokyo.

Preparations for the trip were intense. A special box was constructed for the rear of the car and in it was placed an assortment of parts consisting of practically a new car. Then maps were studied diligently, each day's route planned and the mileage calculated. Olds and Chapin decided that he could make the trip in six days and accordingly set his departure to take place one week ahead of the New York Automobile Show.

Chapin started at daybreak one morning. He was wearing a leather motoring coat and a cap as a concession to the rigorous trip ahead, but for the sake of Oldsmobile dignity he also wore a high starched collar. He had a small suitcase with some extra linen, a nightshirt and a toothbrush.

The route he had planned led through southern Ontario to Buffalo, then along the Erie Canal to Troy on the Hudson River. From there he intended to head south by the Albany Post Road. By the time Chapin reached Syracuse he had given the spare parts depot on the rear of his car a good workout, but he was still on schedule.

Then the rains came. It had been raining a bit for two days but at Syracuse the water came down in a cloudburst. The roads became impassable. Old residents assured Chapin he would never be able to get out of Syracuse for a week.

But Chapin *had* to get to New York. The future of the Oldsmobile and his own future depended on it. He meant to get there if he had to carry the runabout on his back!

Then someone told him that there was one road that was always high and dry, and that was the towpath beside the Erie Canal. Chapin jumped in his not-so-merry Oldsmobile and headed for the canal. There he drove onto the towpath and opened the throttle wide. For the next 150 miles he fought a battle of invective with the mule drivers along the towpath but he finally reached Albany and the Post Road.

Everything looked rosy, then, until he hit a bump in

Hudson, New York. The bump broke an axle, put him more than a day behind schedule and threatened to end his journey for good. But he finally wired Olds at the Waldorf-Astoria that he was once more on his way and would arrive next day.

The day passed and Chapin did not appear. Olds began to worry. He was ruined if Chapin failed. But that young and eager beaver was grimly fighting his way down the Post Road. Despite the broken axle, punctures, broken springs, ignition trouble, a broken feed line and dozens of other handicaps he was slowly approaching his destination, covered with mud and grease which would soon turn to glory.

Then, as the little Oldsmobile putt-putted down Fifth Avenue, tragedy almost overtook it within a few blocks of the Waldorf-Astoria. A skid on a wet pavement bounced it into a curb. But the unhappy Oldsmobile could take it. Only a couple of broken wire spokes resulted. As Chapin threw in the clutch and pulled away from the curb a faint cheer arose from the spectators.

At the Waldorf-Astoria Chapin drew up in front expecting a welcoming salute from the doorman. Instead, he got the bum's rush. No dirty chauffeurs allowed in the lobby of the Waldorf! Move along or get bounced!

Chapin was not to be stopped after coming all the way from Detroit. He sneaked in a side entrance, made his way to an upper floor on a freight elevator, and reported to his boss. The Oldsmobile had made it—Detroit to New York in seven and a half days!

The accomplishment of the little runabout created a mild sensation and the car was the hit of the show. Searching for a well-heeled New York dealer, Olds discovered that A. G. Spalding and Company, the sporting goods firm, was considering selling automobiles. Olds put on a high-pressure campaign and persuaded the New York manager to take on the Olds agency and one hundred cars as a starter. The order was ready and the deal was all set. It needed only the okay of the Spalding company's board of directors.

But when that body met to discuss the matter they made wry faces and canceled all of their manager's oral commitments. The idea of selling one hundred of the jaunty little Oldsmobiles in a city like New York was patently ridiculous. After all, customers for automobiles were to be found among men of money and dignity. If these men bought cars they were more likely to purchase those clean, silent electric machines manufactured in Hartford, Connecticut, not this little chug-chug from Detroit.

After he thought it over Olds was glad the deal had fallen through. He didn't want his car subordinated to baseball bats and croquet sets. He was sure that the automobile dealer of the future would deal in nothing but automobiles. Olds remembered that there was a young fellow named Ray M. Owen who had sold a few Oldsmobiles in Cleveland and who had gone a little goofy over the new runabout. He had claimed he could sell a hundred cars in Cleveland alone and wished he had a market like New York City.

Olds looked up Owen and told him that if he wanted the New York territory he could have it. How many cars could he handle for the coming year?

Owen thought he could swing about five hundred. That was an interesting figure, Olds agreed, but didn't he think that for newspaper publication it might be more exciting to announce that Owen had signed a contract for one thousand new Oldsmobiles?

Owen thought it was a dandy idea and the reporters were called in for the signing. It was the most exciting automobile news of the day. One thousand at a whack! The new Oldsmobile must certainly be a wonder car!

It was. It sold like hot cakes. The factory couldn't keep up with the orders. But Mr. Owen wasn't easily satisfied; the bigger the public appetite the more he whetted it. He drove one of the little runabouts, with a detachable tonneau, down Fifth Avenue, trailing advertising banners and performing spectacular stunts before the homes of New York's society leaders. But he barely avoided running over a bicycle policeman and that was a little too much; he was arrested for reckless driving and disorderly conduct. More publicity and more sales!

When Chauncey Depew, president of the New York Central Railroad, bought an Oldsmobile and allowed himself to be photographed as he drove to his office, the little runabout with the curved dash had finally crashed the Big Time. It was in Society. From then on the sky was the limit.

The Oldsmobile runabout was introduced at the second New York Automobile Show in November, 1901. From then until January first the company sold over four hundred cars. In 1902 Ray M. Owen sold more than seven hundred fifty cars in New York City alone and the company's output was over three thousand—fifteen cars a day!

By 1903 the Oldsmobile factory was turning out twenty-five per cent of all cars made in America. Henry Ford was still trying to get started, but Olds was already a millionaire; he had made Detroit the center of the automotive world; he had introduced mass production to the industry; he was the giant of the automobile business.

Sales increased each year until, in 1905, the total was 6,500 and Gus Edwards wrote his famous song "In My Merry Oldsmobile," giving the car a boost to all-time fame and a special place among such patent Americana as barbershop quartets, mustache cups, five-cent cigars, two-bit haircuts, wooden sidewalks, girlish blushes and the bicycle built for two.

6

THE MOTOR MEN AND THE GIRLS

1900
Production 4,192
Registration 8,000
The steering wheel

AUTOMOBILES WERE FIRST exhibited at the old Madsion Square Garden on January 1, 1900. The event was the annual bicycle show and the only reason a horseless carriage was allowed in the place was because some of the bicycle manufacturers had seen the handwriting on the wall and were trying to ride two vehicles at the same time. Famous bicycle names that were on automobiles, or soon would be, were Winton, Pierce, Rambler, Columbia, Pope, Lozier, Cleveland, Peerless, Waverly and Orient.

For two or three years the crowds at the annual bicycle show had been growing smaller, but the display of horseless carriages that first week of the new century created a new interest in the bicycle show and by the end of the week the old-time crowds were back. But they came to see automobiles, not bicycles.

The promotion manager of the Chicago *Inter-Ocean* happened to be in New York and followed the crowds to Madison Square Garden. What he saw gave him an idea.

If people were that interested in automobiles why not stage a real show for them in Chicago under the sponsorship of the *Inter-Ocean?*

In July, 1900, the newspaper announced its sponsorship of the first auto show devoted exclusively to motor vehicles. It was to be held in September at the old Washington Park race track and was called "an automobile exhibition."

However, some of the big shots around the *Inter-Ocean* must not have believed that a quiet display of horseless carriages was enough to hold the interest of a Chicago crowd. To be on the safe side, America's first automobile show was turned into a sort of three-ring circus. The newspaper's announcement of the coming event gives some idea:

"On the opening day there will be a general parade of nearly five hundred vehicles, with standing and moving exhibitions, when the general public will be allowed to examine the vehicles in and out of the buildings, and ride in them in the parks."

The reporter for the *Inter-Ocean* went on to describe in glowing words the various contests and races that would be seen at Chicago's first automobile exhibit. First, there would be contests for "general practical utility." The rules were strict. Each manufacturer must enter three cars. One was to carry two passengers and the owner-driver; the second was to carry four passengers and a chauffeur in livery; the third vehicle was to be a commercial or delivery type motor car, with a load of not less than one thousand pounds. No specifications as to the driver or his costume.

It was stated that the cars would be put through some mighty difficult tests. For instance, "practical manipulation," in which a "series of dummy figures will be introduced on the track, some constantly shifted, some remaining permanent as the vehicles pass through them, causing frequent stops and turnings."

The idea was to prove that "any intelligent operator" could direct the movements of an automobile as easily as he could drive a horse and carriage. "These tests," the *Inter-Ocean* assured its readers, "should be of inestimable value to the automobile industry."

Races of various lengths and strange purpose were also a part of the program. There were to be speed contests between steam, gasoline and electric carriages, free-for-all races, races with a full complement of passengers, long races, short races, and even a *backward* race.

A novelty race was scheduled to demonstrate that motor cars could be used with safety to carry the United States Mails. This was rather an involved affair in which the contestants raced for ten miles snatching, en route, dummy postal cards and letters from dummy mail boxes located around the track. No effort was made to furnish any sleet or snow or rain.

After that came a contest on "both an incline and decline grade." The idea here was to show "control-ability of the vehicle." But the *pièce de résistance* of the six-day meet was Ladies' Day.

The newspaper announced that "Ladies' Day will be full of interest, as ladies will have the track exclusively in a series of races, which will be run with motor carriages and not racing vehicles. In addition to this, the most dexterous lady operator in dodging the dummy figures, climbing grades, and general manipulation of the vehicle, will receive a special gold medal."

Unfortunately the *Inter-Ocean*'s automobile exhibition ran into a week of rain and the show was more or less of a flop. The *Scientific American* reported:

"The exhibitors of complete automobiles numbered twenty, of whom eleven showed vehicles or cycles propelled by hydro-carbon motors; five exhibited electric vehicles and four steam vehicles.

"The electric vehicles were, by all odds, the handsomest vehicles in the show, judging from the standpoint of a carriage builder.

"The speediest vehicles on the grounds—for any considerable distance, at least—were the gasoline vehicles.

"Among the larger vehicles there was only one machine that made any pretensions to speed sufficiently high to make a showing against the little French tricycles, and that was the racer with which Alexander Winton vainly attempted to win the championship of the world in France this past summer. This machine covered fifty miles in 1 hour 17 minutes and 50 seconds."

A month later the Automobile Club of America staged the first full-scale automobile show in New York City. The *Scientific American* gave the event a big spread and pointed out that "although it was regarded as being something of an experiment, the really first class nature of the exhibits and the excellent attendance stamped this venture as being a thorough success."

Once again, however, the promoters played safe by staging an action show for those who bought tickets. But, as was to be expected, it was a more refined exhibition than was given in Chicago. There were no mail races, or races for ladies, or backward races. However, an oval track had been constructed inside the Garden and this was "given up to the exhibition of automobiles in motion and to various tests of the starting, stopping and steering qualities of the automobile."

The *Scientific American*'s reporter thought that the most spectacular of these events was a contest over an obstacle course in which the drivers "had to steer their way between barrels and other obstructions which had been distributed around the track."

But the exhibition that seems most startling today took

place on the roof of the Garden, where the Mobile Company held hill-climbing demonstrations. The exploits of the Mobile steam car were observed and reported thus:

"Anyone who had doubted the hill-climbing potentialities of these machines would have been greatly impressed with the trial, which was carried out on a specially prepared grade built upon the roof of the Garden. The track, which was carried on trestles, extended with a right-angle turn from the roof of the Garden to the side of the great tower."

Among the attractions at the show were two foreign racing cars. One of these was a Panhard which had won the Marseilles to Nice race in 1897. It was described as a "massive high-power machine, driven by a four-cylindered engine of 24 horse power." This monster had covered one mile on the Guttenberg, New Jersey, track in one minute and 27.8 seconds. The other racer was a small De Dion racing tricycle, winner of the 1900 Paris-Toulouse contest, at an average of twenty-seven miles per hour.

It is rather surprising to discover that the *Scientific American,* at that time an almost unassailable authority on science and invention (but not the objective scientific journal that it is today), apparently preferred steam and electric automobiles. The magazine's automobile editor wrote glibly:

"A striking feature of the exhibition was the evidence of the increased attention which is being paid to steam as a motive power for automobiles. The Locomobile Company had a very complete exhibit. These cars were shown in a variety of styles, all of which are marked by the clean lines and general light and symmetrical appearance which characterizes machines of this make.

"The Mobile Company of America is another concern which has devoted itself with great success to the develop-

THE MOTOR MEN AND THE GIRLS 81

ment of the steam automobile. While the Mobile may be called the first cousin to the Locomobile, it possesses various distinctive details and wrinkles of the kind which are dear to the heart of the automobilist."

There were many more words praising the two steam cars. Then the writer gave a strong plug for electric automobiles:

"The exhibit of the Electric Vehicle Company was one of the handsomest in the Garden. The incorporators of the company have always been strong advocates of electricity for motive power, and all of the carriages but one in their exhibit were of the electric type. They were all marked by the great beauty and finish which characterizes the work of this company. In the exhibits were the Columbia phaeton, runabout, victoria, rear-boot victoria, cabriolet, surrey, a brougham, hansom, and several others. They also exhibited a gasoline runabout with engine of 4 horse power."

Notice the lack of enthusiasm over that little Columbia four-horsepower runabout. The magazine seemed to have little interest in anything driven by gasoline. It had only this to say about the most well-known American car of that day:

"The Winton Motor Carriage Company exhibited several styles of their well-known vehicles. One in particular was a racing machine, splashed with mud and weather-worn, which was driven by Mr. Alexander Winton from Cleveland, Ohio, to Madison Square Garden, 810 miles (November 1 to November 4), at an average speed of 21 miles an hour. The roads during this period happened to be wet and heavy with mud."

This was the second time Winton had made the cross-country trip from Cleveland to New York. The first time, in

1897, it had taken him ten days. The trip from Cleveland to New York in 1900, at an average of 21 miles an hour, was a record worthy of a lead story in the magazine. Instead it was buried at the tail end of the show article.

The Haynes-Apperson car, made by the oldest automobile company in America, was brushed off with the following:

"Another exhibit of interest was that of the hydrocarbon vehicles by the Haynes-Apperson Company, of Kokomo, Indiana. These were substantially built and easily operated. The first hydrocarbon vehicle built by this company in 1893 was on exhibition in the historical section."

Winton and Haynes were both regular advertisers in the *Scientific American* or they probably would have been overlooked entirely, as were Oldsmobile and Packard. What was behind this partiality? Not technical ignorance, surely. The editors definitely knew that in France the gasoline automobile had proved its superiority in every road race that had been run since 1894. And yet the foremost technical magazine of its day gave most of its space and praise to steam and electric vehicles, and especially those manufactured by The Locomobile Company of America, the Mobile Company of America, and the Electric Vehicle Company.

Without implying any villiany in the possession of wealth it is interesting to observe that Locomobile, Mobile and Electric Vehicle were owned by very rich men who were in the habit of making certain, if possible, that their investments paid off.

The Locomobile Company had been formed in 1899 with the purchase, for $250,000, of the steamer patents owned by the Stanley brothers. The Mobile Company was also formed to operate under these patents. Probably another $250,000 had gone into these two companies for plants, machinery, etc. Electric Vehicle must have been even more in the red; probably to the tune of a million dollars, contributed by

Colonel Albert A. Pope and his friends. The men who had backed these three companies expected to get their money back. They would spend more, if necessary, to convince the public that steam and electric automobiles were superior to the gasoline variety. And the quickest way to do that was to get a "good press."

The early New York and Chicago automobile shows saw some strenuous "selling" campaigns. Manufacturers often wooed important dealers with more zeal than they did the ultimate consumer; editors and reporters were wheedled with flattering words, banqueted and lied to, all for the purpose of obtaining a boost in newspapers and magazines.

A few years later, when the competition became as intense and conscienceless as a battle royal, somebody developed a subtle sort of bribery known as the wine, women and song routine. A company with a tough bill of goods to sell might throw a private party during show week that could cost as much as two hundred dollars a plate. The male guests were not only wined and dined in lavish style, but were supplied with charming and acquiescent partners for the occasion.

These "stag" parties were sometimes attended by editors and reporters, as well as preferred customers. Nothing was demanded of the representatives of the press; there were no vulgar suggestions that the news be slanted in any way; but of course a gentleman always spoke well of a generous host. The results of a lively "stag" party were seldom disappointing.

This type of salesmanship reached its peak one year when a certain accessory firm, hard pressed for business, held a banquet in a private dining room, at which the guests were ten important car manufacturers. The ten found their place cards at the table and discovered that each one had a vacant chair next to him. If any of them wondered about the vacant chairs they were not kept long in ignorance. For in a few minutes ten very attractive dinner companions filed in, all as naked as the day they were born.

The technique in Chicago was slightly different. Although official headquarters for the show were at the Coliseum, some of the automobile crowd maintained a sort of second headquarters at the Everleigh Club on South Dearborn Street.

The Everleigh was the most luxurious place of its kind in America. It opened for business in the same year that the first auto show was held in Chicago, and doubtless some of the roistering, hard-drinking, two-fisted men who were drawn into the automobile industry, found their way to the Everleigh establishment that first year. And for the next ten, lush, colorful years of the automobile's early history the Everleigh sisters assisted the industry in its show-time "selling."

The Everleigh bordello was located in a double house at 2131-33 South Dearborn Street. The place was elegantly furnished with thick carpets on the floors, silken drapes at the windows and the most expensive furniture. There were twelve parlors in the house where a gentleman could meet one or more of the thirty beautiful hostesses who dwelt there—besides Minna and Ada Everleigh, who were also young and attractive. The parlors were furnished in different styles and periods; each one named according to its décor. There was the Gold Room, the Rose Room, the Turkish Room, the Oriental Room, the Chinese Room, the Parisian Room, the Japanese Room, etc. There was nothing garish or cheap about the manner in which the parlors were decorated. According to the style of that day they were in excellent taste. Divans, comfortable easy chairs, tables, sofas, lamps and occasional pieces were the best that could be had.

The ladies were dressed as elegantly as the house was furnished. They all wore evening gowns and were instructed not to betray their calling until they retired to their luxurious boudoirs.

Private dinner parties with a girl for every guest were, of course, easily arranged at the Everleigh Club. During show week in Chicago there were private parties most every night in the parlors of the club. Here, after a strenuous day, the motor makers and their important customers relaxed with a midnight snack, a bottle of wine, and a trip up the softly carpeted mahogany staircase to the mysterious, mirrored boudoirs of the Everleigh nymphs.

An evening at the club was expensive. Champagne was twelve dollars a bottle, the colored servants expected folding money for tips, and no one ever insulted a young lady at the club by offering her less than twenty-five dollars for her charms.

It is said that during the week of the show one night was always designated by the Everleigh sisters as Automobile Night at their club, and it required an official exhibitor's badge to gain admittance.

The Everleigh Club closed its doors in 1911, and since then the Automobile Show in Chicago has never been quite the same.

7

FASTEST THING ON WHEELS

1902
Production 9,000
Registration 23,000
The side-door tonneaux

FOR SOME REASON the men with the money were usually wrong about the automobile business. About 1898 Wall Street money started the Electric Vehicle Company. The financiers had it figured out that electricity was the coming rage in the horseless carriage game. Electric carriages were clean and quiet and simple to operate. Obviously a gentleman would have nothing to do with a noisy, greasy, bucking, gasoline buggy.

Then along came the Stanley brothers with their steam car. In 1899 they had one model car, orders for two hundred, some patents and were about to manufacture cars in an old bicycle factory when a syndicate of wealthy men bought them out for $250,000.

That was the smart money, the hard-to-fool money. But when the monkey-wrench engineers in Detroit tried to raise capital, Boston bankers sniffed audibly and looked out the window, while the Wall Street crowd gave them the bum's rush. So Detroit's young inventors had to get dumb money from the local yokels, who weren't bright enough to realize that electricity and steam, not gasoline, were the coming things.

The electric auto never had a chance. Its radius of operation was far too limited; it carried too much weight per horsepower; and it required special, rather expensive equipment to keep the batteries charged.

But the Stanley Steamer was a dilly of a car and in the early days of the horseless carriage the average layman believed implicitly that steam engines would never be surpassed as a means of power. They were quiet, fast, powerful; they needed no cranking, and kerosene, which was their fuel, was safer and cheaper than gasoline. The only drawback to a steamer, according to the drugstore wiseacres and the curbstone critics, was the boiler. Yes, sir! That was something you had to look out for. If you didn't watch the pressure gauge like a hawk the goddam thing would explode and blow you to kingdom come!

Of course, even the early steamers had safety devices to keep the boiler pressure from rising too high, but nevertheless people were suspicious of them, and the explosion bugaboo was something the Stanleys always had to fight.

Doubtless a good many boiler explosions in the past had created this latent fear of steam, for steam engines antedated all others by over a hundred years. A Frenchman built the first steam road vehicle about 1770 for the French army. It hauled a cannon at the rate of two and a half miles per hour. The vehicle is still in existence and may be seen at the Museum of Arts and Trades in Paris.

After James Watt invented his more efficient steam engine British experimenters built several steam stage coaches and it looked as though this new form of transportation might displace horse-drawn coaches, which were slower and more costly to operate.

But the stagecoach operators of England lobbied a law

through Parliament that successfully killed steam coaches and all types of automobiles for the next sixty-five years.

The "red flag law" (explained previously) forced the steam engine enthusiasts to buy their own rights of way, on which they laid rails to operate their steam vehicles; thus the railroads were born and the stagecoaches were driven out of business anyway.

Oliver Evans, a builder of steam engines in Philadelphia, is credited with operating the first steam road vehicle in America in 1805. This ingenious gentleman had a contract to build a steam scow which was to ply the Delaware River. It happened that his plant was across town from the river so when he began to build the scow in his factory yard, the neighbors thought he had gone daffy. When the steam scow with its big walking beam was finally ready to sail, Evans attached wheels to it; then the neighbors were sure that he was off his rocker.

On the day that Evans got up a head of steam half of Philadelphia turned out to see the fun. Everybody said he must be crazy as a bedbug. But when Evans opened the steam engine's throttle, the walking beam started seesawing, the wheels began turning and the damn-fool contraption headed out of the yard and down the street toward the Delaware River. When he arrived there, Mr. Evans ran his amphibian monstrosity into the water, removed the wheels and collected his money. The neighbors went home shaking their heads and talking to themselves.

Light steam road cars were made as early as 1863, and in the 1880's quite a few inventors were making homemade steam buggies. As has been mentioned, R. E. Olds built his first steam machine in 1887 and in 1893 his second, which he sold to a firm in India. By 1895 the French were building steam cars commercially. But it was a few years after that, probably about 1899, before any American steam cars were regularly offered for sale.

The Stanley brothers, who became the big shots of the

steam car business, first saw a horseless carriage in 1896 at a county fair at Brockton, Massachusetts. It was a steamer, of such inefficient construction that it could not make a complete circuit of the half-mile track without stopping to build up steam pressure.

The Stanley brothers were identical twins. They wore identical clothes, and even kept their flowing beards trimmed to identical shape and length. It was also said that their penmanship was identical and some friends insisted that they thought the same thoughts at the same moment.

At the time they saw their first steam buggy, they had already made a modest fortune manufacturing photographic dry plates under a process for which they held a joint patent. On the way back from the Brockton Fair the brothers decided, practically simultaneously, to try their hand at making a steam car. One that would go around the race track not only once but several times, without stopping to build up a new head of steam. They completed their blueprints for this car late in 1896.

Neither of the brothers knew anything about steam engines, so they did what seemed like the smart thing: they ordered a manufacturer of steam engines to build them an engine suitable for a road wagon. Then they went to a boiler factory and ordered a boiler.

To their dismay, when the boiler and the engine arrived at their shop in Newton, Massachusetts, they found the combined weight to be seven hundred fifty pounds. The brothers realized that it was somewhat ridiculous to place all this machinery in the light two-seater buggy they had designed to hold it. But they had bought and paid for the damned engine so they went ahead and installed it. Neither one had ever driven an automobile, but they fired up, climbed in and opened the throttle. The date was September, 1897.

"I shall never forget our first ride," one of the Stanleys

wrote later.* "We went out our alley way onto Maple Street, and turned toward Galen Street. A horse hitched to a produce wagon was standing headed toward Galen Street. He heard the car coming, turned his head around, took a look, gave a snort, and jumped so quickly that he broke the whiffletree, but did not move the wagon, ran out to Galen Street, turned around, took one more look, and then ran up Galen Street, through Newton Square and did not stop running till he reached Newtonville Square."

Next day they tried it again and another horse ran away. The brothers didn't take their steam buggy out much after that. They realized that it was cumbersome and slow, and they were afraid that the heavy engine was too much for the light buggy.

They went back to their friends, the steam engine people, and asked them to make an engine that weighed not more than a hundred pounds and a boiler that weighed maybe one hundred fifty pounds. Couldn't be done, the steam engine people said.

The Stanleys got some books and read up on steam engines. But the books didn't help much, so they hired a young engineer to help them and together they designed an engine that was not intended to push a ship across the ocean, or move a loaded freight train, but only to roll a two-seated buggy along the streets of Newton.

The Stanleys next took the precaution of avoiding their friends, the steam engine people. Instead they went to a brass foundry and a machine shop that knew practically nothing about steam engines. Between the two they managed to get an engine made that weighed only thirty-five pounds, and a boiler that weighed ninety pounds.

Of course the steam engine experts said that their engine was no good. It would probably shake apart, burst, burn out, melt, disintegrate, blow up, or just go phttt!

---

* This and subsequent quotations from Mr. Stanley are from Floyd Clymer Publication—Modern Steam Car.

It did none of these things. It ran like a charm. So the Stanleys built another one, identical with the first and drove around Newton, one behind the other, or sometimes abreast, frightening skittish horses and local inebriates.

The brothers had no intention of going into the automobile business. The two steamers were just a hobby. So when anybody came along and offered to buy one of the cars they turned him down. But one of the brothers had an idea that he could make a still better car, so finally he yielded to temptation and sold his car for $600. That was in 1898.

A month or so after that the brothers went into Boston to see the first automobile show held in New England. It was staged at Mechanics Hall. On exhibition were four cars. The classiest was a De Dion from Paris, which was a low-slung racing car, with the engine in front. The others were American cars and all resembled buggies. There was a Haynes-Apperson gasoline car, a Whitney steam car, and a Riker electric car.

Following the indoor exhibition an open air meet was to be held at Charles River Park, Cambridge, with speed and hill-climbing contests. The Stanley brothers were invited to participate in this meet.

They protested that they were not making cars for sale and therefore weren't interested in competing with the others. However, they were persuaded by the sports editor of the Boston *Herald* that these were purely sporting events and the more the merrier. So F. E. Stanley drove his car to Cambridge for the meet.

There was some talk of turning the contestants loose to race around the bicycle track at the Park, but on second thought this was vetoed as being dangerous and undignified. Instead, each contestant was timed separately as he drove three laps to complete a mile. The three American cars that had been exhibited in Boston were timed first. Then came the De Dion racer from France. It beat the hell out of the first three American cars, negotiating the three laps in two minutes and fifty-eight seconds. The crowd went wild.

Then Mr. Stanley, his whiskers jutting out at a defiant angle, drove his little steamer to the starting line. There, his brother held the car in check as it tried to get away under a terrific head of steam. At a signal from Stanley No. 1, Stanley No. 2 turned the car loose and it shot away from the starting line with a terrific *whoosh!*

The fans in the grandstand oh-ed and ah-ed, then shouted excitedly, for the little Stanley was surely beating the be-jesus out of that damned frog car from Paris. And they were right. Two minutes and eleven seconds for the mile! A newwww worrrrld's rrrrecord!

Then came the hill-climbing contest. An incline had been built with five, ten, fifteen, twenty and thirty per cent grades. The gasoline cars hadn't a chance. They balked on the fifteen per cent grade. Even the Whitney steamer could only get part way up the twenty per cent grade. But our hero opened wide the throttle of his little Stanley Steamer and shot to the top of the thirty per cent grade in the twinkling of an eye.

"Never, before or since," wrote Mr. Stanley, "have I seen such enthusiasm as was created by these two performances of this little car. This was the last event of the day, but we were kept there over an hour answering questions and explaining the construction of the car. And in less than two weeks from this event we had received orders for over two hundred cars similar to the one shown there. It was then, for the first time, we decided to engage in the manufacture of automobiles."

Next door to the Stanleys' dry plate factory was an abandoned bicycle plant owned by the American Bicycle Company. The Stanleys purchased this factory for peanuts, put in the necessary machinery and prepared to make Stanley Steamers.

They had made one car when news reached New York

about the wonderful performance of the Stanley Steamer and the backlog of orders the Stanleys had in their little ex-bicycle factory.

People with money to invest in 1899 seldom knew anything about automobiles, but they knew what a backlog was. That was what Mr. John B. Walker wanted to buy—a backlog. The Stanley Steamer was okay, too, he guessed, but you couldn't go wrong on a backlog.

Walker was the owner of the *Cosmopolitan* magazine. He wanted to sell the Stanleys some advertising and he was hoping to trade advertising for a half-interest in the automobile. But the Stanleys were true Yankees; anything they sold they sold for cash. Besides they didn't believe in advertising. Never bought a penny's worth as long as they were in business. So Walker went back to New York without an advertising contract and without any share of the Stanley Steamer Company. But a couple of months later he was back in Newton and this time he said he wanted to buy the company outright.

The Stanleys went home to think it over; they only had $20,000 tied up in their steamer, so far, but they felt they had a good thing and if they were going to sell they decided to get a whopping big profit. Next morning they met Walker at their office and told him their price was $250,000.

Walker took them up so fast they knew they should have asked for more. He gave them a check to bind the deal and rushed back to New York to dig up the rest of the cash.

A few days later Walker wired the Stanleys asking them to bring their automobile to New York to demonstrate to his millionaire friends. F. O. Stanley drove to Providence and caught the night boat to New York.

Next morning he drove his car off the steamboat at Pier 18 where a friend met him. He described the arrival as follows: "The street in front of the wharf was crowded with trucks and conveyances of all sizes and dimensions, all drawn by horses. The horses were frightened and the drivers hostile, and apparently bent on our destruction. How we ever succeeded in running such a gauntlet without a smash-up I have never been able to figure out. But we did, and we soon found ourselves well up on Broadway, where traffic was light and conditions apparently safe. But we learned what every automobile driver soon learns: that one is not safe when riding in an automobile. For a girl riding a bicycle, coming down a cross street, and looking over her shoulder, ran plump into the side of our car. The girl was thrown bodily into the arms of Mr. Elliott and was uninjured, but the bicycle was a wreck. A policeman was standing quite near and saw the whole incident. A crowd soon gathered. The girl was much excited and the crowd threatening. But the policeman came to our rescue. He severely criticized the girl for being so careless, and drove the crowd out of the way, and we went on without caring to discuss the matter further."

During the next week or so Mr. Stanley took various millionaires joy riding in his car, including two sons of Jay Gould and a Rockefeller, who took two cautious rides before deciding not to invest.

But finally the money was raised and the wily Stanleys turned their factory, patents and backlog over to Mr. Walker and his partners for a quarter of a million dollars. These gentlemen formed the Locomobile Company of America, which was to be one of the leading automobile companies of the country for many years to come. The Mobile Company was also organized to manufacture automobiles under the Stanley patents, but the Mobile car was never successful.

Only a year or so after it went into business the Locomobile Company moved to Bridgeport, Connecticut, changed its policy completely and started making gasoline cars exclusively. So the two country boys, who had sold out to the smart New York crowd offered to buy back their patents as well as the little factory at Newton. But not for a quarter of a million. Oh no! The Stanleys were Maine

Yankees. They got their factory and their patents back for $20,000!

Then, a few months later, the White Sewing Machine Company, which was making steamers in Cleveland, wanted to use some of the Stanley patents; they bought a license for $15,000. So the Stanleys got their business back at a net cost of $5,000.

For a number of years steamers were more satisfactory than gasoline cars and they predominated in numbers. In 1902, for instance, automobile registrations for the state of New York totaled 909. Of this number 485 were steam cars. Among the hundred or more steamers of that time were the Grout, the Tractobile, the Toledo, the Skene, the Waltham, the Prescott, the Lane, the Stearns, the Ross, the Mobile, the Locomobile and the White Steamer.

The Stanley engine consisted of two cylinders, which was all that was necessary to give continuous torque to the crankshaft. It had, according to the Stanley catalogue, only thirteen moving parts. The engine was geared direct to the rear axle. No transmission or gearshift was necessary, for the power could be applied as slowly as desired; and the engine always turned over at the same rate as the wheels. Instead of ignition and carburetor, a steamer had a boiler and a kerosene burner, neither of which had any moving parts. The engine gave out no violent explosions or vibrations; the car was faster than any gasoline car and apparently climbed hills without effort.

The Stanleys for many years averaged about six hundred to one thousand cars a year and never spent a dime for advertising. On the other hand, the White Company, their principal rival, advertised extensively and for a while sold more cars than Stanley.

The price of Stanley Steamers was moderate. The early ones sold for under a thousand dollars. In 1909 the famous Stanley Mountain Wagon, which carried twelve passengers sold for $2,300. The family touring car was only $1,300.

The Stanley Mountain Wagon could climb like a goat. It was designed to travel from Loveland, Colorado, to the Stanley Hotel in Estes Park. This same chassis was also used for the Stanley express truck and the Stanley racing cars.

The Stanleys thought any form of advertising was just a way of cheating the customer out of dollars that should be spent on the product. But they spent a lot of money on racing, hill-climbing and endurance contests.

The first Stanley racing car was shaped like a cigar to reduce wind resistance and was painted red. It was given a number of nicknames by newspaper writers of the period. They called it the "Bug," the "Teakettle," "Whistling Billy" and the "Torpedo." It was first entered in a Memorial Day race at the Readville Track near Boston, in 1903.

The only two cars that F. E. Stanley, the driver, considered serious competitors were a Grout steamer, which reputedly had run a mile in less than a minute, and the "Cannon Ball," a steamer owned by George C. Cannon, a sports-minded Harvard student. The Cannon car was a curiosity in that it required two men to operate it. One handled the steam engine and the other steered.

A Boston paper described the event as follows:

"A trail of steam followed the red-painted machine as it skimmed around the Readville Race Track and overhauled and passed other larger and seemingly more powerful automobiles. The machine resembled somewhat an inverted boat. The top was rounded and from the center could be seen the head of its operator, F. E. Stanley."

The article forgets to mention that Mr. Stanley was wearing a yachting cap and his usual flowing whiskers. It must have been a cheering sight to residents of South Boston, if any were in the grandstand, to have watched Mr. Stanley and his handsome beaver beating the pants off the Harvard youth whose mustache was doubtless both skimpy and blond.

For Mr. Stanley created a new record that day, driving the mile in one minute two and four-fifths seconds.

Stanley's triumph was short-lived, however, for an hour or two later, newspapermen told him that word had been flashed from the Empire City Track near Yonkers, New York, that a fellow named Barney Oldfield had just driven a mile in one minute one and three-fifths seconds. And that the big 80-horsepower gasoline car in which he had turned the trick had been built in Detroit by an engineer named Ford.

But the Stanleys were sure they could build a car that would travel faster than anything on wheels. They completed this car in 1905 and took it to Florida to try for the world's speed record on the sand of Daytona Beach. Fred H. Marriott, a young mechanic working for the Stanleys, said he would bust the record or bust the car trying.

The straight-away, one-mile record was held at the time by a Ross steamer which had used Stanley boilers and two Stanley engines, so after a fashion the Stanleys already held a leg on the record. Now they hoped to make a new one that was all theirs.

Fred Marriott kept his promise and broke the record by something like seven seconds for the mile, traveling the distance at the rate of 127.66 miles per hour. Marriott thereby became the first man to travel faster than two miles a minute.

The 1906 catalogue of the Stanley Motor Carriage Company claimed world's records for one kilometer, one mile, one mile in competition, five miles, and five miles in competition.

The following year another Stanley racer with an improved engine and boiler was sent to Daytona Beach. Again Fred Marriott, the Newton mechanic, was scheduled to break the record. They had geared up the machine so that they figured a speed of three miles a minute was easily possible.

Unfortunately, when it came time for the speed trial, the beach was in bad condition. But Marriott was determined to break the record. In Mr. Stanley's own words, "The crowd was anxious and Fred was desirous of lowering the record. Fred went up about nine miles beyond the starting line. He set the automatic so as to raise the steam pressure to 1,300 pounds. When he crossed the starting line he was going at a rate of speed never before seen. But when he reached the bad place in the course the car left the ground completely for a distance of nearly 100 feet, and it turned slightly in the air and struck at an angle, and of course was instantly smashed. The boiler was torn out, and with a tremendous roar of steam from the broken pipe, rolled several hundred feet down the beach. When first reached Fred was unconscious. He had several broken ribs, a bad cut on his head, and one eye hanging out of the socket, which, had it not been for Dr. Parks of South Boston, would have been removed. But it was put back and later perfect sight was restored.

"When that accident happened, the car was traveling at nearly three miles a minute . . . the most valuable lesson learned was the great danger such terrific speed incurs. So we decided never again to risk the life of a courageous man for such a small return."

Which they never did. That was the last record the Stanleys ever tried for. During the next ten years they continued to do business without advertising or promotion of any kind. They were the leaders in their field and all the business they wanted came to them without solicitation.

In 1917 F. E. Stanley was killed in an automobile accident. His brother, who had been in ill health much of his life, survived him, but he had no more interest in automobiles. The company was sold to Chicago financiers and not until then did an advertisement for Stanley Steamers appear in a magazine.

But apparently it was not advertising or promotion that the Stanley Steamer needed, but the care and devotion of the twin brothers who believed so implicitly in the superiority of their car. By 1925 the Stanley Motor Carriage Company was out of business.

8

HOLD ONTO YOUR HATS!

1905
Production 24,250
Registration 77,400
The windshield

FOR MANY CENTURIES the horse had been man's most popular means of locomotion while sitting down; but about 1890 came the safety bicycle, on which a good man, traveling over a good road, could easily make a hundred miles in one day. If you wanted to go any faster than that you left the public highway and took a train.

Then, in the short space of time from 1895 to 1905, man's speed on the public highways increased from a perspiring ten-miles-an-hour to a roaring mile-a-minute.

No wonder the coming of the automobile raised the devil with things-as-they-were. Our way of life had to be quickly remolded into a more streamlined shape if we were to keep up with the motor car. In the next twenty years the world went through more assorted groans, gripes and convulsions than in the thousand years preceding.

"The Quiet Mile-A-Minute Car." That was the slogan for Colonel Albert A. Pope's famous Pope-Toledo. One wonders at the effrontery of the copywriter who r'ared back and committed that startling falsehood. The Pope-Toledo of 1905 was powered by a four-cylinder engine and possibly could do sixty—with a tail wind. But quietly, never! No car, in those days, traveled quietly at *any* speed.

Nevertheless, it was a very doggy car, especially the touring job with the victoria top, meant to be driven only by a chauffeur in black or gray livery. And the price, $4,000, made it exclusively a vehicle for bankers, brewers and Wall Street speculators.

Then there was the tonneau model, one of the first to eliminate the rear-door entrance. The "new front-door entrance car" did not have access to the tonneau by a door. Instead, the front seat split in two and one of the halves swung out over the side of the car on hinges so that passengers could step into the tonneau from the front. It was considered a wonderful car for a family with children. The kids could be deposited in the rear, where they were well fenced in. No danger of the rear door opening and dropping them into the street.

When going for a spin in the "Quiet Mile-A-Minute Car," Milady soon learned to leave her hat with ostrich plumes at home. She wore goggles, a duster, motoring gauntlets and a sensible hat with only a couple of bird wings and a bunch of cherries for ornaments, the whole anchored firmly in place with a strong veil tied beneath her chin. In later years she wore the popular Mary Pickford motoring bonnet (Sears, Roebuck, $2.39), or the Anita King ladies' motor cap (better department stores everywhere).

One of the unsung heroes of the pioneer days was Charles B. King, who built an automobile in Detroit in 1894.* But Charlie King was a perfectionist. Dissatisfied with what he had built he dismantled it and went to France to see what

---

* The Automobile Manufacturers Association gives 1896 as the date of Charles King's first automobile. But Mr. King claims 1894 as the proper year for his earliest car, and the best evidence indicates that he operated a car in Detroit before 1895.

was being done abroad. In Paris he became interested in art as well as automobiles and stayed much longer than he had intended; but when he returned he was one of the best informed engineers in Detroit. He became the chief engineer and designer of the Northern Manufacturing Company, which was formed in 1903 just in time to become a member of the A.L.A.M.

King put a lot of new and unusual features in the Northern automobile. It was the first car to have a left-hand drive, although Ford is usually given credit for that innovation. It was also the first to place the headlights on the fenders and the very first motor vehicle to be equipped with air brakes. Also King eliminated all side levers, so that complete control was at the wheel and with the pedals. Later King became head of the company which bore his name and which manufactured the King car.

Two more early motor men were Lewis S. Clark, of Ardmore, Pennsylvania, and F. B. Stearns, of Cleveland. Clark built the first Autocar in 1897 and his company is still building commercial vehicles. Autocar was one of the first cars in those days to have a gearshift lever on the steering column. This later became outmoded and then returned, about 1937, with such fanfare one would have thought it was the invention of the year.

Frank B. Stearns was the son of a wealthy man in Cleveland, Ohio, and had a passion for motor cars. He built a four-cylinder car as early as 1897 but it was far ahead of its time, so he abandoned it as too expensive and complicated. In 1899 he built twenty cars and sold them. From that time until 1930 the F. B. Stearns Company built one of America's outstanding cars. In 1912 Stearns brought out the Stearns-Knight, a luxury car of great distinction.

Another early Cleveland car was the Peerless. The first Peerless introduced a new wrinkle in steering wheels. The steering column had a hinge in the middle so that it could be folded forward out of the way while the driver slipped into his seat. However, this jointed steering column was not entirely successful, for if the joint gave way the car was on its own and usually went bouncing over the curb and onto somebody's front lawn.

Among the more familiar names of those early days were: Pope-Hartford, "Be Sure the Name Pope Is on Your Automobile," $750; Lozier, "The Choice of Men Who Know," $5,000; Matheson, "America's Finest Motor Car," $6,000; Elmore Two-Cycle, "The Car That Has No Valves," 3 cylinders, $1,750; Knox Waterless, "The All the Year Round Car," $2,500; Reo, "You Can Do It With a Reo," runabout, $650; Mitchell, "The Car You Ought to Have at the Price You Ought to Pay," $1,500; and Stevens-Duryea . . .

"It Starts from the Seat" was the slogan of the Stevens-Duryea. Even in those days you couldn't trust a copywriter as far as you could toss a Linotype machine. "It Starts from the Seat" meant that you could crank while sitting down. But it was damned awkward and after a couple of tries you usually got out beside the car and gave the crank a spin.

The Stevens-Duryea was designed and engineered by Frank Duryea. For a long time he clung to the idea that anything on wheels should look like a carriage. As late as 1904 the Stevens-Duryea resembled something a horse should have been pulling. It had 28-inch artillery wheels with three-inch tires; the frame was of heavy bicycle tubing; the fenders were made of top-grain leather; at night it was guided by kerosene carriage lights. Standard equipment was a storm apron, to be used in case of rain. This was a large tarpaulin with two holes in it through which the driver and his passenger could thrust their heads. The price of the car was $1,300.

But the Stevens-Duryea was made in Chicopee Falls, Massachusetts, a locality inclined to prefer things as they had been, rather than things as they were to be. In Cleveland and Detroit motor cars were beginning to look like Parisian automobiles and to move just as fast. The rapid changes taking place in those days is illustrated by the famous Winton car. In 1902 the Winton was a 15-horsepower, two-cylinder contraption, boasting a top speed of thirty miles an hour, which it actually attained only under the most ideal circumstances.

By 1904 the Winton was a four-cylinder 40-horsepower job. An advertisement in *Leslie's Monthly Magazine* stated: "All speeds graduating from 4 miles an hour to 40 miles an hour, available by merely pressing right foot on pedal. Easiest controlled car in existence! Can be run by a Youth, after one hour's coaching. Automatic Foolproof Motor. Four upright cylinders, fed by one single Gas-mixer (carburetor) and fired by one single Magneto (electric sparker). Motor instantly accessible, by merely lifting hinged top of hood, which is forward of dashboard."

Then, a couple of years later came the Winton Six, which set the style for power, speed and elegance. The Six would do sixty, and its reputation was enhanced by Barney Oldfield, who raced the Winton Bullet, a record-breaking *eight-*cylinder car.

But the rapid advance of the motor car did not change the appearance of city streets at once. The horse-drawn vehicle still dominated the busy thoroughfares of any city. If you were typical you thought of your new car as something to be used on Sundays or holidays, like a silk hat. Week days you rode the trolley to work.

It was quite likely that you still owned a bike and retained your membership in the League of American Wheelmen. On gala occasions, such as the Fourth of July or the parade in honor of President McKinley, you did team drills with the bicycle Zouaves of your local fraternal order.

By 1904 the Haynes-Apperson had also advanced beyond the carriage stage and was a 35-horsepower, four-cylinder touring car styled for factory managers, prosperous merchants and proprietors of high-class saloons. The catalogue said that it would "run almost in silence—a much appreciated feature." It wasn't quite as classy as a Pope-Toledo but in Kokomo, Indiana, where it was made, you would have had a fight on your hands if you had said so. Its price was $3,000 for the five passenger car, $200 extra for the folding top.

Influenced by Kokomo's fame as the home of America's second gas buggy, more than forty automobile companies mushroomed in Indiana in the early days. Most of these were in Indianapolis which had a number of fine machine shops. Some of the more easily remembered cars that came out of Indianapolis were Overland, American, Cole, Marmon, Duesenberg, Elco, Empire, Frontenac, HCS, LaFayette, Marion, Monroe, National, Parry, Waverly Electric, Pope-Waverly, Roosevelt, Stutz and Premier.

"The Quality Car" was the slogan for the Premier. It was an air-cooled job in 1904, priced at $1,500. The company's ad in *The Horseless Age* proclaimed with simple dignity, "Still, by far, the best car on the market for the price. Graceful, fast, powerful climber, comfortable, beautifully finished, *very* durable."

But by 1907 Premier had abandoned the air-cooling principle and the moderate price range to become a heavier, more elaborate and much more expensive car. As one of the highest priced cars in America it pioneered the electric gearshift, an early-day super-wonder gadget, which never panned out as well as advertised.

At this time the gag writers and joke peddlers were already having a field day with the automobile. Ford jokes soon became so numerous that an entire book of them was published. The Essex, the Saxon and even the high-priced Pierce-Arrow suffered from the jokesters' jibes. But Premier's electric gearshift gave rise to the prize story of its day. Every traveling salesman knew one version or another of the one about the Premier salesman who lisped.

It seemed that this fellow was the world's greatest automobile salesman. He was never at a loss when a prospect asked embarrassing questions and he was so sincere and convincing that, despite his serious speech handicap, he seldom lost a sale.

One day he ran into an unusually tough prospect and was extending himself to the utmost in order to sell his man a Premier with an electric gearshift.

"It maketh dwiving eathy ath pie," said the salesman enthusiastically. "Juth pweth button one, pweth button two, pweth button three and *away* you go! Ith abtholutely foolpwoof!"

"Foolproof, eh?" growled the hard-boiled prospect. "You mean it can't get out of order?"

"Abtholutely not! Never, never!" the salesman assured him. But, he added that if anything ever should go wrong there was a little emergency lever that went with the car. You simply put this lever in a little hole in the floorboard and shifted gears in the regular way.

At this the skeptical prospect roared his loudest. "Foolproof, my foot!" he protested. "If the electric gearshift never gets out of order why do you need an emergency lever?"

"Mithter!" the salesman replied, with smug assurance, "did you ever find yourthelf pwegnant?"

"Don't be silly. Certainly not!"

"O' courth not!" triumphed the Premier man. "But jutht in cathe you ever do, you'll notith the Lord gave you two emergenthy titth!"

Another famous car from Indianapolis was the Marmon. In the beginning it had an air-cooled engine like the Premier but later followed the trend to water cooling. In the early days it had a long, roundish hood, preceded by a pair of brass headlights the size and shape of snare drums. A pair of rakish, uplifted fenders made it look like a mechanical monster that was about to fly. Marmon later developed an exclusive patented feature that must have delighted the company's advertising copywriter. This new feature was *Double Three-Point Suspension*.

"Luxurious cast aluminum body on one frame," explained

the company's advertisements, "entire power plant on another frame, each frame operating independently of the other, each being suspended on three pivotal points. No matter which wheels are raised, no matter which frame is tilted, the power plant, straight and rigid driving shaft and rear axle, are always in perfect alignment, free from twisting and binding strains. This means perfect power transmission and less wear on all parts, tires included."

For a few years Nordyke and Marmon built America's fastest racing cars and the company was one of the most prosperous. At one time Marmon racers held most of the national track records. A Marmon was the first winner of the Indianapolis 500-mile Memorial Day Race and was the last car to be manufactured in the city that had once hoped to be a second Detroit.

The racing cars were going a mile a minute, even two miles in a minute. Was the rest of America accelerating, too? Not yet. There was inertia to be overcome. You still ate Pettijohn's breakfast food. It was served steaming hot with milk or cream. Father ate the stuff because it had become a habit. The kids ate it because mother told them to and no nonsense. Clean up that plate or get your bottom tanned!

Child psychology was the back of a hairbrush. And there were no breakfast foods that popped or crackled or made any kind of interesting noises at all. You didn't get a G-man's badge and a pistol for five box tops and a dime; not even a magic explorer's ring with the secret code word. There really wasn't much fun to eating breakfast—just a big bowl of soft, silent Pettijohn's.

But, still, the inertia was giving way. Things were moving faster. At Coney Island they had a ride called Shooting the Chutes. Talk about speed. Took your breath away!

Even out in Kenosha, Wisconsin, things were moving along. Thomas B. Jeffery, who had made the famous Rambler bicycle, was making an automobile called the Rambler.

In his Surrey, Type Two, priced at $2,000 he introduced a startling innovation. It was a windshield, but he just called it a "plate glass swinging front." The car had a permanent canopy top supported at the four corners by steel rods and by a center pole fastened to the back of the front seat. Concealed around the edge of this top were waterproof storm curtains, neatly rolled, so that they could be lowered quickly in case of rain.

Mr. Jeffery advertised that "the working parts of the Rambler are so simple and so readily accessible through the hinged floor and seat falls that adjustments can be made without the help of a chauffeur, while the methods of operation are so plain they can be learned at a glance. Instruction given without charge to all buyers who wish it. Immediate delivery."

The ghost of the old Rambler still rambles in every Nash that travels the road. For when Charles W. Nash resigned as president of General Motors he bought the Jeffery plant in which to build his Nash car.

Along about 1902 H. H. Franklin, owner of a die-casting business in Syracuse, New York, heard about a new type of air-cooled engine which had been patented by a fellow townsman. He put up the money to build an automobile around this engine and called it the Franklin.

From that day until 1934 the H. H. Franklin Manufacturing Company and its successor, the Franklin Automobile Company, worked vainly to convince the American public that air cooling was more scientific than water cooling.

In 1905 a Franklin car was driven from San Francisco to New York in the middle of August. Later a Franklin was driven non-stop for ninety-six hours to prove that it couldn't overheat. And to top off this performance a Franklin was sealed in low gear and driven 860 miles without stopping.

Despite all these fine stunts a Franklin car still got hot as hell in the summertime. But my father, who manufactured motorcycles, knew that air-cooled engines were more practical than the water-cooled kind, so he bought a Franklin in 1913, because he said it was lighter in weight, more efficient and couldn't freeze up in the wintertime.

He was absolutely right on all counts. The Franklin had a frame made of hickory wood instead of steel, so was much lighter than other cars of its size. It also had what were called full elliptical springs. As a result that car used to jump around like a jackrabbit. At forty miles an hour, on a country road, it was airborne ninety per cent of the time.

In the winter it wouldn't freeze up and that was a fact, but it never warmed up, either. It would splutter and cough for five miles before the engine got rid of its shivers. Even then, on a near-zero day, it would continue to wheeze and gasp like an asthmatic sea lion.

As for efficiency, in the summertime a Franklin air-cooled engine was the most efficient piece of machinery ever made; it was practically perpetual motion. That was because the summer heat helped raise the temperature of the engine to just below the melting point. When you wanted to shut the damned thing off you had to kick the big aluminum ignition switch with your foot. It was too hot to touch with your hand. But after you had kicked the ignition off, the engine went right on running. The heat generated in the cylinder walls would keep firing the unexploded gas fumes in the engine and each time the engine turned over more gas would be sucked into the cylinders, etc., etc. It was the perfect example of a vicious circle.

Sometimes father would have to stop that engine by sheer force. He would pull on the emergency brake as far as it would go, put the car in gear and then drop in the clutch. That would do the job all right, but the Franklin always gave a protesting shudder and a sort of mechanical death rattle. It was pretty ghastly. Mother hated it.

As can be imagined, any car as radical as the Franklin became the butt of many jibes and jokes. Jack Donahue, famous dancer and comic of the twenties, had a favorite gag that always brought a sure laugh. In describing a bucktoothed girl he said, "She wouldn't be so bad-looking only she's got Franklin teeth—they're air-cooled."

The Knox Waterless, the Premier and many other air-cooled cars gave up the fight and went over to water cooling. But not the Franklin. It stuck to its guns until the bitter end.

The year after the first Franklin automobile was built, a couple of bicycle mechanics actually ascended in a flying machine at a place called Kitty Hawk. That was the same year Pierce-Arrow put their gearshift lever on the steering column. And at the Edison Studios in New Jersey a moving picture was made called *The Great Train Robbery*. It had a plot, just like a stage play, but nobody saw much future in moving pictures because the actors couldn't talk. Folks said it was just another fad like the phonograph.

If all the automobile slogans that were coined between 1900 and 1905 had been laid end to end they would have reached the length of Detroit's Woodward Avenue, with a lot of adjectives left over. But of all those fine phrases only one remains alive today. "Ask the Man Who Owns One" first appeared on an advertisement for Packard automobiles in 1902.

Forceful, crotchety Colonel J. W. Packard was a manufacturer of electric cables and supplies in Warren, Ohio. He had a successful business and no interest whatsoever in automobiles until, in 1897, a man named Alexander Winton ordered some varnished ignition cable from him. Later, in Cleveland, the two men met and eventually Packard drove the twelfth automobile manufactured by Winton back to Warren.

Packard was a man who liked an automobile as well as a slogan to be honest, practical and full of solid worth. He had a lot of trouble with the Winton and the next time he saw its builder he told him the machine was no damned good.

The maker of ignition cable and the quick-tempered builder of automobiles were soon in the middle of a rhubarb. If Packard knew so blamed much about automobiles, Winton demanded, why didn't he try to build one? Declared Packard, by God, that's exactly what he would do!

So the Colonel went back to Warren and built himself a one-cylinder car that was the best and the fastest in Warren. It was so good that some of the other big shots in town wanted one just like it.

By 1901 Packard had formed the Ohio Automobile Company to build Packard cars, and in 1902 his New York dealer was bragging that his supply of Packards wouldn't last long for "no machine in this or any other country is more graceful or powerful."

The 1902 Packard was a 12-horsepower job with a demountable tonneau, which one entered through a door in the rear. Standard equipment included two oil headlights, and a bulb horn mounted on the steering wheel, but no top.

Henry B. Joy, a young man from Detroit, who had inherited a fortune from his father, bought one of these cars in New York for $1,500 and had it shipped to his home. He liked the car so well that he went to Warren to talk with Packard about expanding his automobile business.

The Colonel was about to sell his electrical cable business so he agreed to go to Detroit and make automobiles if Joy would raise the money to finance a new company. Joy went back to Detroit and among his wealthy friends raised the money to organize the Packard Motor Company.

Meanwhile, the sale of Colonel Packard's plant in Warren was moving slowly, so Joy went ahead and superintended the building of a factory. Word came finally from Ohio that the sale of Packard Electric Company had been completed but part of the agreement called for Packard to stay and run the business. He apologized to Joy and his friends for ditching their proposition, but they would have to go it without him.

Thus Henry Joy, who knew nothing about manufacturing automobiles, found himself in charge of the new company. He decided to build the finest automobile in America; one that he and his wealthy stockholders could be proud of. So the one-cylinder car that Colonel Packard had made was sidetracked and a four-cylinder machine was designed. Packard, down in Warren, Ohio, heard about the change and wrote Joy that he was out of his mind. Why should he multiply his troubles by four? Stick to the car that had already proved successful!

Joy insisted that the only kind of a car he wanted to make was one that he himself would enjoy driving. If he liked the car, then other people would like it. The first year he built two hundred cars and lost $200,000.

But the company still had a use for its little one-lunger. Three of them were sent on a reliability run from San Francisco to New York City. The first car to finish was named "Old Pacific" and it encountered some brutal roads along the way. At one point the crew mutinied and refused to travel the course that had been laid out for them. They were told that their salary and expense money would be waiting for them only at those towns along the prescribed route. So the pair drove grimly on and reached New York in sixty-one days. It was an outstanding accomplishment in 1903.

Joy announced that in 1904 the company would manufacture four hundred cars; his wealthy friends backed him up with more money. There were a good many pessimists in Detroit who figured that if the company had lost $200,000 its first year, it would lose $400,000 in its second. But about that time the performance of "Old Pacific" and the quality that Joy had insisted on putting into Packard cars began to pay off and soon the company was making money, with a line of cars priced from $3,000 to $10,000. There was no finer automobile in America, and that was the way Henry Joy wanted it.

In 1904 the tempo was picking up. In New York City the subway opened. Darndest thing you ever saw! Shoot you through a hole in the ground at forty, fifty mile an hour!

The first automobile trucks also appeared in 1904. A lot of people just laughed at that idea. You can't teach a milk route to a motor truck, they said. Or make a mechanical engineer out of an Irish teamster.

Blacksmithing was still considered a depression-proof trade. And a good white wing took great professional pride in his skill with the broom and the shovel. Automobiles were a wonderful invention, everyone agreed, but the world couldn't get along without horses.

Just the same the big merchants began to view motor cars with interest. John Wanamaker, for instance, decided to put in a line of automobiles and motoring equipment. He handled cars of all prices but was the exclusive distributor of the Searchmont, made in Philadelphia. It was a car of grim dignity and resembled a French Renault. For extreme safety it had three brakes and the passengers in the tonneau were elevated fully a foot above those in the front seat, giving them an unimpeded view of approaching scenery.

R. H. Macy and Company backed a French car called the Rogers, while Sears, Roebuck and Company put out a Sears Motor Carriage, "The Business Man's Car." Nine models were priced from $325 to $475. Sold on ten days' trial.

But the mail-order houses, as well as the department stores, soon found that they were not automobile merchants. For they were not equipped to give repair service, and service was what those early cars needed the most of.

There were a lot of fine cars with fine slogans that couldn't survive the competition. Quite often it was because they didn't have the right dealers. The Peerless, "Finest Creation of the Day"; the Thomas Flyer, "World's Champion"; the Kisselkar, "Compare With Any Car At Twice the Price";

the Houpt-Rockwell, "You Can't Go By a Houpt-Rockwell, So Go Buy One"; the American underslung, "The Classiest Car"; the Stoddard-Dayton, "Six Cylinders All in Action"; the Velie, "The Climax in Auto Value"; the Apperson Jackrabbit, "Guaranteed Speed 75 Miles per Hour"; the Abbott-Detroit, "Always Up to Date," and dozens of others all disappeared, some soon and some late.

It wasn't a question of fine slogans or performance or price. Low-priced cars fell by the wayside, too, if the buyers couldn't get satisfactory repair service. The Orient, priced at $375, the Brush at $485, the Hupmobile at $750, were all cheaper cars and the latter two were probably better cars than the early Fords. Most of them expired because they had no proper dealer and service policy.

The public in general was a little slow at first, but the young folk soon caught on to the new trend. Mandolin clubs weren't nearly as popular as they had once been; iron stags on the front lawn were objects of suppressed derision; among young gentlemen the hard hat began to be replaced by the Fedora; at co-ed colleges young ladies in bloomers and middie blouses perspired gently as they performed calisthenics or played basketball (ladies' rules).

Cadillac bravely introduced the ladies' coupé, a very upright 10-horsepower car, and young President Roosevelt was often seen riding in an automobile at better than thirty miles an hour, despite warnings from Secret Service men that they considered it a dangerous practice.

The graceful rhythm of the waltz was replaced by the accelerated two-step; soon it would be the one-step, the Turkey Trot and the Bunny Hug. The world was going to hell at a rapid clip. And it was almost time for Henry Ford to bring out his Model T.

In 1903, when Ford and his lucky eleven stockholders formed the Ford Motor Company, Henry was just a monkey-wrench engineer who had been trying for several years to get going. He had been chief engineer of two companies which had folded. The only success he had had with automobiles was as a builder and driver of three powerful racing cars, the most famous of which was 999. He had yet to prove that he could build an automobile that the public would buy.

The Ford Model A of 1903, first called a Fordmobile, was designed to compete with the Cadillac, most popular car of the day, excepting the little Oldsmobile with the curved dash. The price of the Cadillac touring car was $900. It had a one-cylinder engine under the front seat and cranked on the left-hand side. The Ford had a two-cylinder opposed engine, cranked on the right-hand side, was a better-looking car and was priced at $850, later raised to $900.

The advertisements said: "Boss of the Road. The latest and best. This new light touring car fills the demand for an automobile between a runabout and a heavy touring car. It is positively the most perfect machine on the market, having overcome all drawbacks such as smell, noise, jolt, etc., common to all other makes of Auto Carriages. It is so simple that a boy of 15 can run it."

The Dodge brothers, who had one of the best machine shops in Detroit and had been building transmissions for the Oldsmobile, were given a contract to manufacture engines, transmissions and other parts for the new car. Part of their pay was fifty shares each in the Ford Motor Company.

In a building which was rented for seventy-five dollars a month Ford took charge of assembling the new cars. In the office, James Couzens, a bookkeeper, who had bought twenty-five shares of stock, became the business manager. He watched the company's cash, discounted its bills, and sent out a sight draft with every car that was shipped.

The two-cylinder Ford, fifty dollars cheaper than the Cadillac one-cylinder job, was an immediate success. But shortly after Ford began shipping cars, reports came back that the new machines were getting into trouble on hills. Mechanics were rushed out to make changes in those cars that had already been delivered. Ford is said to have tried to close down operations until the difficulty could be corrected in the plant. But Couzens warned him that if they shut down for one week the company would go broke. So they kept on shipping cars and sending trouble-shooters out to change the cars in the field. In the first fifteen months the company sold 1,700 cars and declared a one hundred per cent cash dividend.

Then Ford seems to have started stumbling around in a fog of uncertainty. He couldn't make up his mind what kind of a car he wanted to build. Like so many other manufacturers he wanted to get everybody's money. The original Model A was dropped and four other cars were added to the line. Model B was a four-cylinder, side-entrance tonneau car, selling for $2,000. Model C was an improved Model A with a removable rear-entrance tonneau selling for $950. Then there was a runabout called a Doctor's car, $850. And last came the new Model F, $1,200, which was the Model C dolled up with a side-entrance tonneau. This was the first Ford ever to appear with a running board. Business was good, as usual, but the two-cylinder cars sold the best.

In 1906 Ford made the prize boner of his career, one that could have busted the new company. He added to the already overcrowded Ford line a big six-cylinder car called Model K, priced at $2,500 and later raised to $2,800.

A lot of people have wondered how the genius of mass production could ever have made such a bull. He made his mistake because he was human. It was a terrific temptation, once the money was rolling in, to build something bigger and better than the others. Six-cylinders—a mile a minute!

But the public didn't go for that six-cylinder stuff. It was the little $500 four-cylinder Model N runabout that kept the Ford profits mounting. Even so, Ford was determined to crack the luxury market. In 1907 his ads featured the big Model K. They said, "History repeats itself when each succeeding season proves Henry Ford to have been a year ahead of all competitors. . . .

"The 1907 Model K Ford is the same as that of 1906 but its power (still called 40) has been increased 20 per cent by refinements of details, grinding cylinders and other slight changes. Chrome nickel steel is used throughout—all gears, shafts and even the frame. The Ford dual ignition system, with two sets of plugs has been copied by many makers both in America and Europe—we appreciate the compliment.

"One thing you can always count on—the feature they most criticize in the latest Ford car is the one they copy first. The 1907 K has a lot of features others will adopt for 1908.

"Ford Model K six-cylinder motor; 40 h.p. at the wheels; sixty miles an hour—down to four on the high gear, by throttle control alone. The silence of an electric, the flexibility of a steam engine, the simplicity and economy of a gasoline motor."

Ford tried hard to sell Model K but it was Model N, priced at $500 and Model R, at $750 that did business. At the end of 1907 the company had made a profit of a quarter of a million dollars. If it hadn't been for Model K they might have made half a million.

For some months Ford had been growing sick and tired of that big expensive six-cylinder car that wouldn't sell. Just when he got the flash that resulted in the Model T no one knows. But sometime in 1907 he decided to junk all the cars the company was making and concentrate on one car, built strictly for service. It was to be a better Model R. There would be nothing fancy about it but it would contain the very best steel that money could buy; it would be built to outlast all other cars, to run in mud or sand or across open fields; it would be for the farmer and the working man.

It came out in 1908. There were just two models—the touring car for $850 and the roadster for $825. It was as plain as a shoe box. Color, black, period! It might have been designed by a ten-year-old boy who was a little backward in his drawing class. Its belly rode high off the ground, so that it could straddle hogback roads and tree stumps. It was light in weight in contrast to its power, so that neither sand nor gumbo could conquer it. Its power plant and all of its mechanical contraptions were as simple as two-plus-two, so that any farmer, given time, some baling wire, a handful of bolts, a wrench and a hammer could keep it in repair.

In its first year eleven thousand people bought the new Model T and the company declared a stock dividend of one thousand per cent!

9

MAN WITH A MAD ON

1906
Production 33,200
Registration 105,900
Demountable rims

Mr. Henry Ford could be as soft as sponge rubber or as hard as chromium steel. And when he was hard he was the most hard-nosed, contrary, immovable character in all Christendom.

When a poor man is that way he is called a stubborn old galoot. When a rich man is a stubborn old galoot he is called a rugged individualist, a man of indomitable courage, a Rock of Gibraltar, a son-of-a-bitch. Most of his life Henry Ford was called those things and a lot more by the rest of the automobile industry. And it all started in the summer of 1903 when Mr. Ford applied for a license to manufacture automobiles under the Selden patent.

At this point let us digress for a moment. By 1903 the Electric Vehicle Company's Association of Licensed Automobile Manufacturers was running along very smoothly. No trouble at all. Just one big happy family. Sort of a gentlemen's club with the Electric Vehicle Company making the rules.

There had been a few troublesome episodes but these were now in the past. Alexander Winton, for instance, had put up a short fight against paying royalties to Selden and his Wall Street friends. When he was sued he hired important lawyers and gathered together considerable defense evidence. Then he went into court and filed a demurrer, contending that it required no exercise of the inventive faculty to substitute a gas engine for a steam engine in a self-propelling vehicle.

The court found, however, that Selden's patent described an "ingenious and complicated machine" and that it could not be maintained that "the construction of such a machine required no inventive skill." The demurrer was overruled, with costs, and Winton was told that he must defend the infringement suit.

Winton and his lawyers apparently grew worried. A couple of days before the trial was to start, the suit was settled out of court and Winton accepted a consent decree. But Winton's lawyers made a pretty good deal for him. He got a credit of $50,000 against future royalties and, in turn, gave to the Electric Vehicle Company all the defense material his attorneys had gathered.

The next rift in the solid structure of Electric Vehicle Company's auto trust was started a few years later by the manufacturers in Detroit. R. E. Olds, owing $130,000 in royalties, got together with Henry Joy of Packard and Henry Leland of Cadillac and formed a bloc to fight the size of the pay-off. As a result, the royalty, which had once been a straight five per cent, was reduced to 1.25 per cent, and eventually to .8 per cent.

But long before this, in March of 1903, the leaders of the automobile industry signed the agreement of the Association of Licensed Automobile Manufacturers and thereby banded together to maintain the Selden patent and to prosecute infringers. Thirty-two signed up before the end of the year

MAN WITH A MAD ON   121

and by 1910 there were eighty-six. The original signatories were:

Electric Vehicle Co.	Columbia
Olds Motor Works	Oldsmobile
The Autocar Co.	Autocar
The George N. Pierce Co.	Pierce-Arrow
Packard Motor Car Co.	Packard
Apperson Bros. Automobile Co.	Apperson
Searchmont Automobile Co.	Searchmont
Knox Automobile Co.	Knox Waterless
Locomobile Company of America	Locomobile
The Haynes-Apperson Co.	Haynes
The Peerless Motor Car Co.	Peerless
The Winton Motor Carriage Co.	Winton
U. S. Long Distance Automobile Co.	Long Distance
Waltham Manufacturing Co.	Orient
International Motor Car Co.	International
The J. Stevens Arms and Tool Co.	Stevens-Duryea
H. H. Franklin Mfg. Co.	Franklin
The Commercial Motor Co.	Plymouth
Berg Automobile Co.	Berg
Cadillac Automobile Co.	Cadillac
Northern Manufacturing Co.	Northern
Pope-Robinson Co.	Pope-Robinson
Elmore Mfg. Co.	Elmore
E. R. Thomas Motor Co.	Thomas Flyer
The Kirk Manufacturing Co.	Kirk
Buffalo Gasoline Motor Co.	Buffalo
Pope Motor Car Co.	Pope-Toledo
Sandusky Automobile Co.	Sandusky
Crest Manufacturing Co.	Crestmobile
Studebaker Automobile Co.	Studebaker
The Buick Motor Co.	Buick
The F. B. Stearns Company	Stearns

These were the top makers of automobiles in America. The only important manufacturer who was not a member of the A.L.A.M. was Mr. Thomas Jeffery, who made the Rambler. The association expected to round him up eventually but he was hard to get at, located as he was, in a place called Kenosha. The officers of the Electric Vehicle Company weren't very sure where Kenosha was. But they were biding their time and as soon as Mr. Jeffery came out of the woods they intended to slap a suit on him.

Meanwhile, according to the contract the members of the A.L.A.M. had signed, they were supposed to exchange ideas and patents, to prevent any outside manufacturer from infringing the Selden patent, and to keep fly-by-night stock promoters from giving the automobile industry a bad name.

A former official of one of the member companies of the A.L.A.M. has stated that it was not the intention of the Electric Vehicle Company to create a closed trust; that any legitimate manufacturer was to be allowed to join the A.L.A.M.

However, the *Scientific American,* in 1909, pointed out that one of the most important clauses in the articles of agreement of the A.L.A.M. stated that only firms which were actually engaged in the manufacture of autos on or before the date of its organization were eligible to membership, and, as the industry was hardly in its first swaddling clothes in the early part of 1903, it was apparent that many important companies entering the field later were barred nilly-willy.

A notable example of this was found in the organization of the Selden Motor Car Company in 1907, with George B. Selden as president. In order for the inventor himself to get into the A.L.A.M. the Electric Vehicle Company arranged for him to acquire the license of the Buffalo Gasoline Motor Company, which was about to go out of business. But this, apparently, was a very special kind of deal not available to any Tom, Dick or Harry.

It was shortly after March, 1903, that Henry Ford approached an officer of the A.L.A.M. and inquired about joining their exclusive club. Unfortunately Ford had already been connected with two unsuccessful companies. The big guns around Detroit and Cleveland, such as the Olds Motor Works, Packard, Cadillac, Peerless and Winton, considered Ford an unreliable and tricky operator. Before taking him into the fraternity they suggested that he had better demonstrate that he could build something more than an 80-horsepower racing machine. They doubted whether the Ford Motor Company would ever amount to anything.

Mr. Ford did a slow burn. The more he thought about it the madder he got. He got himself a mad on that was to last for the rest of his life.

Just as the date of Henry's first car has often been wrongly cited as 1893, many historians have mistakenly put the cart before the horse and claimed that the A.L.A.M. first came to Ford and asked him to join and that he and Couzens turned them down.

There is no doubt that late in the summer of 1903 the A.L.A.M. had changed its mind and was anxious to have Ford in their organization, for by that time he was selling cars faster than he could make them. So Ford was invited to become one of the brothers, but it was too late. He had been snubbed when he had come to them with his hat in hand. Now he was a man of indomitable courage, a rugged individualist, a success. He turned them down. They could take their license and go jump in the Detroit River. He'd fight them from hell to breakfast before he'd pay a penny of royalty!

Any doubt as to the fact that Ford was turned down by the A.L.A.M., before he turned them down, was dispelled by the testimony of Edsel Ford in 1938 before a Congressional Committee. Edsel said, under oath:

"My father inquired of one of the officers of the association if it were possible to join this association and become a member as the other motor car companies were. He was told, I understand, he had best go out and manufacture some motor cars and gain a reputation and prove that he wasn't a fly-by-night producer, before he should ask for a membership in this association."

Mr. Ford was a man who never forgave unless it was good business. Later in life he would forgive America for going to war and he would forgive the Jews for being Jewish, because it was good business. But in the fall of 1903 he elected not to forgive the A.L.A.M. nor any of its members because they had suggested a few months before that he was a fly-by-night.

He may have thought that a fight with the A.L.A.M. would be good advertising and sell more Fords. Or it may just have been that he picked a fight simply because he was a hard-nosed, contrary, immovable character. In any case, there was nothing for the Electric Vehicle Company to do but bring him to heel. Late in 1903 they brought suit in the Federal Circuit Court of New York against C. A. Duerr and Company, Ford's New York distributor.

The suit was also directed against the Ford Motor Company, Ford's advertising agents, John Wanamaker, a Ford dealer, the manufacturers of the Mercedes and the Panhard automobiles and their New York dealers. But it was the Ford Motor Company that the Electric Vehicle Company was after. Once the big fish was caught the others would also be in the net.

It takes time to bring an important law suit to trial. The case of Electric Vehicle Company *vs.* C. A. Duerr and Company was continued and continued again. It dragged on for six years while both sides built up supplies of ammunition and deployed for battle.

Meanwhile, a sort of guerrilla warfare was carried on in the newspapers and trade journals. In a full-page advertisement in *The Automobile,* "manufacturers, dealers, importers, agents and users of gasoline automobiles" were warned that the members of the A.L.A.M. were the pioneers in the industry and that they had commercialized the gasoline vehicle by many years of development and at a great cost. "They are the owners of upwards of four hundred United States Patents," stated the ad, "covering many of the most important improvements and details of manufacture. Both the basic Selden patent and all other patents owned as aforesaid will be enforced against all infringers . . . any person selling or using machines made or sold by any unlicensed manufacturers or importers will be liable to prosecution for infringement."

The Ford Motor Company replied in the same issue of the magazine:

"NOTICE to Dealers, Importers and Users of our gasoline automobiles. We will protect you against any prosecution for alleged infringements of patents. Regarding alleged infringement of the Selden patent we beg to quote the well-known Patent Attorneys, Messrs. Parker and Burton: 'The Selden patent is not a broad one, and if it was it is anticipated. It does not cover a practicable machine, no practicable machine can be made from it and never was so far as we can ascertain. It relates to that form of carriage called a FORE CARRIAGE. None of that type has ever been in use, all have been failures. No court in the United States has ever decided in favor of the patent on the merits of the case, all it has ever done was to record a prior agreement between parties.'"

This sounds as though Mr. Couzens were speaking. The lower half of the advertisement was probably Mr. Ford speaking. It reads as follows:

"We are pioneers of the GASOLINE AUTOMOBILE.

Our Mr. Ford made the first Gasoline Automobile in Detroit and the third in the United States. His machine made in 1893 (two years previous to the granting of the Selden patent, Nov. 5, 1895) is still in use. Our Mr. Ford also built the famous '999' Gasoline Automobile, which was driven by Barney Oldfield in New York on July 25th, 1903, a mile in 55 4/5 seconds on a circular track, which is the world's record.

"Mr. Ford, driving his own machine, beat Mr. Winton at Grosse Pointe track in 1901. We have always been winners.

"Write for catalogue."

Ford knew that the public wasn't interested in what Messrs. Parker and Burton, the famous Patent Attorneys, had to say. So he added something a little more exciting: some fiction about his first automobile, the glamorous name of Barney Oldfield and his own race against Mr. Winton, who happened to be a member of the A.L.A.M.

This advertisement, in October, 1903, was probably the first time Ford fabricated the 1893 date in connection with his 1896 automobile. But anything was fair in this war. He meant to make it a fight to the finish and the stakes were too large to worry about a white lie or two. He intended to gain public sympathy by making the suit against him look like a rank injustice.

Ford was something of a genius when it came to garnering favorable publicity and in this fight with the A.L.A.M. he made his competitors suffer. In a short time the public thought of the A.L.A.M. as a gang of pirates who were trying to put honest Henry Ford out of business. There stood Henry, his back to the wall, fighting for his very life—but also for humanity, for all those people who wanted to buy Ford cars. Even though he was outnumbered 34 to 1 Henry would stand up and battle that wicked old giant, the automobile trust, to the bitter end. It was David Ford against A.L.A.M. Goliath.

At the same time, the Association displayed a remarkable lack of judgment in its public relations. It tried to bully people into not buying Ford cars. Its advertisements said, "DON'T BUY A LAW SUIT WITH YOUR AUTOMOBILE," then went on to warn prospective purchasers that under the law, the buyer of an unlicensed automobile could be prosecuted.

Americans don't like to be bullied. They scorned the A.L.A.M. warnings and went right on buying Fords. Possibly a few people bought Ford cars just to show the trust that nobody could dictate to them.

So the A.L.A.M. decided to make an example of somebody. Slap a suit on some private individual for driving an unlicensed car. But that was ticklish business; it might be hard to get a jury to bring in a verdict against an ordinary taxpayer. The problem was solved finally by bringing suit against a fellow named Charles T. Barney, who had paid $7,000 for an unlicensed Daimler Mercedes car.

They knew Ford wouldn't care what happened to the buyer of a Mercedes, and surely the public wouldn't feel sorry for a millionaire who had bought an expensive foreign car.

Barney's lawyer asked for a stay to restrain prosecution of the suit until the Ford-Selden case was settled. But the judge denied the motion.

The way was then wide open for the A.L.A.M. to make an example of the buyer of this unlicensed automobile—to prosecute and collect damages from Mr. Barncy. The newspapers carried the story and everybody agreed that it was an open-and-shut case.

What happened? Ford announced that henceforth he would issue a bond with every Ford car sold, if the buyer wished it, guaranteeing him against loss. The bonding company, worth six million dollars, and the Ford Motor Company, worth another six million dollars, stood behind every Ford and every honest American who bought one.

Only fifty buyers of Ford cars ever asked for a bond. The public as much as announced that they were with Henry, win or lose. He didn't have to supply any bonds. They liked Fords and they were going to buy Fords and to hell with the law!

So the A.L.A.M. allowed the case against Mr. Barney and his Mercedes to go unprosecuted in the federal courts.

Meanwhile, warned that Ford would try to prove in court that Selden's "paper patent" could not be built into a workable automobile, the Association decided to build a Selden automobile. In all these years there had never been anything more concrete to Selden's idea than some drawings in a patent application. But now, at last, Selden's car was to come to life, some twenty-one years after being conceived.

Mr. Henry Cave, of the Electric Vehicle Company, was given the task of building a workable machine from George B. Selden's patent drawings. His instructions were to follow the drawings as closely as possible but to produce something that would run.

A patent drawing is crude, at best, usually developed from an early model. But there had never been even a mock-up model for Selden's drawings. Except for the early engine he had made, Selden's drawings came entirely from his imagination. And they were so far behind the automotive art of 1903 as to seem ludicrous, especially the Brayton two-cycle engine.

But Mr. Cave was an able engineer and a man of inexhaustible patience and resourcefulness. After a good many months and the expenditure of thousands of dollars, he built a machine that not only ran but looked so much like Selden's patent drawings that anyone who did not know might have thought Mr. Selden had been hiding this gas buggy all these years in his cellar. As the crowning touch, the Electric

Vehicle Company's paint shop inscribed the date "1877" on the side of the contraption.

It took considerable ingenuity to start the engine, and then the machine would move no faster than a man could walk, but it did move; it was an automobile and had been made from Selden's drawings dated 1877.

Mr. Ford, meanwhile, produced any number of ancient vehicles that ran by steam and electricity, also stationary gas engines that had been operating for years, clutches, transmissions, differentials and experts. They had experts by the dozen who were ready to state that there was nothing new about Selden's automobile.

Finally the battle of words began. The result was some thirty-six volumes of testimony and depositions. There were so many volumes of evidence that Federal Judge Charles M. Hough, in his final decision, entered a plaintive plea asking Congress or the Supreme Court or somebody to stop this nonsensical gathering of words by the millions, lest the country's system of jurisprudence collapse from sheer verbosity.

Judge Hough then went on to say that Selden had contributed little to motor car advancement in the United States and nothing at all abroad. All American cars, in the judge's opinion, had been modeled on French ideas, using engines descended from Otto through Daimler, and not from Brayton through Selden or any other American.

"In short," said Judge Hough, "this American patent represents to me a great idea conceived in 1879, which lay absolutely fallow until 1895, was until then concealed in a [Patent Office] file wrapper and is now demanding tribute from later independent inventors who more promptly and far more successfully reduced their ideas to practice."

There was, however, a "but" in the judge's opinion, and it was a very large BUT. Regardless of all the things Selden had failed to do, and regardless of the blamelessness of other inventors in their infringements, the law was with Selden.

The Patent Office had granted him a patent which was good for seventeen years, and in the judge's eyes it was a valid patent.

For instance, in the third claim of his original application Selden had described his new device thus: "The combination in a road locomotive provided with suitable running gear and steering mechanism, of a gas engine, traction wheels, and an intermediate clutch or disengaging device . . ."

This was Mr. Selden's claim in 1879. "And in that year," inquired Judge Hough, "just how stood the art—what was known of the horseless carriage industry, either at home or abroad?"

The answer, His Honor pointed out, was that in 1879 there was no such industry, the art existed only in talk and hope; no vehicle even faintly fulfilling the requirements as described by Mr. Selden had ever been built and there was no competent and persuasive evidence that any gas engine experiment had ever moved one hundred feet, or revealed an organization of mechanical parts warranting the expectation that it would ever do so.

In other words, Mr. Selden had been first to conceive a practical gasoline automobile, regardless of the fact that he had only described it in a patent application and drawn pictures of it and had never built it. His patent was valid and Mr. Ford was infringing it!

The cries of joy in the A.L.A.M. camp were long and loud. But as far as Henry Ford was concerned the fight had just started. He had a mad on that was good for another twenty or thirty years. He would carry the fight to the United States Supreme Court, if he had to. Besides it was good advertising. So the war continued in the newspapers and his lawyers prepared an appeal.

As for the public, were they frightened by Judge Hough's decision? Not by a tonneau full. The demand for Model T's doubled. In the year 1910 the Ford Motor Company grossed something like $20,000,000.

By this time the Ford-Selden fight had become something of a *cause célèbre*. And ironically enough Selden was thought of as a bloated millionaire milking the public, while Ford was the underdog suffering at the hands of big business. Actually Selden had received about a million and a half in royalties, while Ford was worth at least six million and the Ford Motor Company had become by far the biggest big business in Detroit.

But no patent fight had ever been so completely aired in the newspapers and argued about by the man in the street. Few of them understood the legal battle, but every potential automobile buyer in the country was sure that he would save a lot of money if Ford won the case.

It is not difficult to believe that even the judges of the Appellate Court might have been unconsciously swayed by their desire to render a decision for the public and against the so-called Automobile Trust. For at that time, anything vaguely resembling a trust was in bad repute.

Was the Selden patent a detriment to the development of the automobile industry? Was the A.L.A.M. an octopus strangling the newcomer and oppressing the little man? Was it to the best interests of the public to render ineffective this "paper patent" held by a man who had never built an automobile and controlled by a group of Wall Street millionaires? Thoughts of this sort must have gone through the minds of the judges as they considered Ford's appeal from the lower court's decision. In any case, the final decision of the Appellate Court was a most interesting one.

In January, 1911, almost eight years after suit had first been filed, the court ruled that Selden's patent was valid, but that his combination of engine, running gear, clutch, etc., contained the wrong type of engine and that it therefore did not cover the modern automobile. Consequently

Henry Ford was not infringing the Selden patent and the lower court was reversed.

Public interest notwithstanding, it seems quite obvious today that the learned judges of the Appellate Court did some very involved reasoning to arrive at their decision. Either that or they were unfamiliar with things mechanical. What the court said, in effect, was that a mule pulling a wagon has no relation whatever to a horse pulling a wagon. For that is a parallel example of the difference between a vehicle propelled by a Brayton gas engine and a vehicle propelled by an Otto gas engine. If Selden had been the first, what did it matter what kind of a gas engine he used? The combination of gas engine, running gear, clutch, etc., was what Selden had been granted a patent on and there was no proof that anyone preceded him in his concept.

Besides that, even though Selden's drawings indicated that he was concerned only with the Brayton type engine, his patent application stated: "Any form of liquid hydro-carbon engine of the compression type may be employed in my improved road locomotive." This certainly covers the Otto engine as well as the Brayton.

However, the reversal of opinion finished the A.L.A.M. for it relieved all the members from paying any more royalties. The fight might have gone on, but the patent had less than two years to run and there was very little chance of getting the United States Supreme Court to review the case.

The much-abused Selden patent was actually a great boon to the automobile industry. It brought the manufacturers together for several years in a strong trade association. It also brought together the automotive engineers in what was called the Mechanical Branch of the A.L.A.M. They set up standards for parts, materials and manufacturing practice that were invaluable to the growth of the industry. This cooperation between executive forces as well as engineers proved so mutually satisfactory that after the A.L.A.M. was dissolved the old members formed the National Automobile Chamber of Commerce—later to be called the Automobile Manufacturers Association—while the Mechanical Branch of the A.L.A.M. became the present Society of Automotive Engineers.

The cross-licensing agreement that had been set up by the A.L.A.M. was thus continued for a number of years and helped advance the industry during its formative period. Since the Selden decision, infringement suits within the industry are practically unheard of. But Henry Ford never joined the ranks of the old members of the A.L.A.M. When Mr. Ford got a mad on it was a dandy.

It has often been stated that removal of royalty restrictions gave a terrific boost to the automobile business. This is complete nonsense. The royalty paid on the Selden patent in its later years was very moderate. If the Appellate Court had upheld the lower court a Ford would have cost about $695 instead of $690.

Ford, the white knight, fighting the good fight for the man in the street, was the only one who gained much by beating the Selden patent. Mr. Ford became richer by two million dollars.

10

TURN RIGHT AT BLACKSMITH SHOP

1907
Production 43,000
Registration 140,300
The magnetic speedometer

COLONEL ALBERT A. POPE, whose Pope Manufacturing Company once employed more than three thousand men in the manufacture of bicycles, was a man with a magnificent growth of whiskers and a roving eye in search of a passing dollar. He also had the foresight to get into the automobile game at an early date and his numerous companies at one time made the most and the best automobiles in America. The Columbia, the Pope-Hartford, the Pope-Toledo, the Pope-Tribune, the Pope-Robinson and the Pope-Waverly were manufactured in Pope plants in Massachusetts, Connecticut, Maryland, Indiana and Ohio.

As early as 1880 Colonel Pope realized that the new sport of cycling and the success of his new bicycle factory depended on good roads, so he became the most ardent advocate of the well-paved street and the hard-surfaced highway in America.

He was available as a speaker for most any occasion, provided he could talk about America's need for good roads. He wrote articles for such popular magazines as *Munsey's*;

his handsome features and words of wisdom appeared in such high-class journals as *Harper's* and *World's Work;* he headed various committees bent on improving America's mud roads; and he spent large sums promoting bicycle and touring clubs.

In 1880, as part of his uphill campaign, he published *The American Bicycler,* a cycling book written by the editor of *The Bicycling World, A Journal of Bicycling, Archery, and Other Polite Athletics.* On the last page of the book Colonel Pope modestly advertised, "Having had two years' experience in the manufacture of bicycles, and the benefit of all the best English machines to guide us, we now claim to make the best finished and most durable bicycle ever put upon the market in any country."

Twenty years later Colonel Pope would be one of the leaders of American industry and a multi-millionaire.

The American Bicycler, printed in 1880, is pertinent to the development of the automobile only because its pages give the first hint of our country's hectic, mobile future—of the time when, on a Sunday afternoon, along New York's Bronx River Parkway, or Cook County's Skokie Road, or Los Angeles' Ventura Boulevard, it would seem that most of America was trying to get some place else, as fast as possible, while sitting down.

The title page of *The American Bicycler* described the little book as a "manual for the observer, the learner, and the expert." It gave the history of cycling, described all the bicycles then available, instructed the beginner in the mysteries of mounting and dismounting, explained the laws and courtesies of the road and listed many useful cycling facts. But most important of all were the eighty-five touring routes described in the book.

Before the advent of the bicycle nobody went touring just for the pleasure of taking a ride. You might take a Sunday drive in a buggy with your best girl, but that was something inspired by the biological urge rather than lust for the open road.

With the coming of the bicycle, however, things changed, for a cyclist on a strange highway immediately envisioned adventure ahead. Doubtless there were a few lewd fellows who went pumping along a country lane seeking the ubiquitous farmer's daughter, but the cyclists whom *The American Bicycler* had in mind were gentlemen of the highest order, interested only in a tussle with a stiff hill or the elements and not stray females.

There was no doubt that a bicycle was a remarkable vehicle of pleasure; grandfather will tell you that it was fun just to get on and ride. It gave him a feeling of power and exhilaration that he could get in no other way. And when safeties and tandems appeared it became an instrument of social importance. For it was then, for the first time, that America began dashing off in all directions at once, while sitting down.

And in New England, at least, one was likely to be guided in his dash by *The American Bicycler*. Its most popular Sunday trip probably was Route 1—Boston to Milton and Quincy—which was as follows:

"From the Common, by Boylston and Dartmouth Streets, mostly macadam, and Columbus Avenue, asphalt (1.25 m.), Chester Park (to the left), macadam (.6 m.), Albany Street, &c. (cobble-stone for short distance), Sweet Street, macadam (1.2 m.), then Boston and Columbia Streets (to right and on to Washington Street), macadam and gravel (2.75 m.), Washington Street (to left), down Codman Hill with care, good gravel roads (2 m.), to Milton Lower Mills; thence across the Neponset and up Milton Hill (pretty stiff, and rideable only by the experienced) and along Milton Avenue, good gravel roads (2.75 m.), to East Milton, and thence by main road, smooth gravel (2.25 m.), to Quincy ("Robertson House"); making in all a run of 11.8 miles, over varied and very good roads, and through fine scenery. The views from Mount Bowdoin and Milton Hills are charming."

Thanks to the bicycle, by the time the touring car was introduced to America we were already a nation of tourists. This was evident in the touring booklets issued by the League of American Wheelmen, which described such long-distance jaunts as Philadelphia-to-Washington and Hartford-to-New York City. Only the hardiest of souls actually took such bike trips, but many dreamed of taking them and once they owned a touring car they grabbed their Wheelmen's touring guide and headed for the open road and the adventure that was waiting over the distant horizon.

Colonel Pope's efforts to improve the country's roads had borne little fruit except in the environs of Boston, New York and other large cities. Despite that fact the intrepid purchasers of Columbias, Pope-Hartfords, Pope-Toledos and other cars were not in the least deterred. They formed automobile clubs along the lines of their bicycle clubs and made mass treks in the form of picnics and Sunday outings. On these club tours a repair car often followed in the wake of the motorists just in case somebody needed special mechanical aid. In the course of a fifty-mile trip it was seldom that any car went unscathed and sometimes the repair car itself would need assistance.

But your true enthusiast considered mudholes, sand, broken springs and blowouts part of the game. These touring hazards only made the adventure more of a lark.

Many motorists of those days experienced as much trouble with the language of motoring as with its discomforts. Some time before 1900 the august French Academy had coined the word "automobile." Although the editor of *The Horseless Age* felt that "motor carriage" was more elegant, most magazine editors accepted "automobile" without a struggle. Other French words also found favor with the journalists of the day. For a time anyone at the wheel of a car was a "chauffeur." A woman driver was a "chauffeuse." A runabout was often called a "voiturette." But the word "garage" did not at once find favor. "Automobile stable" was preferred for quite some time. Public garages, which began to appear as early as 1902, were "automobile stations."

Motor club bulletins and minutes spoke gravely of automobilism and automobiling. It was possible in those early days, at least in the public prints, to automobilize down Fifth Avenue.

But after the neophite automobilist had enjoyed automobilism, for a month of two, with the other automobiliers of his club, he usually struck out on his own. The Sunday drive with mother and the children became almost routine in many homes.

Females of the early twentieth century still possessed a large measure of Victorian frailty. In the open cars of that period, with no windshields and with springs of doubtful flexibility, thirty-five miles, round trip, was about all that mother—and sister, too, for that matter—could endure. Women almost invariably returned from a Sunday afternoon drive devoid of hairpins and dignity. No doctor in his right mind would allow an expectant mother to set foot in a touring car. It was considered foolhardy for the average female, even in the best of health, to take a trip of more than sixty miles. For she was likely to be left in a state of exhaustion and disrepair that would surely require professional care. And the same for the car, of course.

Consequently, a Sunday drive in the early 1900's was seldom long, though often of considerable duration. If you lived in New York you might drive to Yonkers to visit Aunt Minnie, or to Cousin Hal's at Rockville Center. But even drives of this distance were not to be taken lightly. In preparation father was likely to spend Saturday afternoon repairing tubes and casings, tuning up the engine and polishing the car's eighteen-coat, baked-enamel finish.

Later, after mother became somewhat inured to the

hardships of automobilism, father might, at vacation-time, attempt an overnight trip as a means of reaching some destination in the Berkshires.

On both Sunday and overnight drives, motoring dress was essential. Father wore a linen duster, a linen cap and goggles. Mother wore a duster, goggles and a utilitarian hat tied in place with a veil.

Some women refused, on esthetic grounds, to wear goggles. When entering a dust cloud these fastidious females simply shut their eyes tight and held a perfumed handkerchief to their nostrils.

Any motoring trip usually necessitated the packing of a luncheon. Wicker touring hampers, which strapped to the side of the touring tonneau, could be purchased as additional equipment for any car. Also buffet chests with ice compartments and a set of dishes and flatwear for six, eight or a dozen.

Of course, one never started on a trip of any kind without tow ropes, tire-patching outfits, a kit of tools that was practically a traveling machine shop, and reserve cans of gas and oil.

Among the younger or devil-may-care set, in those days, were automobilists who were practically professionals at the game of touring. It was in their blood, like some tropical fever; they toured America with the intensity of big game hunters off on a safari in darkest Africa. One of these indomitable souls, writing in the *Scientific American,* in 1902, gave a vague idea of the perils of touring, in an article entitled, "A Practical Automobile Touring Outfit." The tourist-author wrote:

"Quite naturally touring has become a favorite pastime with those who patronize automobiling not as a fad, but as a healthful, pleasurable sport—a class of automobilists, by the way, that is constantly increasing, not only abroad but also in this country. In spite of the wretched conditions of

American roads, extended touring in the United States is not only possible but probably more fascinating because of the additional obstacles that are continually presenting themselves to be overcome. . . .

"There is really no such thing on the market as a practical automobile touring outfit. Nobody makes it; nobody sells it, and yet there is an unprecedented demand for it by experienced auto-tourists. . . . Everyone is familiar with the black leather clothing worn by most chauffeurs. For all-around use this is the proper and most practical clothing, and for long distance trips it is the only kind which has been found to be convenient and satisfactory.

"Such leather clothing is usually made from calfskin, but the very best grade obtainable is invariably taken from the hide of the kangaroo—the skin being more pliable, and on account of its rather oily substance it will shed rain a good deal easier than calfskin. The latest style leather clothing is lined, not with corduroy, but with a strong, thick flannel, especially manufactured for this use.

"The proper automobile cap, with an extra long face-mask and goggles combined, and a pair of earmits, ought to keep any head comfortable during fast going on cold days. The hands are best protected by fleecelined buckskin gauntlets with cuffs wide enough to take the sleeve and hold it in.

"As a rule the novice chauffeur will do a great deal of thinking to make his initial tour a success, and generally he returns to his starting place—unless the railroad carries him—finding that he has been doing his most sagacious thinking on the wrong side of the problem. He thought of rain storms and took a machintosh with him; he thought of a scorching sun and provided himself with a monster Panama hat; he thought of cold feet, and added a footbag of furs to his inventory. Now as a matter of fact, a mackintosh is a most irritating kind of garment when automobiling in a rainstorm. It has a tendency to fly up over the knees, interfere with the quick handling of levers, and is invariably stepped on or torn, on leaving the vehicle hurriedly.

"In place of the mackintosh, which only affords partial protection, get a seaman's suit of oilskin clothes, which is sure to protect you completely under the most adverse weather and road conditions, while it is out of the way at all times.

"Instead of the fur bags or similar contrivances for keeping the feet warm during the cold season, it is advisable to dress the feet so comfortably that they will be able to retain their natural heat even in frosty weather. The men employed in the ice-harvesting business on the Great Lakes have solved this problem in a very thorough manner. Adopt their footwear and you need never bother with fur bags, soapstones and such encumbrances.

"Briefly described, this footwear consists of a coarse, heavy-soled rubber, laced boot, into which is slid a sort of thick felt stocking reaching to the knee. The leg is thrust into the felt stocking. This arrangement affords a rubber covering to fight off dampness, a felt shell to fight off the cold, and a trouser-leg and a pair of woolen stockings to retain the heat of the limb. Heavy woolen or flannel underwear under a sporting suit and a heavyweight sweater ought to give comfort, especially when a corduroy-lined leather coat is the outer garment.

"During the summer season, instead of the Panama, the Japanese palm-leaf sun-hat will be found more practicable, since it will not fly off during the swiftest pace. The regulation auto cap, of extra light stock, would be the ideal headgear, if such caps could be had with the sweatband constructed in the same manner as that of the English army sun helmet—the hatters have yet to dream of this. A khaki suit with trousers cut on the cavalry order, so as to permit of canvas gaiters or leather leggings on the legs, would be one of the most practical things for summer wear.

"Next in importance to practical clothing comes such luggage as the chauffeur may care to take along, either for his personal comfort or for camping by the roadside. The best of sportsmen in Europe are already beginning to patronize the 'camping-out' idea.

"To fit out an automobile for a long continuous tour, camping by the roadside, is equivalent to making the machine your nomadic home for the time being. There is nothing impracticable about it, for when a soldier is able to carry on his back his entire camp outfit in addition to his weapons, the smallest automobile on the market ought to carry everything needed to make its passengers comfortable in camp.

"Breakables should be avoided entirely. Things that may be duplicated in any country store should not be given space unless 'unknown regions' are to be invaded. Combustibles are to be discountenanced. A canvas tent on the military order with a folding center pole will house two people in good shape. . . .

"Before going to bed, be sure to lock the manipulating devices on your automobile so that no one may appropriate the carriage while you sleep. You might also place a good six-shooter under your pillow. You will sleep just as well, and it might come in handy.

"When you wake up in the morning, your breakfast is, or ought to be, in the basket you are carrying with you strapped to the stern body of the vehicle. A better auto basket than any of those retailing from fifty to two hundred dollars can easily be improvised for a small amount of money. A wicker basket of the size of a small steamer trunk will do. Have a water and dust-tight cover of rubber made to fit snugly with leather mounting on the corners. Arrange straps on the inside of the lid to hold several plates, forks, knives, cups, saucers, etc., together with the necessary cooking utensils for making meals readily and conveniently. All such utensils should be of aluminum.

"A moderate supply of spices and groceries may be packed in a wooden box so as not to be mixed up with the other contents. If the tour is through a hunting or fishing region, the chauffeurs ought to be able to supply their own 'table' by some skill with the rod and the gun. In fact, this would give a genuine zest to the entire undertaking, and afford the intrepid sportsman a solid feeling of having gone to the bottom of the matter.

"If the tour is through populated country districts, most of the camping is likely to be done in village inns, while the cooking, in such a case, would be intrusted to the innkeeper's 'chef.' To make an automobile camping trip a success you must choose an out-of-the-way route that will compel you to camp out and 'do' for yourself.

"Something that is almost always invariably overlooked in making up an outfit is a supply of drugs, medicines and plasters. Accidents are liable to happen in a hundred unthought-of ways and sometimes minor bruises and scars from slipping or falling become quite annoying from not being attended to promptly.

"A canvas folder with pockets for various-size bottles, boxes and rolls, containing drugs and medicines, would in the majority of cases be found to be of practical use.

"The personal effects of two passengers could easily be packed in two portmanteaus, as all that is needed, besides the clothes they are continually wearing, is changes of underwear and stockings, handkerchiefs, extra pair of shoes, and such little extra items as the taste of the chauffeur may fancy and the season of the year may require. The point should be to take along as little as possible and yet be comfortably fitted out."

Motorists, in those days, who confined their driving only to city streets had trouble enough with bicycle policemen who arrested them for venturing into Central Park or charged them with reckless driving if they exceeded twelve miles an hour. But the touring motorist was beset by all manner of contradictory and cockeyed regulations imposed by different counties and states, and enforced by antagonistic constables and magistrates.

In Missouri, to name the worst offender against the tourists' pursuit of happiness, each county charged a two dollar fee for operating a motor car within its boundaries, and St. Louis charged ten dollars. The red tape and the expense of traversing Missouri in an automobile made the state anathema to tourists, which was probably what its farmer legislators wanted.

Speed limits in most states were from eight to fifteen miles per hour and speed traps were numerous. Michigan was considered the finest touring state in the country because it recognized out-of-state licenses and permitted a speed of twenty-five miles per hour.

Roads were abominable everywhere except in proximity to large cities and in a few sections of New England. And the rural population preferred to keep them that way so that automobiles would stay away and not frighten their horses and livestock.

It was these conditions that drove nine of the largest automobile clubs, in 1902, to form the American Automobile Association, an organization dedicated to the cause of better motoring. The A.A.A. campaigned vigorously against unjust automobile legislation, and the petty racketeers who operated small-town speed traps. It promoted good roads and governed the most important races, hill-climbing events and endurance contests of early days.

But most important of all, it worked to make automobile touring more pleasant, by establishing official garages, hotels and inns where tourists could spend a comfortable night, and official routes between most every city and village in North America.

The approved routes of the A.A.A. were described in six thick volumes, known as *The Official Automobile Blue Books*. They consisted of Vol. 1, *New York State and Canada;* Vol. 2, *New England and Eastern Canada;* Vol. 3,

Pennsylvania, New Jersey and the South; Vol. 4, *The Middle West;* Vol. 5, *Mississippi River to Pacific Coast;* Vol. 6, *The Pacific Coast.* (Price, $2.50 each.)

These books were an elaborate version of the brief cycling routes first seen in Colonel Pope's *The American Bicycler.* Tourists of all kinds found them indispensable. Unless you wished to travel by the stars any trip into unknown country called for assistance from the A.A.A. official *Blue Books.* One of them was sure to contain maps as well as a detailed description of the proper route you should follow to reach your destination. With *The Blue Book* to guide you it was virtually impossible to get lost. Nevertheless you usually did.

Some families would get out their *Blue Book* a week or two in advance of any extensive tour and study its directions with pleasant anticipation as they formerly had studied the pamphlets advertising railroad excursion tours. If there was a choice of routes, each one would be examined for a maximum of macadam as well as for a plentiful supply of official garages and hotels. And, of course, there was always a last-minute check with the Auto Club to learn of any washed-out bridges or hazardous detours that might be encountered.

When finally ready to go, the person seated next to the driver was automatically custodian of *The Blue Book.* This usually turned out to be the driver's spouse and hers was always a nerve-racking job. She had to keep one eye on the book, one eye peeled for the landmarks it described, and a third eye on the mileage as indicated by the odometer. Somewhere en route she was sure to relax for a moment to enjoy the scenery. That was always the very moment when she should not have; for, during that brief period, a red schoolhouse on the left or a white church on the right would flash by unnoticed and the family would soon be lost in a rural wilderness. When that happened it often took sheer genius, a large bump of direction and several hours to get back on the proper route.

For the benefit of those who have never taken a trip with the aid of *The Blue Book*, let us go for a little spin from Chicago to Ottawa, Illinois. We will take Route 22, *via Aurora on good gravel all the way.*

   0.0 CHICAGO, Michigan & Jackson Blvds. Go west on Jackson Blvd. to entrance of
   4.7 GARFIELD PARK; enter park and bear right across trolley at Madison St.
   5.3 Turn sharp left past Robt. Burns' Monument and refectory, going almost straight out of park onto Washington Blvd.
   7.9 AUSTIN AVE., low concrete chapel on far right; turn left 1 block and then right on Madison St., picking up trolley.
10.0 DESPLAINES AVE.; turn left around saloon with branch trolley, crossing RR. and 3d rail.

(This was the most hazardous moment on route 22. In the space of a few yards the trolley, the RR., the 3d rail and the saloon all ganged up on the unsuspecting tourist. He had to have his wits about him to get safely past this intersection.)

10.3 FOREST PARK. Straight ahead between numerous cemeteries.
15.0 End of the road; jog left and immediately right.
17.4 End of road; turn left with poles, following good stone on winding road. Curve right and left around old mill 19.3. Jog left and right through 4-corners at Fullersburg 19.6.
20.0 Right-hand road, RR. just ahead; turn right.
20.6 HINSDALE, station on left.
     Hinsdale Auto Co., Chicago Ave. & Washington St. Go ahead following poles across RR. 24.2; through Downers Grove 24.9. CAUTION for sharp upgrade

TURN RIGHT AT BLACKSMITH SHOP 147

28.8, continuing ahead with heavy poles. CAUTION for downgrade into

32.1 NAPERVILLE, iron water trough on left. Turn left across iron bridge.

32.2 Right-hand road just after crossing bridge; turn right, curving left and right around pond.

32.6 Fork; bear right, jog left and right, following good macadam to center of

40.8 AURORA

(At this point things get all bawled up. The trouble is— no macadam. *The Blue Book* fails to state that although the county road commissioners had promised that there would be good macadam by the time the book was printed, something went wrong and they decided to put the macadam off for another year or two. So, in searching for the good macadam, you even miss AURORA! But of course there is always a way to get back on the road to a big city. You just follow the poles. So you follow the poles for an hour or two and finally you never find AURORA 40.7 but you do get back on the road because you come to DANWAY 74.3.)

75.6 Fork, slate-colored barn on left; bear right with poles.
83.0 Just after crossing canal, turn right at blacksmith shop.
85.0 OTTAWA, Madison & LaSalle Sts.
New Clifton Hotel, Madison & Columbus Sts.
Ottawa Garage, Opposite Hotel.
For city map, see page 144. For diverging routes, see index map, page 144.

Nothing to it. Only four hours out of Chicago and there you were in Ottawa, thanks to *The Blue Book*.

11

DON'T USE A LIGHTED MATCH!

1908
Production *63,500*
Registration *194,400*
Ignition locks

IN 1902 A musical comedy opened on Broadway entitled *Beauty and the Beast*. It was an entertainment of no great importance but it holds a significant place in the history of the drama because it was the first time in America that an automobile had ever been seen on the stage. It was used as a means of escape by a comedy crook, but the car broke down at the psychological moment, creating considerable suspense and a scene described as hilarious.

That same season two cars appeared in a society drama. The title of the play and the stars are forgotten, but the plot revolved around a gasoline car that broke down on a country lane, leaving the heroine stranded; she was rescued however, by the hero, driving a jaunty Columbia electric.

One New York critic suggested that the theater could use a good melodrama climaxed by a thundering automobile race, something like the chariot race in *Ben Hur*. He offered the idea gratis to any producer who wanted it. The records fail to reveal whether or not his suggestion was acted on, but after 1902 the automobile became an important prop, plot device and the subject of a multitude of jokes and songs for the vaudeville stage. The motor car, as a theatrical device, reached a pinnacle of prominence in 1921 with the production of a comedy-drama entitled *Six Cylinder Love*. This was the story of a nice young couple who got in with a fast, motoring crowd; in their efforts to keep up with this high-living automobile set they mortgaged their home and bought a six-cylinder car. Things were in an awful mess for a while but finally got straightened out.

Along about 1903, Virginia Earle, starring in *The Belle of Bohemia* sang one of the first motoring songs, "My Mobile Gal." My Mobile gal drove a Mobile steam car, of course, and was quite a dashing figure sitting on her little runabout. Later the terrific popularity of the Oldsmobile brought on Gus Edwards' smash hit, "In My Merry Oldsmobile." The song gave the car a million dollars' worth of advertising and every automobile company hoped for a similar boost but never quite got it, even though there were a score of songs written, such as, "Ray and His Little Chevrolet" and "The Little Ford Rambled Right Along."

But an automobile song almost as popular as "In My Merry Oldsmobile" was "He'd Have to Get Under—Get Out and Get Under," sung by the popular vaudevillian Bobby North. The song had a laugh appeal for everyone. The people who didn't have automobiles liked to laugh at those who did; on the other hand, a motor-car owner in the early 1900's could chuckle complacently at motoring discomforts, like a millionaire laughing at an income-tax joke. For those were the days of cash-on-the-barrelhead, and any owner was considered more or less a capitalist.

But regardless of financial standing, any automobilist who did not employ a chauffeur spent a large part of his motoring hours getting out and getting under. That was part of automobile ownership and you had to accept it.

Almost as soon as you bought a car you discovered that you needed an instruction book which would tell you how to repair your new machine. There were many experts who authored monographs for the neophyte motorist. Among these, an outstanding authority was L. Elliott Brookes. His manual *The Automobile Handbook* * gave complete instructions covering everything from the radiator to the tail light. It went through numerous editions and was revised every two years to keep up with new wrinkles.

Mr. Brookes was nothing if not thorough. He started off with instructions on how to drive your new car. For instance:

"GEAR-CHANGING. In changing gears the autoist should endeavor to have the motor and car moving at nearly corresponding rates of speed before the clutch is engaged. With the planetary type of gear any mistake in estimating the rates of the car and motor is of little consequence, but with the sliding type severe strains and shocks have to be taken up by the clutch, and are usually transmitted in part to the gear if the clutch is not slipped.

"In changing from a lower to a higher gear it will be necessary to speed up the motor by means of the throttle in order to store up enough energy in the flywheel to furnish the work needed to accelerate the car to its new speed. As the speed of the car increases the higher gear should be engaged."

As Mr. Brookes points out, though his language is obscure, it was no trick to change gears with the planetary type; that was one reason Henry Ford kept them on his car until 1927. But sliding gears were for experts. Changing from first to intermediate to high was not, as it is today, a mere twist of the wrist. There was no patented synchro-mesh device beneath your feet to synchronize the gears so that they would

---

* Published by Frederick J. Drake & Co. Quotations are by permission of the publishers.

mesh together as silently as a cat treading on velvet. No indeed! It sometimes took months to learn how to shift gears without making a noise like a pneumatic drill. Some drivers *never* learned. And you couldn't switch from one car to another without learning all over again. For each car had its own peculiarities which only its master understood.

Your expert gearshifter, changing from one gear to another, depressed the clutch pedal and waited just the right fraction of a second before he eased the gearshift lever into the proper slot. Then he tried it tentatively, cautiously, his sensitive fingertips meshing the gears together like some Jimmy Valentine manipulating the tumblers of a safe; finally, triumphantly, he jerked the lever home.

Ah yes, gearshifting was an art!

After Mr. Brookes had discussed the problem of getting from low speed into high he took up some of the finer points of gearshifting:

"REVERSE—BACKING UP. Among other things connected with driving which is apt to be neglected, is reversing, or driving a car backwards. Steering a car when running backwards is diametrically opposite to that when running forward. A turn of the wheel to the left steers the car in the opposite direction to the right, and vice versa. The autoist should remember that the reverse gear of a sliding change-gear should never be engaged until the car has been brought to a full stop."

Mr. Brookes gives this last instruction because gears were not as tough in those days as they are now and were easily stripped. He goes on to discuss the car's brakes:

"BRAKES, PROPER USE OF. Next to the motive power in importance come the brakes. There are a number of points regarding brakes that every autoist should know and remember. First and most important is the fact that brakes vary in effectiveness and therefore should be tested frequently with the car in motion, the pedal or hand lever being applied until the car slows or stops. The distance covered in making this test should be noted, and a greater distance allowed in making stops on the road."

The spark lever does not exist on today's cars, but before the advent of the self-starter, in 1912, it was imperative for the driver to know how to adjust the spark. Mr. Brookes tries to impress this on the beginner:

"SPARK—REGULATION OF. Upon the proper use of the sparking-device depends the economy of the motor, and in many cases the safety of the driver. When starting, the spark should be retarded in the case of battery ignition, to prevent backfiring, and slightly advanced to a certain point, depending on the motor and magneto, in the case of magneto ignition.

"In ordinary running, a position of the spark lever can be found which will give fair average results through a considerable range of speed without changing its position, and this position varies with each motor, and can be found by experience. When a high rate of speed is desired, the throttle is opened and the spark advanced gradually.

"If a grade is to be negotiated it should be 'rushed' if possible, the throttle being opened full and the spark well advanced until the motor begins to slow down and 'knock,' when the spark should be retarded to correct this.

"Always retard the ignition before starting the motor, and take great care that the ignition is retarded and not by mistake advanced. . . .

"If, in starting the motor, the ignition-device is set to operate before the piston reaches the end of its stroke, backfiring will occur, resulting in reversal of the operation of the motor and possible injury to the operator. (See Commutators, Ignition. p. 245)"

Mr. Brookes seemed to be a little over-technical at this point, or perhaps he hesitated to reveal to the beginner what serious perils lay ahead. For the truth of the matter was that an automobile ride, back in those by-gone days, was a pretty grim affair. The risk to life and limb started even before you drove out of the barn. Mr. Brookes really should have given a more explicit warning that the moment you set about cranking your car you were in serious danger.

After you had set the spark lever at the third notch, which you had learned from long experience was neither too advanced nor too far retarded, you went to the front of the car, bent over, put your shoulder to the radiator, grabbed the crank and turned the engine over twice while holding the choke wire. Then you released the choke, gathered together your full strength and spun the crank. As the first explosion came from the engine you dropped the crank and dashed for the wheel, where you advanced the spark a few notches and opened the throttle wide to race the engine until it warmed up.

Of course, if you happened to forget and left the spark advanced when you cranked your car, the engine would backfire, knock you flat and probably break your arm into the bargain. It was a hazardous undertaking. Only the brave and the strong could manage an automobile in the days preceding self-starters.

Before taking a weekend drive, in those good old days, it was wise to follow Mr. Brookes' suggestion and give the car a thorough inspection. There was no turning the car over to a service station with instructions to give it a lube job and tune up the engine. You did it yourself. You had to get under—get out and get under!

For instance, you got underneath and checked the fuel line. It often developed leaks in those days from excessive vibration and abrasion.

Next you examined the brake rods or cables to see that they were not faulty, and you checked the steering connections very, very carefully. It was not at all uncommon to have a steering connection go haywire, which left your car wandering along a country highway without any control on your part. A most disconcerting sensation.

Another pleasant job was to clean out the mud-pan which was under the engine. This was important for two reasons: it reduced the fire hazard and it turned up any parts that might have dropped off the engine.

While you were underneath there you usually lubricated the springs and saw to it that the grease boot on the driveshaft joint was filled with grease.

After that you probably checked the clutch. A clutch was almost always either slipping or what was called "fierce." A slipping clutch was very bad in hilly country. Halfway up a hill you started slipping down again—and backwards, of course.

Most clutches were of the cone type, faced with leather. To improve a slipping clutch you took a coarse file and roughed the glazed surface of the leather. If the clutch facing was too far gone you soaked a piece of belting in neat's-foot oil, overnight, and replaced the old leather.

A "fierce" clutch was often worse than one that slipped. It would sometimes grab so violently as to shear off the bevel driving gears. The best remedy was to soak the entire clutch overnight in castor oil. This was a sure way to cure a "fierce" clutch and, also, to stink up your car.

Of course, you always checked all tires and tubes and prepared for at least one puncture or blowout. If it was a hot day you might have to repair two or three blowouts. So you tested your jack and oiled your pump before you started out.

The last thing you did, before going to bed in preparation for an early start, was to check your tool kit. Brookes was very emphatic in assuring the inexperienced motorist that the fewest tools he could safely get along with on the road were the following:

Monkey wrench, 9 inch
Machinist's screwdriver
Ball-peen hammer, one pound
Combination pliers, 8 inch
Set of double-end, or "S" wrenches
Flat file, mill cut
Three-cornered file
Round file, six inch
Center punch
Prick punch
Drift punch, flat-ended
Offset, or "bent-end" screwdriver
Cold chisel, three-quarter inch
Spark plug wrench
Small wire-cutting pliers
Emery cloth
Cotter pin puller
Wire brush for spark plugs

But of course any old hand at weekend touring had a tool box with a much larger assortment than this. Your supply of automobile tools grew like a pen full of rabbits. You were always buying something recommended by a friend or some special tool that would make some odious job easy instead of difficult. These super-tools were usually elegant, nickel-plated affairs with special left-handed screws and universal joints and hooks and fingers of hardened steel.

About 1910, there was a greater variety of wheel and gear pullers than there were wheels and gears. These were sold by all supply dealers. There was also a standard and very popular tool for removing flywheels. Unfortunately it was not adjustable to all flywheels.

Some of these super-tools were designed to do only one job on one brand of automobile. For instance, Rambler owners needed a special tool to remove the wheels. It was a rather cumbersome device which had no other earthly use.

The Pierce-Arrow automobile also needed a special wheel puller in its tool box; this tool was completely different from the Rambler puller. Oldsmobile had a gear puller which was the most exclusive device in motordom. It removed just one special gear on the Oldsmobile; and, of course, it served no purpose at all for any other car.

The wise motorist always carried an assortment of other odds and ends in his tool box, or his pocket. My father always carried chewing gum, rubber bands, a short length of two-by-four, a coil of iron wire and fifteen or twenty yards of strong twine. The two-by-four was useful in blocking up broken springs. The others had multiple uses.

It is interesting to see that Mr. Brookes strongly advised carrying twine in the tool kit and suggested that a length of twine "can be put to various uses about the car, such as reinforcing weak spots in tires, protecting chafed wires, and binding together split sections of the steering wheel."

Yes, motoring was rugged in those days, but if you were armed with your *Blue Book,* to guide you along the proper road, and your *Automobile Handbook* to help keep your engine running you seldom got into serious trouble.

Suppose, for instance, you were touring in a Pope-Toledo, with big acetylene headlights and a chain drive. Just suppose one of the chains broke. What to do? Mr. Brookes gave you the answer right on page 72. Just fasten the idle sprocket with a piece of wire or some of that twine from your tool kit. Then proceed carefully homeward on one drive chain.

Or suppose you found yourself out in the sticks with a dry differential casing and no garage around to supply you with differential grease. Mr. Brookes tells you that a pound of beeswax may be used as a substitute. And a pound of beeswax, of course, was easy to find.

What if you broke your gas line? Mr. Brookes said that you must always carry a piece of rubber tubing for just such an emergency. When it had been forced over the broken ends, all was well. But, he warned, since gasoline attacked rubber, too much dependence should not be placed on the rubber tubing.

If you had trouble locating a leak in the gas line, you just rubbed it with soap suds, then blew through it and looked for the soap bubbles.

To find out which of your two or four cylinders was missing, you touched each one with the business end of a kitchen match. The cylinder that wouldn't light the match was the one that was misbehaving, of course.

Mr. Brookes told you how to fix broken gear teeth, how to loosen rusted nuts and screws, how to repair bent axles and broken springs, how to bring a dead coil back to life, how to repair a broken steering rod, and how to jack your car up if you happened to be without your jack. (Get your puncture near a rail fence.)

If, by chance, your weekend drive kept you out after dark you had to turn on the acetylene generator in order to light the headlights. (About 1905 came Prest-O-Lite—a small tank of carbide gas under pressure.) The acetylene generator was usually found on the running board of the car and sometimes under the hood or even fastened to the dashboard. It consisted of a small water tank over a gas chamber which held calcium carbide. A valve was opened so that the water dripped very slowly into the calcium carbide, which released acetylene gas. The gas then flowed along rubber tubes to the headlights. There a match was applied and a dazzling white light resulted. Also an unpleasant stench.

After being used, the acetylene generator always had to be cleaned and prepared for the next after-dark venture onto the highways. The carbide chamber had to be washed out and thoroughly dried; there were special brushes to clean the valves and outlets which were likely to become clogged with lime. Then new calcium carbide was added to the gas chamber and water placed in the tank.

Of course, while you were at it you checked the tail light and side lights to be sure that they had plenty of kerosene.

And when you got back from that long weekend drive, Mr. Brookes had a lot of other odd jobs for you. He thought it was a good idea to inject a little kerosene into each cylinder to clean the rings. This kept them free of carbon deposits and insured proper compression.

He also thought it was a good idea to give your engine a complete physical checkup after any long run. He found that a valuable aid for this job was a flexible speaking tube "such as is commonly used with phonographs." One end of the tube could be held to the ear and the other moved about from cylinder to cylinder in a search for knocks.

Or, if you suspected a knock in a certain cylinder, you could take a light iron bar, press one end against the spot where the knock was suspected and the other end against your teeth. According to Brookes the knock would be clearly transmitted to your teeth. This, of course, was not the cure, but merely the diagnosis.

Winter driving in those days created very special hazards, of course. Many motorists preferred to jack their cars up and drain the radiator the moment snow was in the air. But there were other more hardy souls who fought it out with the ice and sleet—and usually lost.

Except in California and the Deep South the automobile business collapsed by November. Agencies often closed entirely and automobile factories laid off most of their employees. In December of 1905 Studebaker's advertisement in *Munsey's* magazine featured snow, holly and Studebaker Sleighs. A footnote said: "The new Studebaker Electric Victoria-Phaetons and the improved 2 and 4 cylinder gasoline touring cars will be ready for inspection in April."

Those early-day cars didn't like cold weather worth a damn. On a sub-freezing winter morning, the job of getting a gas car started was often monumental. My mother always had a teakettle full of boiling water ready for father to use on cold mornings.

DON'T USE A LIGHTED MATCH! 159

On his way out of the house father would grab the teakettle and a couple of old rags that mother would have laid out for him. In the barn our 1909 Marmon would have its radiator bundled in heavy blankets and lap robes, which had been placed there the night before. When these had been removed and the hood raised, father would wrap his rags around the carburetor, then pour on the boiling water. When the rags were steaming hot father would dump the remaining water over the engine. This probably did no good but father didn't like to waste all that hot water.

If it was not too cold the boiling water on the carburetor might cause sufficient vaporization of the gasoline so that the engine would start. But if it had been around zero during the night it might take more extreme measures. In that case, father dove into his tool kit under the rear seat and got out a can of ether, which all experienced motorists carried for winter starting.

Then the petcocks on top of each cylinder were opened and a few drops of ether was inserted into each one. (If your car didn't have cylinders with petcocks, you might have to buy special spark plugs with built-in petcocks.) The ether vaporized in any temperature and was as explosive as gasoline so after that father could usually get the car started with only two or three backbreaking spins of the crank. After the engine had been warmed up for five or ten minutes father was ready to head for his office.

When all other methods of warming up the engine failed father could manage it with a vocabulary of super-heated adjectives that burst from the barn like flames from the mouth of a cannon. Mother always cringed during father's verbal pyrotechnics and could hardly bring herself to face the neighbors for the rest of the day.

If you were going for a winter drive of any length you usually took along a charcoal footwarmer, or put a hot soapstone on the floor of the car and used a couple of heavy lap robes to hold in the warmth.

There were no very satisfactory anti-freeze solutions for your radiator. Alcohol and water was the most common, or a mixture of glycerine and water and alcohol. But the cooling systems were not very efficient so the alcohol would boil out every few days. Unless you checked your radiator almost daily with the hydrometer which you kept in the barn it would freeze up and your engine would overheat.

When this happened the car would usually start steaming. But sometimes there would be no steam. Instead there would be the smell of hot metal, the engine would begin to knock and, if you didn't know enough to stop the car, the motor would eventually freeze.

The test for serious overheating was to spit on the engine. If it sizzled for a moment, all was well. But if it instantly turned to steam you had a very hot engine on your hands.

Then you had to take out the spark plugs and turn the crank a few times to draw cold air into the engine. If the pistons were frozen tight you squirted some kerosene into each cylinder until they were free. Then you poured boiling water over the radiator to thaw out the ice. Once you got water flowing through the cooling system you were ready to try your luck again with Jack Frost.

The Automobile Handbook explained all these matters to the inexperienced so that he could try winter driving if he wished, but the book wasn't very encouraging. You felt that Mr. Brookes thought it wisest to drain the radiator and wait for spring. But just in case you were a cold weather fanatic he covered the subject. In fact, there wasn't much about an automobile that he failed to tell. You had to be pretty doggone stupid not to be able to take care of your car with L. Elliott Brookes practically at your elbow. His final advice to the beginner was in the form of a few pointed and succinct *don'ts*, to wit:

"DON'TS. In the first place don't forget to ascertain the fact that the ignition mechanism is retarded before cranking the motor. Many a sprained wrist and plenty of broken heads or arms have been caused by neglect of this simple precaution.

"Don't forget to fill the gasoline tank before starting.

"Don't smoke while filling it.

"Don't take out all the spark plugs when there is nothing the matter, except that there is no gasoline in the tank.

"Don't forget to always have an extra spark plug on the car.

"Don't fill the gasoline tank too full, leave an air space at the top or the gasoline will not flow readily.

"Don't have any open hole in the gasoline tank. When the car is washed water may run in this hole, mix with the gasoline and cause a lot of trouble.

"Don't keep on running when an unusual noise is heard about the car, stop and find out what it is.

"Don't start or stop too suddenly, something may break.

"Don't forget to examine the steering gear *frequently*.

"Don't fail to clean the motor and all wearing parts of the car occasionally.

"Don't forget to oil every part of the motor where there is any friction.

"Don't use a lighted match to see if the gasoline tank is empty. Something unexpected may happen."

And with this sly witticism, Mr. Brookes completed his instructions.

12

FIVE CYLINDERS AND EIGHT WHEELS

1909
Production *127,731*
Registration *312,000*
Left-hand drive

EVERYBODY WANTED TO get into the act. From 1900 to 1915 more than a thousand varieties of automobiles were offered to the American public. Some say more than two thousand. But many of these were strictly "paper" cars, designed by smart promoters who were interested primarily in selling stock certificates. There was hardly a city of any size that didn't have its automobile factory, or at least a blueprint of one. From San Francisco to Boston, from Minneapolis to Shreveport *everybody* wanted to get into the act!

Most bicycle and buggy manufacturers were losing business to the new little giant; they tried assembling automobiles in an effort to get off the dime and onto the gravy boat. The Elkhart Carriage and Harness Manufacturing Company put a car together called the Pratt. The Kentucky Wagon Manufacturing Company assembled a job called The Dixie Flyer. The Columbus Buggy Company made the Firestone automobile, which they dubbed "The Mechanical

FIVE CYLINDERS AND EIGHT WHEELS 163

Greyhound." The Fuller was put out by The Fuller Buggy Company of Jackson, Michigan. And there were dozens of others assembled by the panicky carriage makers. Few people are aware that the giant "General Motors," was founded by a former buggy maker. But the only name from the buggy business that survives today is Studebaker.

Of course, machine shops were the natural places for new cars to originate. The first Haynes was built in the machine shop of the Apperson brothers. The great Marmon car came from the shops of Nordyke and Marmon. Often a car built in a machine shop became the first tangible asset of a new automobile company. But there were a hundred machine shops that built cars in those early days with names that have long been forgotten. Automobiles like the Gale, for instance, built by The Western Tool Works, of Galesburg, Illinois.

And numerous marine engine works tried to get on the band wagon. The New Era car was made by The Auto and Marine Power Company of Camden, New Jersey. The Valley Boat and Engine Company, Saginaw, Michigan, built a car called the Saginaw.

The J. I. Case Threshing Machine Company, of Racine, manufactured the Case automobile. The Standard Steel Car Company, a subsidiary of the Pennsylvania Railroad, put a Standard automobile on the market. The Moline Plow Works made the Stephens Salient Six; The Lewis Spring and Axle Company manufactured the Hollier 8.

The Tribune, the Lozier, the Rambler, the Pierce-Arrow, the Peerless, the Columbia, the National were all manufactured in bicycle factories. And for every machine shop, buggy plant and bicycle factory that switched from its original purpose to the manufacture of automobiles there must have been two more that toyed with the idea or even went so far as to make a car or two that never were placed on the market.

My father's first car, for instance, was manufactured in the old Rambler bicycle plant, in Chicago, after it had been purchased and absorbed by the American Bicycle Company. As the company's western jobbing representative he was able to buy this mongrel machine at what he thought was a bargain price. It turned out, however, that the little one-lunger had a tendency to catch fire and spurt flames from beneath the rear seat.

Father sardonically named this orphan from the Rambler plant The Bullet, after Barney Oldfield's famous Winton, which also belched flames. By some hook or crook father managed to get his hands on an ingenuous character from Peoria, Illinois, who was looking for a bargain in motor cars. He got The Bullet.

About this same time another Chicago bicycle factory was on the verge of going into the manufacture of automobiles. This was Arnold, Schwinn & Company, today the outstanding bicycle manufacturer in the United States. Shortly after the turn of the century, Ignaz Schwinn, the company's founder and chief engineer, was undecided about the future of the bicycle. The industry's sales had dwindled from a million a year to about half of that. In 1896 he had designed and manufactured, for his own use, one of the first electric automobiles seen in Chicago. Then he had experimented with two one-cylinder gasoline cars. By 1902 Schwinn was seriously interested in building an automobile for the market. He designed a four-cylinder touring car with all of the latest improvements: sliding gear transmission, shaft drive, high tension ignition and side-entrance tonneau. Two of these cars were completed in the summer of 1905—a seven passenger model, which was for Schwinn's wealthy partner, Adolph Arnold, the meat packer, and a five passenger model for himself. The Schwinn bicycle was called, at that time, the World, so that was the name Schwinn gave his two automobiles.

Arnold was rather pleased with the experimental World that his partner had built for him, but he had no faith in the motor car business. He was a man who loved horses. He owned half a dozen blooded animals, three carriages and a couple of sleighs.

Schwinn, on the other hand, was a mechanic and an engineer. He thought that he could combine the bicycle and the automobile business as many of his rivals had already done. In the winter of 1905-06 he held a conference with Arnold in which he outlined his plans for going into automobile production.

Arnold was against the idea from the beginning. The initial costs were too high and the risk too great, he protested. But Schwinn insisted that the automobile had come to stay and that horse-driven vehicles were doomed.

The argument had already grown heated, and at this remark Arnold burst into a rage. Seizing his partner by the elbow he propelled him to the window of his second-story office and pointed down into the street where the Arnold sleigh and a team of beautiful black horses, attended by a footman, was waiting for him.

"Do you mean to stand there and tell me that any rattling, stinking, dangerous contraption like an automobile will ever drive those beautiful animals off the street?" demanded Arnold. Then before his partner could reply, he added, "You must be crazy!" And with that he jammed his bowler hat on his head and slammed out.

That ended the argument as to whether Arnold, Schwinn & Company would manufacture automobiles. A few years later, Mr. Schwinn bought out his partner and began making the Excelsior motorcycle, but he never again considered making motor cars.

Today Arnold, Schwinn & Company is the only bicycle manufacturer in the United States that has remained continuously in business since 1895. Doubtless if Adolph Arnold had not been so fond of horses one of the important automobiles on the street today might be called the World.

In the early 1900's there were few standards to go by in

the automobile business. Every screwdriver genius in the business had some new idea up his sleeve that he tried to incorporate in an automobile. As a result, the freaks and white elephants of the early automobile business were very nearly as numerous as the practical workaday cars.

Around 1900, Uriah Smith, of Battle Creek, invented what he called the "Horsey Horseless Carriage." It was just any old horseless carriage with an imitation horse's head attached to the dashboard. Uriah contended that real live horses would not be frightened by the approach of a "Horsey Horseless Carriage." He also recommended that the space inside the phony horse's head could be used for a gasoline tank.

About 1905 a certain citizen of Jessup, Iowa, constructed a freak machine that reached an all-time high for goofy conveyances. This one looked like a row boat on three wheels. It carried three passengers and had a three-cylinder engine. It was amphibious, having paddles mounted on the two rear wheels. The inventor said that he had also used it as an ice boat with special spiked wheels and a sled runner in front.

In the automobile show of 1901 the "auto-quadricycle" was one of the most interesting exhibits. This was a four-wheeled vehicle which somewhat resembled the wheeled chairs seen today on Atlantic City's Boardwalk. Two passengers could ride in front, on an upholstered seat, while the chauffeur sat behind on a saddle.

That same year the Automobile Forecarriage came in for very favorable comment at the show. This was an engine attached to a pair of wheels surmounted by a king-pin-and-tiller. You took the front wheels off your brougham and replaced them with the forecarriage. Thus your old-fashioned carriage was converted to gasoline in a trice.

The Model Automobile Company of Peru, Indiana, figured out a way to save you from getting out and getting under to look at the engine, which was secreted beneath the front seat. They had a tonneau which was hinged at the back end. All you did was unfasten a couple of hooks and *presto!* you could lift up the whole body just as easily as you could lift a piano.

In 1903 an engineer with the Fairbanks-Morse Company got up the water-gasoline engine and actually built a car around it. The water-gasoline engine used water as well as gasoline for fuel. Finely atomized water was sprayed into the engine at the same moment the gas fumes were introduced. The water turned to super-heated steam and expanded at the same moment the gas exploded. Double action—get it?

The Adams Company in Dubuque, Iowa, had a daisy of an idea in the Adams-Farwell Revolving Air-Cooled Five-Cylinder Engine. The five cylinders were under the rear seat and over the transmission and rear axle. The advertisements said it took no skill to operate.

A cousin to this one was the 1908 Gyroscope car, with a horizontal engine and flywheel, "giving gyroscopic stability in running—no skidding—takes turns at any speed." Anyway that's what the advertisement of the Gyroscope Automobile Company, Gyroscope Building, New York City, said. It also said that top speed was thirty-five miles per hour.

There was a real genius behind the Carter Twin-Engine car, manufactured by the Carter Motor Car Corporation of Washington, D.C. This one had two 35-horsepower engines under the hood. Same idea as a twin-engine plane. If one motor conked out, you could still get home on the other one. But of course it was as expensive as two cars. Price $5,000.

The Carter Twin-Engine is not to be confused with the Cartercar which was manufactured in Pontiac for a number of years. The Cartercar was a bit of a freak, too. It had a friction transmission and a chain-in-oil drive. The Cartercar advertised "no clutch to slip, no gears to strip, no bevel gears, no noise." Nice meter but as an automobile it was a flop.

Ten years after the Carter Twin-Engine died, a variation of that idea came along in the Enger Convertible Twelve. This car had a V-12 engine which could be converted into a six by just pushing a lever. It may have worked fine but it didn't sell. A year later they were out of business.

Sometime before 1900, while Hiram Maxim was building experimental Columbia cars for the Pope Manufacturing Company, one of his main problems was to try to reduce the number of foot pedals and hand levers that were necessary to drive a gasoline car. His bosses wanted him to combine the operation of the clutch and the throttle so that his gasoline car would operate as simply as an electric automobile. They felt that the average person could not learn how to coordinate the movements of his feet and hands so as to be able to handle the clutch, the spark, the throttle, the brake and the steering wheel simultaneously.

At this time Mr. Justus B. Entz, chief engineer of the Electric Storage Battery Company, makers of Exide storage batteries, came to Maxim with a revolutionary invention which eliminated the clutch pedal from a gasoline car.

Mr. Entz' idea was a magnetic clutch which operated as smoothly as today's Hydra-matic clutch. The power of the gasoline engine was transmitted through this clutch, which in itself became an electric generator that sent power to a booster motor attached to the drive shaft.

Mr. Entz spent a lifetime trying to put his idea over. After the Pope Company abandoned it, he went to Cleveland where the makers of the White automobile experimented with it for a while, then gave up. But an automobile using Entz' patents was finally perfected. It was called the Owen Magnetic and was manufactured by The Baker, Rauch and Lang Company in 1915. The latter company was a consolidation of two manufacturers of electric automobiles. They hoped that the Owen Magnetic might recapture the customers they had lost to gasoline.

But although Mr. Entz' invention was a wonderfully clever

FIVE CYLINDERS AND EIGHT WHEELS 169

device it was not nearly as simple and light and trouble-free as a gearbox. And by this time motorists had learned to coordinate their hands and feet so that they didn't need the help of a magnetic clutch. After six years of red ink the Owen Magnetic was finished.

The Elmore car, which first came on the market in 1900, was the most persistent of the two-cycle automobiles. George B. Selden's 1895 patent on the automobile pictured a two-cycle engine, but when Selden himself started building cars he used a four-cycle engine. However, the two-cycle advocates had a good pitch. They pointed out that each time the piston of a two-cycle engine reached the top of its stroke it was propelled downward by an explosion, while in a four-cycle engine the explosion only occurred on every other stroke of the piston. Also, there were no valves in a two-cycle engine, consequently fewer repairs.

There were other cars besides the Elmore which espoused the two-cycle cause, but none were as successful. The company was purchased by General Motors in 1909 and almost immediately the two-cycle principle went out of date.

Among the almost unbelievable freaks of early motordom were the Octoauto and the Sextoauto. These two cars were the ingenuous dream of one M. O. Reeves, a banker of Columbus, Indiana, who should have stuck to his counting house. The principle behind the Octoauto was that an automobile, like a railroad car, needed lots of wheels—eight to be exact—four in front and four behind. All these wheels were supposed to allow the car to travel over a road full of chuckholes without ever disturbing its gliding horizontal movement. Mr. Reeves found that four wheels in front rather complicated the problem of getting around sharp corners, so he eliminated one pair of front wheels and called his new machine "the Sextoauto, sister of the Octoauto."

Mr. Reeves' advertisement said: "Rides like a Pullman Palace Car. No shock, no jolt, no bounce, no rebound. An old and accepted principle to accomplish easy riding applied to the automobile. It's a phenomenal car and bound to revolutionize automobile construction where comfort in riding is a consideration."

The records seem to indicate that Mr. Reeves was in and out of the automobile business in one year flat.

The accessories of those old days were as varied and as imaginative as some of the cars. Take, for instance, the detachable tonneau. The idea of this invention was to give you two cars in one. You could buy a roadster and later turn it into a touring car by purchasing a tonneau. These tonneaus came in various styles, with and without doors. Some had rear doors and some had side doors. If you didn't care for the kind that the manufacturer of your car supplied, you could buy a dozen different kinds made by other companies. They fastened to your car with hooks and bolts, though there was no guarantee that they would stay fastened. A favorite sight gag of the early cartoonists and silent movies was the detachable tonneau becoming detached at top speed.

Before tops were created for automobiles someone invented storm aprons. A storm apron was simply a tarpaulin with head holes cut in it. If you owned a two passenger car you had a storm apron with two holes. If you had a five passenger job you carried a five-holer.

Another device which added extra seating accommodations to your roadster was the Swan patented, folding, *dos-à-dos* seat. These were priced from ten to twenty dollars depending on upholstery and finish. Although they were made primarily to fit the bustle on the Merry Oldsmobile they also could be attached to a number of other roadsters.

In those days the state did not furnish you with a license plate; it furnished you with a number. You could paint this number on a shingle and hang it on your car, if you wished. But usually you went out and bought a tailored license number. The most stylish were white leather numbers on black patent leather, or vice versa. And, of course, you bought your own kerosene tail light and a special bracket which attached to the tail light to hold your license plate.

The Klaxon appeared at the same time as the storage battery. It was a raucous, motor-driven, ratchet horn that turned many a pedestrian's hair white. They were forbidden in some places as more of a menace than a warning.

The Jericho and the Aermore horns, on the other hand, had dulcimer tones and operated from the exhaust. They sang with a siren note that almost tempted the pedestrian to meet the oncoming vehicle with open arms.

Before 1910 no manufacturer supplied a windshield on his car. This was an accessory. They came in various styles. The Metzger Automatic Windshield was very popular. It sold for twenty-five to forty dollars, depending on type and size. Its frame was brass, with brass rods that fastened to the fenders to brace the windshield. The upper half of the automatic windshield could be set at an angle or folded down to allow the breeze to hit you full in the face. The advertisements proudly stated: "Up or Down with One Hand Without Stopping the Car."

Shock absorbers were also something additional that you had to buy for your car. They sometimes called them "snubbers." One inventor called his shock absorber the Hotchkin Anti-Jolt Device.

Speedometers were also extra equipment. They began to come in about 1906. No car was equipped with them regularly until the Haynes came out in 1910 with a completely furnished dashboard. It was an overnight sensation! Automobile row was agog!

The Boyce MotoMeter was a gadget that practically no motorist attempted to do without. It was a thermometer which attached to the radiator cap. From the driver's seat you could peer out at the MotoMeter and read the temperature of the water in your radiator. Of course you never thought of peering until the car started steaming. Then you looked at the MotoMeter and sure enough, the red column in the thermometer had mounted to the line marked "DANGER."

Drop brakes were a safety feature that you could attach to your car in case you lived in hilly country. They consisted of a pair of sharp iron spikes protruding from the rear of the car and hinged to the axle. If your foot brake and your emergency brake failed while on a hill, you just released the drop brakes and the two spikes jammed into the road and held the car. Drop brakes were sold mostly to the type of customer who wore both a belt and suspenders.

Before demountable rims appeared most motorists carried a small tire repair shop in their car. You always had spare "boots" and "shoes" to take care of blowouts, and a vulcanizing outfit to repair punctures and damaged casings. You carried a double-action pump to inflate your tires, or a compressed air bottle, or an engine pump which worked off the engine. You had to have your own air gauge to check the air pressure, which in the early days was from sixty to eighty pounds. And when you had finished changing a tire you got out your rubber washbasin with its own water supply. "Absolutely watertight. Water enters basin only when valve is opened. Convenient to carry, folding up like an opera hat when not in use. In cold weather it is filled with hot water and used as a foot warmer."

The problem of cranking a car without getting out of the seat was another challenge to inventors of that day. The Star Safety Crank was one answer to this challenge. It consisted of a lever which came up through the floorboards and a steel cable that ran through a number of pulleys to a reel-and-ratchet arrangement at the front end of the crankshaft. To turn the engine over, you seized the lever and gave it a jerk.

My father installed one of these devices on his first Model T Ford about 1910. It worked all right when the engine was hot, but not at all when it was cold. For a cold Model T needed spinning to get it started and so did most cars. One day father was cranking the Model T with the Star starter, when the cable leading to the crankshaft broke. He snapped his neck so hard he couldn't turn his head for three days. When he recovered he removed the Star Safety Crank and threw it onto a junk heap in our barn.

When the Model T Ford first came on the scene, as bare of accessories as a newborn babe, a whole new industry sprang up to correct this deficiency. Gadget-minded inventors, of which America has always had two in every garage, had a field day with the Model T. The gadgeteers created for Henry's child an array of additions which Henry himself could not have dreamed up. Wings for the radiator cap, sun visors, dash lights, braces for the steering column, special oil to prevent clutch-chatter, running-board cans for gas, oil and water, rattle silencers, pedal pads, rear-view mirrors, windshield wipers, accelerators, anti-shimmy rods, running-board lights and a hundred other refinements to make the Model T as fully equipped as more expensive cars.

Naturally the easy money in the auto accessory game made many manufacturers scratch their heads and try to get in on the big boom by switching their products to fit the needs of motor cars and motoring. Joseph N. Smith and Company, of Detroit, manufacturers of bicycle-seat posts, created special brass rails with which to trim and beautify an automobile. Manufacturers of eyeglasses for the optical trade shunted that business into a side room and were soon working night shifts to supply the demand for automobile goggles. Glovers designed automobile gauntlets, clothiers created special ulsters, dusters, leather suits, leather caps, and ladies' motoring hoods with isinglass panels in the front. Makers of kerosene carriage lamps switched to powerful gas headlights. Makers of cornets and slide trombones created special horns for automobiles that worked by squeezing a rubber bulb.

Even the makers of patent medicines flipped a ride on the merry-go-round. The Murine Company, of Chicago, for instance, put forth determined efforts to equip every motor car with a bottle of Murine. Full-page Murine ads were to be seen in every motoring magazine and the company's advertising agents combined sex, drama and poesy to sell their bill of goods. The following is the copy that went with one of their 1907 advertisements, illustrated with pen-and-ink drawings reminiscent of Charles Dana Gibson's beautiful women and handsome men:

Charles the Chauffeur

Charles, the chauffeur, and milady, Juliet,
The dashingest pair of the autoist set,
All primed for adventure, are out for a spiel,
On this fine country road, in their automobile.

As they dash down the pike, without quaver or hitch,
The farmers in front of them take to the ditch,
And the cohorts that follow are trailing afar
Like the Netherby clan after young Lochinvar.

After climbing a long grassy slope, at the top
The pulsing machine has been brought to a stop,
For the silt of the air, and microbic flies
Have reddened the lids of milady's bright eyes.

And Charles, at the signal, has stopped the machine
And passed back the bottle containing Murine;
So milady leans back, and looks up at the sky
As the magic "two drops" are dropped into each eye.

Now again they are off, at a forty mile pace,
With vision restored and new zest in the race;
And woe betide him who opposes their gait,
For he's booked for a serious tussle with fate.

The automobile, by some unwritten code,
Has won, in fee simple, all rights to the road;
And quite as true title indisputably lies,
To the trite, but true saying, "Murine cures eyes."

FIVE CYLINDERS AND EIGHT WHEELS 175

*Murine Is A Tonic For The "Auto Eye"
Soothes And Quickly Cures Eyes
Inflamed By Exposure To Strong Winds and Dust.* *

Auto eye became a fashionable malady for beautiful young ladies, and the handsome Charles and Milady Juliet sold many gallons of Murine.

* Used by permission of The Murine Company, Inc.

13

THE SUPER-SELLERS

1910
Production *181,000*
Registration *468,500*
One-man tops

AFTER THE AUTOMOBILE was once on its way those geniuses of American commerce, the super-salesmen, began to emerge as leaders of the industry. Today it is rather confusing to know whether they were really super-salesmen or whether there was a superabundance of buyers. But we do know that of the thousands who tried to be automobile tycoons there were only a few, brash, determined, strong-willed men who are remembered today, because they succeeded where the others failed.

In comparing the quality of the cars and personalities that played important parts in the drama of the auto industry, it seems very likely that the men who succeeded were willing to give fifteen hours a day to their god-on-wheels, to think, dream and talk of nothing else, and to die before they were sixty in order to achieve their success. Not all of the talented men who made and sold motor cars were willing to give quite that much. Most of those missed the boat but lived to reminisce.

It is said that John North Willys was the sort of salesman who could have peddled electric refrigerators in Alaska, steam radiators in the jungles of Africa and brassières in Bali.

In 1900 Willys had a sporting goods store in Elmira, New York, where he sold everything from fishing tackle to bicycles. That year, on a trip to Cleveland, he saw his first automobile. It was a Winton, and Willys, just as most of America soon would, went automobile crazy. He would probably have taken a Winton back to Elmira with him, except that none was available at the moment.

When Willys returned home he discovered that a local doctor had just brought an automobile to town—it was a Pierce Motorette, manufactured in Buffalo and powered with a De Dion single cylinder 2.75-horsepower motor. The Motorette had a light Stanhope body with bicycle wheels and a frame of bicycle tubing. This looked even better to Willys than the Winton.

Apprehensive lest someone get there first he caught the train for Buffalo and went straight to the George N. Pierce Company, manufacturers of the Pierce-Arrow bicycle. George Pierce was experimenting with automobiles but was not yet in production. The car he had sold to the doctor in Elmira was the first he had made.

But the Willys gift of gab was not to be denied. He persuaded Pierce to sell him the next car he turned out and to give him the Pierce-Arrow agency in Elmira.

In 1901 Willys sold two cars. In 1902 he sold four. There was no holding him now. He went to Kenosha and obtained the agency for the Rambler car. He had to have that big Rambler surrey with the storm curtains and isinglass windows that rolled up and fastened under the permanent top.

Willys, the little Motorette and the Rambler went to town; in 1903 he sold twenty cars. But the factories had trouble in those days making enough cars to go round to all their dealers. So Willys took on another car, the Detroit, manufactured by the Detroit Auto Vehicle Company in, strangely enough, Romeo, Michigan. But even with three suppliers Willys couldn't get enough cars, for by this time he had opened a sales agency in New York City. At the end of 1906 he had a stack of orders that were still unfilled.

He knew by this time that he could sell any car that would run, so he looked around for a factory that could supply his needs. In Indianapolis he found it; the Overland Automobile Company, an outgrowth of the Standard Wheel Company, had been making automobiles since 1903. The company was just barely keeping its head above water, but there was nothing wrong with the Overland car that a vigorous sales policy would not cure. For 1907 the company was planning to build just two models—a runabout and a touring car. Both were to have a two-cylinder, vertical engine of eight horsepower; the price was to be $600 and $700.

Willys, hungry for cars, contracted for the company's entire output. This may sound like a lot, but the Overland was being made under antiquated conditions and the entire output of the company for 1907 was forty-seven cars. These, added to the cars that Pierce-Arrow and Rambler apportioned to him, gave Willys a healthy bank account and a terrific appetite for more merchandise. He estimated that for 1908 he could handle five hundred cars. To help Overland increase its facilities he paid down $10,000 against those five hundred cars and headed back for Elmira, confident that he had made a smart deal.

But he had hardly returned home when word arrived that the Overland Automobile Company was in financial trouble. As a matter of fact the whole country was in trouble. The Knickerbocker Trust Company of New York had failed, precipitating the panic of 1907.

Willys hopped a train and headed back to Indianapolis to save his $10,000. When he arrived he discovered that

Overland was in much worse shape than he had ever imagined. The company's bank balance was so low that some of the salary checks that had been issued on Saturday were bound to bounce on Monday.

Willys saw himself out $10,000 as well as the profit on five hundred cars, plus the down payments on a hundred or so that he had already accepted. If Overland went bankrupt he would go bankrupt with it! He got the officials of the company together and learned that all that was needed to cover the payroll checks on Monday morning was $350.

That was simple; he would write a personal check for that amount and deposit it on Monday, thus bolstering the company's account. But it was not quite that easy, he was informed, because the Indianapolis banks were not accepting out-of-town checks. He would have to deposit cash.

That was a problem. Hard money and currency, too, had gone into hiding. It was so scarce that much retail business was being carried on with Clearing House certificates. The only place Willys might be able to cash a check was the hotel where he always stopped when he came to town.

He explained his predicament to the owner and appealed to his civic pride. Overland would go broke unless the hotel cashed Willys' check for $350. So the owner hoarded cash receipts for Saturday night and Sunday until he could cash the check. On Monday morning the $350 was deposited at the bank and the company was temporarily saved.

But that was only the beginning. The Overland employees had to be sent back to work and another week's payroll met. They had to keep turning out cars. That was what Willys wanted—saleable merchandise.

He held a meeting with the company's board of directors and demanded a chance to rescue the company. They didn't think he could do it but they told him he was welcome to try. Then the treasurer revealed that the company owed $80,000 and its creditors were demanding immediate payment.

Eighty thousand dollars was hard to lay hands on in the midst of a financial panic. Banks were calling loans rather than making them. People who had money were hiding it in mattresses and burying it in the cellar.

Probably Willys' greatest selling job came when he faced those Overland creditors. They came to the meeting expecting to get a good part of their money, for it was rumored that Willys had been able to find some cash. But the total amount he had raised was only $7,500—a most disappointing sum. The creditors looked grim and uncompromising until Willys went to work on them. The super-salesman promised that he would put the company back on its feet if they would give him a chance. All they had to do was extend Overland more credit!

Willys must have been a man of great persuasion, for they bought his proposition. They not only gave him more credit but promised to help him establish credit elsewhere. After that he was made president, treasurer, sales manager and purchasing agent of the rejuvenated Overland company. During 1908 he pushed 465 cars through the Overland factory. That gave the company sufficient capital to improve its production methods and in 1909 more than four thousand cars, now called Willys-Overland, were built and sold.

From then on it was a breeze. For it so happened that in 1910-11 those firms that were doing well were going great guns, while those that were slipping found themselves headed toward a precipice. More than twenty leading automobile manufacturers went bankrupt during that period. They probably lacked the kind of super-salesmen and super-producers who were willing to die before sixty. One of them was Pope-Toledo, with a big, well-equipped plant at Toledo, Ohio.

Willys bought the plant with all machinery and material on hand for $285,000. The Indianapolis plant of Willys-Overland was then moved to Toledo and in the next few years the company absorbed a number of other firms such as Electric Auto-Lite, New Process Gear, Duesenberg Motors, Morrow Manufacturing Company and others.

In 1913 Charles Knight invented the sleeve-valve motor; Overland acquired the rights to this engine and produced the popular Willys-Knight. In 1915 the Willys-Overland Company built 91,780 cars; it was the second largest automobile company in the world.

In the early days, when Willys was selling more bicycles than automobiles, R. E. Olds in his Oldsmobile factory was unconsciously siring a whole fleet of future cars. For out of the Olds organization came the men who helped to found the companies that made Maxwell, Thomas-Detroit, Chalmers, Hudson, LaFrance, Hupp, Reo, Dodge, Northern, King and EMF. And some of these were the forbears of later cars. Out of the moribund Maxwell plant, for instance, came the beginnings of the great Chrysler Corporation, while EMF spawned the Flanders and itself became the Studebaker.

It was Olds who first departed from the Olds Motor Works to establish the Reo Motor Car Company. Once the boss had gone, the young group, who had helped him make Oldsmobile the leading car of its day, soon began to try their wings with projects of their own.

Two of these were Roy D. Chapin and Howard E. Coffin. The latter was a young engineer who had contributed much to the success of the Oldsmobile. Chapin was the Horatio Alger character who, in 1901, had started the curved dash Oldsmobile on its way to fame by driving it from Detroit to New York, and who, at the age of twenty-four, became sales manager for the Olds Motor Works. A good many years later he was to be appointed Secretary of Commerce under Herbert Hoover.

But in the year 1906 Chapin's pal, Coffin, had designed a new car to sell for $2,750. Chapin, the salesman, was so certain the car was a winner that he resigned his job at Olds Motor Works and began looking for capital to build Coffin's car. Eventually he went to see Edwin Ross Thomas, president of the E. R. Thomas Motor Company. Thomas was an ex-bicycle manufacturer who had built his first Thomas-Flyer in Buffalo in the same year that George N. Pierce had started making Pierce Motorettes. In six years Thomas had grown wealthy and was wintering in California. Roy Chapin followed him there, showed him the blueprints of Coffin's new automobile. Soon he had persuaded Thomas to back them and to sell the new car through the Thomas-Flyer sales organization.

Thomas became president, Chapin general manager, and Coffin, of course, was made chief engineer. They named the car the Thomas-Detroit, thus capitalizing on the Thomas name, but still distinguishing it from the more expensive Thomas-Flyer which was still made in Buffalo. In their first year they manufactured and sold five hundred cars, at that time a sensational beginning.

But Chapin wanted to sell a thousand cars in one year, maybe even two thousand! He looked around for the most talented sales manager he could find. His eye lit on Hugh Chalmers, of Dayton, Ohio, another character out of Horatio Alger, who in ten years had advanced from office boy to vice president and general manager of the National Cash Register Company, and a salary of $72,000 a year.

However, it was rumored that Chalmers was dissatisfied, that he wanted to have a business of his own. Acting on these rumors Chapin went to Chalmers with a proposition that was too flattering for any super-salesman to resist. Chapin offered Chalmers a block of stock in the E. R. Thomas Detroit Company, also to change the name of the car to the Chalmers-Detroit!

Chapin and Chalmers were both twenty-seven years old; Chapin was a man of great administrative ability and judgment while Chalmers was one of the most dynamic personalities in the business world. And they were both willing to live their lives on a treadmill. Together they should have made an unbeatable team. But Chapin had grown up in the automobile business and Chalmers was a cash register man. They found that they could not see eye to eye.

The eventual result was that Chapin and Coffin sold out to Chalmers and formed a new company. The man who put up most of the money for this new enterprise was J. L. Hudson, owner of the Detroit department store which bears his name.

Chapin and Coffin created a great new car—a big, sporty-looking automobile that was to sell for under a thousand dollars. To honor their financial backer they called the car the Hudson.

On July 3, 1909, the first Hudson "Twenty" rolled off the production line and the big rush started. Never before had an automobile company been so successful in its first year. Four thousand cars were sold, and Chapin—at the age of twenty-nine—was a millionaire.

The relationship of Oldsmobile to Studebaker is more complex but none the less real, and a genealogist would even point to a few drops of Cadillac and Ford blood flowing in the Studebaker line.

This crossing of strains was due to three men named Everitt, Metzger and Flanders, who joined talents in 1910 to manufacture and sell a car called EMF. It became one of the ten-strikes of the industry.

Bernard F. Everitt was a buggy upholsterer and later a body manufacturer, who did work for the early Olds Motor Works.

William E. Metzger had Detroit's first automobile agency, then became the original sales manager for Oldsmobile and in 1902 became the first sales manager for Cadillac.

Walter E. Flanders was the production man who turned out Ford's first Model T's. He had had a small factory where he made crankshafts for Ford. Henry was so impressed with Flanders' ability to produce goods on schedule that he offered him a salary of $1,000 a month and a bonus of $20,000 if he would step up Ford production to ten thousand cars in one year.

Flanders was a big, two-fisted roughneck who had a genius for getting things done. But he was no Horatio Alger hero. Not Flanders. He loved hard liquor, women and a good fight. And when, at night, he was through with a hard day's work he usually went out and found all three.

He took on the Ford job and in a few weeks completely revamped the plant's production methods. The whole interior of the factory was rearranged, new machinery installed, workers given new jobs. It was not assembly line production, which was to come later, but it was the most efficient production system that had been introduced in Detroit up to that time. In the final assembly, for instance, each workman had specific jobs to perform. Each group of assemblers had runners to keep material always on hand; and there were helpers who supplied small tools at the exact moment they were needed. There was no hit-or-miss assembly as there had been before. Everything was done systematically, and thus the job of putting Fords together was considerably speeded up.

Two days before the end of the year Ford production passed the ten thousand mark. Flanders won his $20,000 and an unprecedented reputation for turning out automobiles. But Flanders was unhappy working for the non-drinking, non-smoking, non-chasing Ford. The moment he had earned his bonus he quit. And shortly thereafter, standing at the bar of the Hotel Pontchartrain, where the auto makers of that day did their drinking, Everitt and Metzger and Flanders completed plans for the EMF car.

Everitt and Metzger put up the money and Flanders supplied the know-how and the drive. He was given a block of stock and carte blanche to build the EMF "30," selling price $1,250, and the Flanders "20," to compete with Ford.

The joining together of such a triumvirate was big news. From the Pontchartrain bar, gossip spread through the lobby, across Cadillac Square, along Woodward Avenue and then fanned out over the city. Inside of a few hours everybody in the industry knew that another important automobile was being born. And then a Studebaker agent spread the news to South Bend, where the Studebaker brothers had been building vehicles since 1852.

Now the Studebaker company had made its first automobiles in 1902 when it sold twenty electrics. Then in 1904 the company sold its first gasoline-powered automobiles, but these were assembled jobs. The motors and chassis had been manufactured by an outside company; only the bodies and the wheels were made by Studebaker.

It was still company policy, in 1908, to assemble its cars. By that time the tremendous Studebaker sales organization needed more cars than the factory at South Bend was turning out. Studebaker needed badly to have its own complete factory but the company was old and conservative; it was still dubious about the automobile's future and hesitated to build a factory of its own. So instead, when news of the Everitt-Metzger-Flanders combination reached South Bend, Studebaker sent for EMF's Sales Manager Metzger.

No newborn automobile company ever made a more lucrative deal; Studebaker took the company's entire output of EMF and Flanders cars. Although the old wagon-making company immediately began selling cars in large quantities the arrangement was not entirely satisfactory for either company. Studebaker didn't like the EMF transmission and asked for a broader guarantee to protect Studebaker customers. EMF said that might be the way they did things in the buggy business but not in the automobile game.

Studebaker then offered to buy out Everitt and Metzger. But neither one was very interested in selling, so a satisfactory price could not be agreed on. Studebaker then went to

The Garford Company, at Elyria, Ohio, and made a contract to purchase Garford chassis to which Studebaker bodies would be added, the car to be called a Studebaker-Garford. Then, in the middle of the season, Studebaker notified EMF that it would need no more cars.

The EMF organization was taken by surprise. Metzger was in Europe and Everitt knew nothing about creating a distributing organization. But Walter Flanders, the big roughneck with a genius for getting things done, was undismayed. Trouble was his meat. He loved problems. He mapped out four areas with central distribution points and inserted full-page ads in the newspapers announcing that distributor and dealer franchises were available.

The EMF and the Flanders names were magic. Prospective dealers began arriving in Detroit on every train and Flanders began signing up the best of the lot, many of them Studebaker's own dealers.

Studebaker discovered, too late, that its sales organization was being raided. It tried to stop Flanders but the wagon-making firm was too big and too ponderously slow. Its efforts were futile. In two weeks Flanders had his national sales organization functioning. By the time Metzger arrived on the run from Europe the crisis was past and the infant EMF, less than two years old, was swaggering around like an old-timer.

Studebaker suffered. The Garford car was not to the public's fancy. Sales began to dwindle and the Studebaker family realized that wagons and carriages would soon be a thing of the past. Once more The Studebaker Brothers Manufacturing Company, which in its time had made more than a million vehicles, offered to buy the infant EMF; and this time Flanders and his partners could name their own price.

Everitt received $1,800,000, Metzger got an even million and Flanders, who had never put up a penny, was paid $250,000.

Then the big, bull-necked Flanders, super-salesman, super-producer, and walking proof that right living was not a recipe for success, slammed his hat on his head and went out to find a drink, a girl and perchance a good fight.

14

DOUBLE OR NOTHING!

1911
Production *199,319*
Registration *618,727*
Closed bodies

HE WAS A crapshooter. Probably the best and the worst the industry ever knew. He could keep a dozen bets in mind. He knew the odds down to the last decimal point. But he never drew down. It was double or nothing! Let it lay! Shoot the works!

That was Billy Durant, a brilliant, cocksure optimist who couldn't believe that it was possible for him to roll "snake eyes," and who won and lost some of the biggest pots in the history of American finance.

He was the greatest super-salesman of them all. He could charm a cowhand out of his horse; he could sell straw to a scarecrow. And besides, when the chips were down he could frighten Wall Street with every roll of the dice.

Durant has been called a genius, a vain, arrogant slave driver and other names both endearing and uncomplimentary. Whether he was a genius depends on your definition of the word. At best he may have been half a genius; the other half was childlike, and unconcerned with reality. For the founder of General Motors apparently had little or no mechanical skill. It would seem, from some of the mistakes he made, that he had no clear understanding of the principles behind the clutch, the transmission, the four-cycle engine or the differential—and these were what made an automobile.

Durant was of the horse-and-buggy age, founder of the Durant-Dort Carriage Company; so he wasn't supposed to understand automobiles. But he was a millionaire and not yet forty when a group of men in his home town of Flint, Michigan, asked Durant to rescue them from an automobile venture in which they had sunk some money.

The car these men had so foolishly invested in was the Buick, with the valve-in-head engine. David Buick had been a manufacturer of plumbers' supplies. He had discovered a way to fix porcelain on cast iron and had created a fancy bathtub, which made him quite a lot of money. Then he began to experiment with gasoline motors. Poor Dave Buick should have stayed in the bathtub business. It was not as potentially rewarding as automobiles but on the other hand plumbers were not as rough and tough as super-salesmen, who were willing to work fifteen or even twenty hours in a day. Buick eventually lost all his stock in the company and when he died he was a teacher in a trade school.

Durant knew nothing about automobiles, but he drove one of Buick's two-cylinder cars over half of lower Michigan before he decided to take over the company. He knew by then that it was a good car.

In 1904 Durant reorganized Buick and in one day sold half a million dollars' worth of stock to fellow citizens of Flint. Mr. Durant was indeed a super-salesman; almost the moment he took charge of Buick its business began to improve. For success breeds success and everybody knew that Billy Durant had been a terrific success for over twenty years.

In the fourth year after Durant took charge, 8,487 Buicks

were manufactured and sold and the company's net worth had increased to $3,417,142. Most men would have been satisfied with this accomplishment, but not Durant. He decided it was time to shoot the works. Double or nothing!

Another big-time operator of that day was Benjamin Briscoe, who had made a fortune with a sheet metal plant in Detroit and later had formed the Maxwell-Briscoe Motor Company to manufacture a car designed by John D. Maxwell. Durant went into a huddle with Briscoe and laid plans for a huge corporation which would merge the four largest automobile companies in the country. They were Buick, Maxwell-Briscoe, Reo and Ford. But at the very first meeting called to discuss the plan Ford tossed a monkey wrench in the works by announcing that he wanted $3,000,000 in cash for the Ford Motor Company. Olds said if anybody was going to get cash Reo would have some of that, too. But Durant had no idea of buying anybody out for cash. He had meant to accomplish his giant merger by issuing stock. So the conference broke up.

Another attempt by Durant and Benjamin Briscoe to set up a holding company, with the aid of J. P. Morgan and Company, collapsed when Durant refused to do business with a Morgan lawyer, or perhaps it was vice versa. In any case it is estimated that the disagreement cost Morgan and Company over $200,000,000.

But Durant was determined to have his holding company, to play for bigger stakes. In 1908 his lawyers incorporated the General Motors Company of New Jersey. A few days later the new corporation absorbed Buick by exchanging General Motors stock for Buick shares.

At this time Oldsmobile had ceased to be one of the leading automobiles in the United States. The company's sales had dwindled from over 6,500 cars in 1905 to 1,055 cars in 1908. Ranny Olds was out of the company and running Reo and most of the young men who had given the company its original impetus were now with other companies; the Olds Motor Works was, in fact, on the verge of bankruptcy.

So Durant, off on his first buying spree, was something of a lifesaver when he offered to buy the company with stock in General Motors. It was a good deal all around. Durant got the best known name in the business and the stockholders got off a sinking ship and onto a vessel that appeared to be seaworthy and heading somewhere. This was late in 1908.

In January, 1909, Durant absorbed the Oakland Motor Car Company, manufacturers of the Oakland, a very good car, which was losing money for the company. Later it was to be called the Pontiac.

It was all right to buy a good name here and a good car there and hope that a year later the companies would be making money. But the real trick was to pick up firmly established moneymakers, like Buick. Durant had his eye on one of these, but it took him a while to land his quarry. The name was Cadillac.

In 1909 Cadillac had been in business for all of seven years, an old-timer in the industry. After a fashion it, too, had been an outgrowth of Oldsmobile. When the Olds plant burned down in the spring of 1901, Olds was forced to find someone to build engines for him. He chose the Leland & Faulconer Manufacturing Company, the best precision machine shop in Detroit.

Henry M. Leland, head of the firm, had been for twenty years with the famous New England firm of Brown & Sharpe, makers of precision gauges and tools. He was a fanatic on precision manufacture. Not satisfied entirely with the performance of the one-cylinder engine he was building for Olds, Leland experimented to improve it. He changed the timing system, increased the size of the valves, machined the cylinders and pistons to much finer tolerances. When Leland finished his experiments he had increased the horsepower of the one-cylinder engine from 3.7 to 10.25. But when he took the new engine to Olds and suggested that it be incorporated in his car, Olds turned him down. His reason was that he had all the business he needed and any changes would have slowed up his production.

That left Leland with a beautiful engine but no car to put it in. However, in 1902, when Henry Ford was let out as chief engineer of the Detroit Automobile Company, its backers sought out Henry Leland for advice on how to proceed and he suggested that they build an automobile using his newly developed motor. From the ashes of the Detroit Automobile Company the Cadillac Automobile Company was incorporated, in the summer of 1902, and eventually it merged with Leland & Faulconer to form the Cadillac Motor Car Company, with Leland as president.

Six years later Cadillac won the Dewar trophy, awarded by the Royal Automobile Club of London, for the greatest advance by any motor car during the year. The award was won by demonstrating Cadillac's interchangeability of parts.

Three Cadillac cars were disassembled, their parts mixed, then reassembled. After which the three cars were driven on a 500-mile endurance run over the Brooklands track, finishing with a perfect score.

This was something of a revelation to the British and European manufacturers, who made their cars entirely by hand. It showed that standards of accuracy could be maintained even in a factory geared for quantity production.

It was this famous automobile and factory that Durant coveted. But Henry Leland and his son, W. C. Leland, were too wily to take General Motors stock. They insisted on cash and their price was $3,500,000, good for ten days. They shook hands on it.

Then Durant went out and scurried around for the money. He had plenty of General Motors stock but very little loose cash. In six months he returned, ready to buy. But Cadillac was now running at capacity and the price had gone up. The Lelands asked $4,125,000. Mr. Durant went scurrying off for more money. When he came back again

Brown Brothers

Mother and a mule seem to have taken charge of this embarrassing situation, while father has retired to the back seat completely subdued.

Brown Brothers

The owner of this Reo, about 1906, is beset by a chronic auto ailment of the day—tire trouble. Any trip of 75 miles without a blowout or puncture was a major miracle. A tire that lasted more than 3,000 miles was a worthy museum piece.

A thousand mile race at Grosse Pointe, Michigan, race track. The Packard, Grey Wolf, is in the lead.

The three gentlemen in the derby hats are representatives of the Pope Manufacturing Company. The car is a Pope-Toledo. The Prest-O-Lite tank on the running board suggests that the date is about 1906.

Proper garb for Miss Automobilist of 1905.

Brown Brothers

Even in 1909 the best automobile advertising technique always included a pretty girl at the wheel. But there were few professional models. This young lady doubled as a stenographer in the office of the company.

Cadillac, about 1908, with a bevy of brave ladies on a motor-club tour somewhere in New Jersey.

Brown Brothers
William Howard Taft was the first president in the White House to own an automobile, a White Steamer. Taft and Mrs. Taft are seated in the rear with son, Charles, and John Hays Hammond, famous mining engineer. About 1909.

First family ever to motor across the United States were the Jacob M. Murdocks, in 1908. Their time from Pasadena to New York, 32 days, 5 hours, 25 minutes, set a new transcontinental record for a single car driven by the same driver.

Touring Europe by auto in 1905 was strictly for millionaires with shaggy fur coats and a stand-by chauffeur to take over when a tire needed to be repaired.

Close view of the steering wheel and dashboard of a 1909 Fiat racer. Notice the serpent horn operated by a bulb, which may be seen just inside the rear fender. Note also the speedometer just in back of the large gas headlight. This Italian-made car was the forerunner of the Stutz Bearcat. It will still do 140 miles per hour.

Moe Leiter

Keystone View

A daring lady at the wheel of a Columbia with a detachable tonneau.

One day's production leaving the Overland plant, at Indianapolis. The year is 1909. Later the company moved into the old Pope-Toledo plant at Toledo, Ohio.

These four female motorists of 1909 are driving a brand-new Maxwell. Notice the covers for the headlights. The photographer has managed to arrange a pennant displaying the initials M.B.M.C. They stand for Maxwell Briscoe Motor Company.

This publicity pose of 1911 is a phoney, but the costumes and the vehicles are authentic. The car is a Packard. The motorcycle is a four-cylinder Pierce-Arrow.

Collectors of old cars today hold special meets and endurance runs in their ancient automobiles. Here a member of the Horseless Carriage Club of Los Angeles poses for news photographers during the club's annual Easter parade.

This dashing car was Billy Durant's dream baby. It made Buick one of the leaders and became the first car in General Motors' stable.

No wolf of 1916 was complete without a Stutz Bearcat. Here we see a rising young movie actor, Adolphe Menjou, playing the part of a dashing cad with intentions strictly dishonorable. But Miss Lillian (Dimples) Walker preferred to walk.

The author, with his mother and father. They are bound for French Lick Springs, Indiana, in a Marmon, about 1909.

This pretty chauffeuse, as lady drivers were often called, is at the wheel of this long-forgotten Anhut automobile. The acetylene generator on the running board indicates that it was probably manufactured before 1910.

In 1910 New England still had numerous toll roads and bridges.

A Thomas Flyer and a Packard in a match race on the open highway. These two rivals were leaders in the high-priced market.

Brown Brothers

Two society matrons of Newport, Rhode Island, in a Maxwell runabout, about 1906, have parked on the left-hand side of the street. The policeman is trying to make up his mind what to do about it.

Brown Brothers

At Newport, the electric hansom cab was a great favorite with society folk of 1905. This car was one of those manufactured by the Electric Vehicle Company.

Ewing Galloway
This Model T made the farmer's lot a much happier one and Henry Ford the richest man in the world.

Brown Brothers
The gentleman at the wheel of this British Napier car is Charles J. Glidden, who started the famous Glidden Tours of early days. About 1910.

In 1912 the Lincoln Highway was a red line on a map showing the most direct route to some of the worst mudholes in the country.

Underwood & Underwood
This brave gentleman from Maine with his wife and five beautiful back-seat drivers is at the wheel of a Lozier.

This millionaire's sleek electric cab caused a stir in 1912, even among blasé New Yorkers.

Underwood & Underwood

These electric cabs were a common sight on New York streets the first decade of the twentieth century.

Petite Anna Held, actress of milk-bath fame, poses for a publicity shot in the door of her milk-white limousine.

Here are the Hot Rods. The scene shows members of the Southern California Timing Association joining the National Safety Council.

the price had risen to $4,500,000. But Durant had foreseen that possibility and he accepted with alacrity. It was probably the best buy he ever made.

Now the double-or-nothing fever possessed Durant like a narcotic. He was infallible; he was a genius; everybody around him said so. Some of them believed it. He dashed from factory to factory, making instant decisions, talking by long distance telephone to New York, San Francisco, Minneapolis, dictating letters, issuing orders. He delighted in rising at seven o'clock and working until two the next morning—while a host of sleepy satellites and sycophants hung on every word, every lightning decision, every command.

The story is told that he once made an appointment with one of his executives for the next day at 1 a.m.

"You mean one p.m.," said the executive.

"No, I mean one a.m.," Durant replied. "You're on the night shift."

This little man who weighed barely more than a hundred pounds could work twenty hours a day. Four hours of sleep were all he required. He drove and dominated men who were physically twice his size. He wore them out in platoons. Not only those around him but those in General Motors plants and offices from San Francisco to New York. His monthly long distance telephone bill was always a small fortune; in one especially hectic week it is said to have totaled $25,000.

Of course, like all administrators who are in charge of too many projects, he sometimes gave orders that were virtually impossible to carry out, and yet he always expected results. Because he had many devoted and capable men beneath him, the impossible sometimes came true, giving Durant the aura, not only of a genius, but of a miracle man.

But he had faults by the score and enemies by the hundreds. During office hours he would give audience to five or six callers at once. His advertising agent, the president of a corporation, his attorney, the sales manager of a steel mill, the head of one of his subsidiaries might all be ushered into his office at once, there to sit before him like five petitioners before an indulgent, feudal lord. Oftentimes men of considerable stature found themselves embarrassed by this whim of Durant's; and even the least of his callers resented having their private business with him treated so lightly.

Regardless of any enemies he might make, Durant ran his domain as he wished; and what he wished was to strut, to show his stuff, on his own stage in his own theater—his Irish blood turning him into a ham actor, whose audience either loved and cheered every word and gesture or found his performances to be in extremely bad taste.

But Durant's admirers and detractors alike agreed that he had a mind like a calculating machine and a phenomenal memory for details, so that he could keep the facts and figures of a dozen pending deals all in his mind at once. Which was fortunate, since he hopped from one important oral commitment to another so fast that written records were often a week or two behind his actual accomplishments, and many of his purchases and stock manipulations depended entirely on his memory of vital figures.

During the year following the purchase of Cadillac, Durant, in a burst of activity that surely has never been equaled in the history of any corporation, purchased or secured control of the following companies:

    Champion Ignition Company
    Weston-Mott Company
    Reliance Motor Truck Company
    Rainier Motor Company
    Michigan Motor Castings Company
    Welch Motor Car Company
    Welch-Detroit Company
    Jackson-Church-Wilcox Company
    Michigan Auto Parts Company

Rapid Motor Vehicle Company
Cartercar Company
Ewing Automobile Company
Dow Rim Company
Northway Motor & Manufacturing Company
National Motor Cab Company
W. F. Stewart Body Company
Elmore Manufacturing Company
McLaughlin Motor Car Company
Brown-Lipe-Chapin Company
Oak Park Power Company
Novelty Incandescent Lamp Company
Heany Lamp Company
Randolph Motor Truck Company

He also bought stock interests in Maxwell-Briscoe, the United Motors Company and Lansden Electric. And he tried to buy the Ford Motor Company and the E. R. Thomas Company, manufacturer of the Thomas Flyer. These purchases were, in fact, approved by the General Motors board of directors subject to arrangements whereby the deals could be financed.

Both buys fell through because cash was required and the bankers were not inclined to lend money for the purchase of automobile companies. The big money men were no fools; they knew that the automobile business was too risky; any moment the bubble might burst!

Ford and Couzens are said to have agreed to take $8,000,000 for the Ford Motor Company. They also had agreed to make it easy on Durant—$2,000,000 down and the balance in one and two years.

But those smart Wall Street bankers couldn't be wangled into a deal like that. They shook their heads when Durant tried to borrow the money. Twelve months later Ford grossed over $20,000,000 and the following year the company's gross leaped to $40,000,000!

But even so the bankers' mistakes were not as stupid as Durant's. He seemed possessed by a desire to absorb every automobile company, good or bad, that could be enticed into his holding corporation. Such cars as Ewing, Rainier, Welch, Cartercar and Elmore were of little value and had to be abandoned soon after they became a part of General Motors.

The purchase of the latter two indicated Durant's appalling lack of technical knowledge; and also his gambler's tendency to rely on hunches rather than turn to engineers for any advice. Elmore was the only car on the market with a two-cycle engine. It controlled certain two-cycle patents. The Cartercar had patents on the friction transmission. Durant thought that he was putting a small bet on a long shot, when he bought the two companies. He reasoned that two-cycle engines and friction drive might prove to be better than four-cycle engines and selective transmission. In that case General Motors would be sitting pretty. But a jury of competent engineers could have told him that neither device was efficient nor ever would be. His purchase of Cartercar and Elmore was a display of almost childlike naiveté.

But these two mistakes were minor compared to the bull he made when he purchased the Heany Lamp Company. John Albert Heany, in 1907, was granted a patent on a tungsten filament light bulb. Not long afterward General Electric sued Heany claiming priority on the invention. And in that same year Heany, his attorney and a Patent Office clerk were charged with altering Heany's original application so as to permit later applications to be classed as revisions. The clerk and the lawyer were convicted and sent to prison, but Heany was acquitted.

The civil suits over Heany's patents were still pending when Durant went before his board of directors and persuaded them to purchase the Heany Lamp Company, in order to gain control of Heany's disputed patents. They paid Heany over $7,000,000 in General Motors stock to take over all of his electric companies, which owned little more than a doubtful patent.

Of course Durant must have believed that Heany's patent was good; he undoubtedly had the advice of his attorneys. But it is still hard to understand how he could have felt justified in doing business with Heany, under the circumstances.

Someone has guessed that this may have been a desperate long-shot gamble by Durant. It was one roll—double or nothing! He figured it was a way to pull General Motors out of a hole. Because if Heany's patents were upheld Durant would be sitting pretty. He could dictate to General Electric on light bulbs; he could go to the bankers and borrow millions. For the bankers knew that electric lights were here to stay. They weren't a gamble, like automobiles.

But Durant played in hard luck; the United States Commissioner of Patents voided the Heany rights and eventually the Heany Lamp Company and other Heany companies were written off as a total loss.

The Heany fiasco left General Motors in a very unhealthy condition. In May, 1910, construction on a new Buick plant stopped. Even Cadillac, soundest company in General Motors, had a hard time meeting a payroll. But even so, Durant was negotiating to buy Willys-Overland! When the directors heard this they wondered whether the Little Giant was cracking up.

Perhaps it was a bluff on Durant's part, or perhaps he thought that talk of acquiring the money-making company run by Willys would help him with the bankers. But it didn't. The bankers were still suspicious of automobiles. After all, look what had happened to the bicycle industry. Saturation! That was a word they dreaded. How could bankers guess that the United States would eventually have 33,261,454 passenger cars and 7,227,380 trucks operating within its boundaries, and no saturation point in sight?

Not even Durant, with his abounding optimism and his

insistence that the industry would some day sell a million cars in one year, not even he could guess that in a few years Ford alone would turn out ten thousand cars in a single day.

The irony of the whole thing was that for 1910 General Motors showed a net profit of over ten million dollars, but still it was in a precarious cash position. And in order to keep running, to meet payrolls and discount bills a company must have cash.

For a while a group of Chicago bankers considered loaning the corporation enough money to get by, but lack of a unified bookkeeping system for the corporation had resulted in a scramble of figures that were difficult to analyze. Nobody seemed to know just how much cash General Motors needed. So the Chicago money bowed out.

Durant tried the banks in Detroit, Kansas City, St. Louis. Apparently the deal was too big for any of them. He finally was forced to go to Boston and New York. There the banks agreed to see General Motors through its difficulties, but the terms they laid down were highway robbery.

Events proved that $8,000,000 would probably have been all the company needed, but the bankers wanted to be generous under the circumstances. They set the loan at $12,750,000 at 7 per cent interest, plus a $2,250,000 bonus, plus a stock bonus, plus a voting trust, placing complete power in the hands of the two banking firms that made the loan.

And in addition Billy Durant, who had made General Motors great and then almost wrecked it, was forced to step down from the presidency and become a mere member of the board.

The little man with the driving ambition and the fanatical belief in the future of the automobile stepped down, but he was still cocky and still self-assured. He wasn't through, not that one; he was just waiting until he could get his hands on the dice again.

15

THE SPEED DEMONS

1912
Production 356,000
Registration 901,596
Electric starters

No PRODUCT OF industry ever improved so rapidly as did the American motor car. By 1912 four-cylinder cars with 20- to 40-horsepower rating were standard, and there were also quite a few six-cylinder cars with 60-horsepower rating and higher. The Apperson Jackrabbit was not concerned with such mumbo-jumbo as horsepower; it simply guaranteed that the Apperson could travel seventy-five miles per hour. Of course you first had to find a road that would stand such speed.

By 1912 most open cars were equipped with windshields and a few companies were making closed bodies. All cars came equipped with demountable rims, gas headlights, oil side and tail lights and a bulb horn; Cadillacs were equipped with electric self-starters, while some of the others listed compressed-air starters as extra equipment, or Prest-O-Starters, which were part of the regular Pres-O-Lite gas lighting system.

The frames, the springs, the brakes, the clutches, the transmissions, the ignition systems, the methods of lubrication and even the quality of fuel for automobiles improved almost daily. The reason was that no product had ever before been subjected to such strenuous competition. It was not just the rivalry of the market place, but actual physical competition that took place in race meets, hill-climbing contests and endurance tours.

At speed trials held at the Empire City Track, Yonkers, in July, 1903, Barney Oldfield had driven Henry Ford's 999 one mile in 55.8 seconds, a new track record.

Later that year a Packard racer traveling a straight course on the sands of Daytona Beach made a mile in 46.4 seconds.

Henry Ford, meanwhile, had revamped his 999 for a speed trial on Lake St. Clair, near Detroit. A mile straightaway was cleared and covered with cinders, and on January 12, 1904, with Ford himself at the wheel 999 covered a mile in 39.4 seconds.

The record was short-lived, however, for a couple of weeks later William K. Vanderbilt, Jr., driving an 80-horsepower Mercedes covered a mile in 39 seconds flat, or about 92.31 miles per hour.

And so it went. The record for the mile changed hands almost monthly, especially in the winter, when the professionals gathered on the smooth sands of Daytona Beach. In 1906 the record was up to 127.66 miles per hour, held by Fred Marriott and a Stanley Steamer. By 1910 the speed mark was 131.72 miles per hour, made by Barney Oldfield in his famous Blitzen Benz.

And by that time there was probably not a day in the year that a motor car contest of some kind could not be found somewhere in the nation. Most manufacturers tried to win recognition in as many of these contests as possible. Naturally the pace was brutal, so the larger companies with the best crews of mechanics and drivers usually took the cream. These were Winton, Marmon, Lozier, Knox, National and several others, not one of which is in existence today.

Of course, the poor consumer got pretty confused trying to keep up with all the world's records and perfect scores and unbeaten champions that he met in the advertising pages of the automobile magazines.

For instance Winton's Bullet No. 2 was a special racing car with a straight 8 engine that rested beneath the frame of the car. In 1903 it claimed world's records from one up to fifteen miles.

Peerless in 1905 claimed that its Green Dragon was the "holder of *all* world's records."

In 1907 Ford announced that his new six-cylinder job had just won the 24-hour race at Detroit, "breaking *all* world's records."

Marmon named five important races which it had won in 1909-10, and also claimed *all* national track records from five miles up to two hundred miles.

The Knox claimed to have won some twenty-six races during 1909.

Lozier declared in 1911 that it held *all* world's records from twenty-five to one hundred miles on a one mile track.

Stutz, in 1911, announced it had made an amazing five hundred miles in 442 minutes in the first Indianapolis International Sweepstakes. Which was probably true, but the Stutz advertising failed to state that Stutz did not finish in the money and that at least ten cars in the race bettered the Stutz time.

Harry Stutz was a brilliant engineer, however, and created for public consumption a high-speed sport-racer which captured the imagination and affection of the youthful motoring enthusiasts of that day. This car was known as the Stutz Bearcat. It was a low, rakish car whose owner was required, by all the complex laws that govern proper attire for the younger set, to wear a raccoon coat and a plaid motoring cap. Princeton, Harvard and Yale were the home base for numerous Stutz Bearcats, complete with raccoon coats and plaid caps. But somehow that particular clientele was not sufficient to support an automobile company and eventually the Stutz Bearcat became only a memory on the college scene.

Probably the two most important hill-climbing contests in the country were conducted at Eagle Rock, New Jersey, and at Algonquin, Illinois. But there were hundreds of other hill-climbing events from Massachusetts to California. Every famous grade in the country was subjected to test both by gasoline and steam.

Reo made much of having won a hill climb, in 1905, on Pecowsic Hill, near Springfield, Massachusetts.

In 1906 Buick named all the cars it had beaten at Algonquin, but conveniently forgot about those it had not beaten.

The Correja Speed Runabout, which sounded suspiciously like the bait in a stock-selling promotion, claimed to have won every hill-climbing contest entered in 1911. These were at Bridgeport, New Haven, Ossining, Port Jefferson and Plainfield.

It should be pointed out that hill-climbing contests were always broken down into various classes determined by horsepower, weight, price and other factors. Seven or eight classes often resulted. Some such class as cars of 14- to 22-horsepower, weighing four hundred to one thousand pounds, priced below $1,500, might have only two entries. Therefore, it was possible for a hill-climb "winner" to have beaten exactly one car; but it still took a gold medal and a full-page advertisement in *The Horseless Age*.

Sometime after 1903 reliability and endurance contests became so popular that the American Automobile Association was hard pressed to govern them all.

Easily the most famous of these was the Glidden Tour. Charles J. Glidden, a Boston millionaire, offered a rather ornate and valuable loving cup to be competed for annually in a tour of not less than one thousand miles. It was open to all members of the American Automobile Association or any other automobile club in the world that was recognized by them.

Obviously Mr. Glidden's intent was to promote a gentlemanly competition for motoring enthusiasts, but the manufacturers jumped into this affair from the opening gun and by their frantic efforts each year to win made it the big prize contest of its day.

Since the rules required that the drivers should be members of the A.A.A. the entry list in the early years consisted largely of two or three top executives from every important automobile plant in the United States.

The first Glidden Tour had such important contestants as John D. Maxwell, driving a Maxwell, Walter C. White, in a White Steamer, R. E. Olds, piloting a Reo, and Percy B. Pierce, son of George N. Pierce, driving a Pierce-Arrow.

The opening tour was run off in the summer of 1905 over a difficult course with thirty-three cars entered. It was not considered a race, but the pace was rugged. Every car was expected to reach a certain town each day, in a specified number of hours, depending on the size and speed of the individual car. Any breakdowns or any trouble encountered reduced the contestant's score.

Twenty-eight cars finished the tour and were all awarded certificates of performance, but the Pierce-Arrow, driven by Percy Pierce, had the best score and was awarded the Glidden trophy. Four years in succession Pierce-Arrow won the tour. The publicity from these four wins made Pierce-Arrow almost an automatic choice for people of wealth. And for some reason it also became standard for hearses and funeral limousines.

The Glidden Tour was undoubtedly the grand prix of reliability runs, but there were many others each year held by motor clubs from Boston to San Francisco. And the scoring in these contests was such that a dozen cars might win gold medals. Consequently there were few automobiles worthy of the name that could not boast a perfect score in some reliability run and thus claim a "win."

But for students of equivocation, the most interesting "contests" were the special one-car affairs in which the sponsoring company could not possibly lose. There was inevitably a favorable result; either the car created a new speed record, a new record in its class, a record for economy and reliability or just a "record." The following are a few examples:

In 1906, a two-cylinder Reo, in something called the New York Economy Test, carried four passengers a distance of 682 miles, at a cost of $3.38 per passenger. Since no mention was made of what it cost other cars to make this run, it is to be presumed that either Reo was *not* the most economical, or that there were no other cars in the competition.

In 1907 a Premier drove non-stop between New York and Bridgeport until the car had covered 4,906 miles, which, the Premier ad stated, was just like going from New York to San Francisco and back to Omaha—a new non-stop record!

In 1908 Maxwell found a way to practically win the Glidden Tour without entering it. A full-page ad in *The Automobile* challenged the winner of the tour to an endurance run from New York to San Francisco.

Naturally the winner spurned the Maxwell challenge, which gave Maxwell dealers the opportunity to claim the race by default. But just the same Maxwell kept working at it until they won the Glidden Tour by having four of their entries finish with a perfect score.

In 1909 Rambler claimed to have broken the record from Los Angeles to San Diego, making it in 10 hours and 32 minutes, with no stops for repairs.

Columbia claimed a new record from Chicago to New York, at least in its class—24-horsepower.

The American underslung made a new record by going from Indianapolis to Boston and return, carrying four men.

THE SPEED DEMONS

Doubtless no car had ever before made that same trip, so a new record was a certainty.

In 1910 Studebaker-Flanders sponsored a fantastic but sure-fire "record" tour. Two boys, both under fifteen, drove a Flanders from Denver to Spokane. There were no age limits or driver's licenses in those days, of course. The boys carried letters from city and state officials. The newspapers didn't say to whom.

This frantic activity on the part of manufacturers hoping to capture "records" for their cars seems a little ridiculous today; but the fact is that these efforts to win races and hill climbs and endurance runs were one of the best things that could have happened to the industry. For the weak points of every car were quickly exposed and as soon as possible were corrected.

The high point in foolish contests came in 1908 with a combination race and endurance contest of gargantuan proportions. Up to that time Europe had had a monopoly on long cross-country races. In France, where Napoleon's network of fine military roads were still doing business, the one thousand-mile road race had been a part of local mores since 1895. And in 1907 *Le Matin* of Paris conceived a super road race to be run from Peking to Paris for a prize of 100,-000 francs. *Mon Dieu! Magnifique!* Yes, indeed, especially in view of the fact that *Le Matin*'s editors were not aware that no complete vehicle road from Peking to Paris existed. As a consequence the contestants had to disassemble their cars and have them packed across a mountain range by Chinese coolies. But the race was completed and won by amateur sportsman Prince Borghese, of Italy, driving an Itala car.

So, in 1908, *Le Matin,* or someone, conceived the idea of a still more sensational contest—a so-called Around-the-World Race. Actually the race was to be from New York westward to Paris, but that was practically around the world; at least it was a hell of a long way in an automobile.

Le Matin and the New York *Times* co-sponsored the race, and on February 12, 1908, six intrepid daredevils of the open road assembled in Times Square ready for the starting gun. The contestants were two De Dion cars of 40-horsepower, a French car called a Moto-Bloc, 40-horsepower, a lightweight French Sizaire-Naudin, 12-horsepower, an Italian Zust, 40-horsepower, a German Protos, 60-horsepower, and a Thomas Flyer, 60-horsepower. Each car was allowed two drivers and a mechanic. In addition, the Thomas Flyer carried a *Times* correspondent.

According to an insider of those days, the E. R. Thomas Company, builder of Thomas Flyers, was in financial difficulties and the race was actually cooked up by the Thomas crowd as a method of recapturing prestige for a car that was losing money. This may explain why no other American manufacturer entered the race. It also explains why the Thomas Flyer company is supposed to have spent $100,000 on that one race.

It is said that from New York to San Francisco the Thomas was never out of touch, for more than twenty-four hours, with a traveling machine shop and parts depot that crossed America by rail, while the Thomas battled across by road. Spare parts, mechanics and machinists were always near at hand in case the car ran into serious trouble.

In all probability the Thomas crowd was primarily interested in winning the race from New York to San Francisco. That would give the company enough publicity to sell a year's record output of cars and then some. If they went on from there and arrived in Paris first, so much the better.

The racers got away from Times Square on schedule, headed up the Albany Post Road and were soon in trouble, for New York state was knee deep in snow. But the Thomas made 116 miles the first day while the others were strung out behind it.

One of the French contestants wired back to its New York agency: "I am sure to win. I shovel very hard."

Another wired: "The race has become a snow-shoveling contest. But we only have 19,995 miles to go."

It took two weeks for the Thomas to reach Chicago, at which point it was leading the way by twenty-four hours. The Thomas distributor threw a party attended by the mayor and other local big shots. There was a great deal of speech-making and much champagne. The Thomas team started westward next day with a hangover.

In Iowa the rains came and they learned about gumbo. But the Thomas crew had plenty of cash and numerous farmers' teams pulled them through. Then came more snow and a couple of mountain ranges, but the traveling machine shop was always waiting at the town just ahead, in case of a breakdown.

The Thomas' progress across the continent was a tour of triumph. They received 22-gun salutes, the keys to various cities and the cheers of throngs that lined the streets of every town they passed through. At last, after forty-two days of rugged travel the Thomas reached San Francisco. The Zust was still in Utah, one of the De Dions was in Granger, Wyoming, and the Protos was undergoing repairs in the neighborhood of Laramie. The other two cars had dropped out.

At San Francisco, the Thomas was put aboard a ship bound for Alaska. And then the race went slightly haywire. For it seemed that the promoters, whether the *Times* and *Le Matin* or the E. R. Thomas Company, had imagined that the contestants could cross from Alaska to Russia on the frozen Bering Sea. Not until the Thomas reached Alaska did anyone think to tell the sponsors that the Bering Sea hadn't frozen solid within the memory of man and that any part which did freeze always resembled the canyons of the Rocky Mountains.

So the Thomas crew received orders in Alaska to turn around and come back. The judges of the race then decreed that all would continue from Seattle to Vladivostok by ship, and there resume the race, at which point the Thomas would be credited with the lead it had over the others at the time it reached San Francisco.

At the Russian port the driver of the De Dion decided that his car was not in shape to attempt to combat the wilderness that lay ahead, so the three remaining cars headed for Moscow neck and neck. They traveled by the stars at times, through country where an automobile had never before been seen. It finally developed into a race between the Thomas and the German Protos.

In Russia the Thomas was without its traveling repair shop so the going was much more difficult. They encountered undreamed-of hardships, and by the time St. Petersburg was reached, the Thomas was four days behind the Protos, while the Zust was trailing by more than a week. The cars stayed in that position all the way across Europe, the Protos arriving in Paris on July twenty-sixth. But although the German car reached Paris first, it was badly beaten in total elapsed time, for it had been judged thirty days behind the Thomas in America. Thus the Thomas won the race by twenty-six days.

But the Protos could claim a European victory, and even the Italian Zust, which finished two weeks after the Thomas, had nothing to be ashamed of in its performance, since it was a much less powerful car than the other two. Doubtless it claimed a record for its class.

As for the Thomas Flyer, by the time it reached Paris the factory in Buffalo was already so far behind on orders that it was running day and night. The Thomas advertisements were exceedingly condescending toward all other cars, especially the winners of Glidden Tours. Prospective purchasers were advised to get in line as soon as possible if they wanted to get behind the wheel of the world's champion. "We are perfectly disinterested," the ads stated, "in advising you to confer as soon as possible with your Thomas representative." Incidentally, a Thomas Flyer cost $4,000, cash on delivery.

The New York to Paris race was a freak and nothing like it was ever repeated. But the shorter road races of the early days were very popular for a while and were invaluable in teaching automotive engineers their errors and in helping to develop the speed and endurance of gasoline engines. The outstanding road races were the Vanderbilt Cup Races, the Elgin Road Races and the American Grand Prix.

William K. Vanderbilt, Jr., an enthusiastic gentleman auto racer, who had participated in most of the important motor races in Europe, presented the American Automobile Association with the $1,000 Vanderbilt trophy for an International Cup Race to be run annually over a closed course for a distance of approximately three hundred miles.

Vanderbilt intended to establish a race for amateur sportsmen, but eventually the manufacturers barged in and took it over as they did the Glidden Tours. The first race, run on October 8, 1904, seems to have been about what Vanderbilt had in mind. The course was on Long Island and was approximately triangular in shape. Starting at Queens Village it ran westward via Jericho Turnpike to Jericho, then turned south through Hicksville to Bethpage Turnpike and from there returned to the starting point. This distance was 28.44 miles. The race was ten laps long.

According to newspaper accounts, the course was crowded by five o'clock in the morning. At six the first contestant was given the gun. The others followed at two-minute intervals.

The American entries were two Pope-Toledos, a Royal Tourist, a Clement Bayard, a Packard, and a Smith and Mabley Simplex. The foreign makes were two Mercedes cars, a De Dietrich, a Panhard, a Fiat and a Renault. But apparently all the foreign racers were owned by American sportsmen and there were only a few professional drivers. George Heath, an American, driving the French Panhard, won that first race with an average speed of 52.2 miles per hour.

But amateur drivers soon disappeared from the Vanderbilt

Cup Race, and in a couple of years the American manufacturers were pointing their whole racing program toward winning that one race. It was the big plum of American competition, even though the prize was only a silver and gold loving cup. A French Darracq won in 1905 and an Italian Fiat in 1906.

In 1907 a Locomobile finally snared the cup for America. Three years later, with the foreign cars outnumbered five to one, American cars took the first three places. They were the Alco, the Marmon and the National, names that are today only a memory.

In 1911 Ralph Mulford driving his famous Lozier took the cup, and that was the last time America won it. From 1912 on the German Mercedes and the French Peugeot ran rings around the American cars. Their drivers were Ralph De Palma and Dario Resta, and they made the Vanderbilt Cup their exclusive property until closed-course racing finally ended in 1916.

But meantime the road race had become an anachronism in America. Dangerous for spectators and drivers alike, difficult to watch, impossible to patrol, its demise was long overdue. For in 1909 Carl Fisher, who had made a fortune with Prest-O-Lite gas lighting systems for automobiles, had conceived the idea of a huge 2.5-mile track in which big-time automobile racing could be conducted under conditions that would be more or less ideal for both the spectators and the drivers.

The Indianapolis Speedway was completed and opened in 1909. The first Memorial Day 500-mile race was run in 1911. It was won by Ray Harroun in a Marmon with the first rear-view mirror.

This race took place about ten years after the A.A.A. conducted its first automobile speed contest—a fifty-mile road race on Long Island. The winner of that contest was A. L. Riker, gentleman driver, and future president of the Locomobile Company. He drove a Riker Electric racer and his average for the fifty miles was slightly better than twenty-four miles per hour.

Ray Harroun's average for five hundred miles was 74.6 miles per hour. In ten years the speed of the automobile had more than tripled. There would never be another ten years like that in the automobile business.

16

A ROAD FOR HONEST ABE

1913
Production *461,500*
Registration *1,190,393*
Wire wheels

THE GOOD ROADS movement, with Colonel Albert A. Pope as its principal proponent, had its beginnings about 1880 and by 1912 had flowered into a beautiful dream, in a class with universal peace, socialism and a cure for the common cold.

There were almost a million automobiles in the United States by that time and their owners were all in favor of good roads. But there were fifty million farmers and miscellaneous taxpayers who couldn't see any sense in building expensive highways when a network of railroads already connected the big cities.

Of course, a lot of people who didn't own automobiles believed in good roads, but road building, for the most part, was in the hands of the counties, so even if one county built some good roads they might be completely surrounded by bad roads. For that reason there were absolutely no good roads of any length in the entire country.

The best and longest road of uniform quality was the Long

Island Motor Parkway. This was a fifty-mile concrete highway extending from Flushing to Lake Ronkonkoma. It had been built in 1907 by William K. Vanderbilt, Jr., and several of his wealthy friends whose homes were scattered along its length. The road bridged every intersection, no carriages were allowed on it and there was a toll charge of one dollar to drive on it. Never a financial success, it was abandoned in 1937. But in design it was far ahead of its time, and fully twenty years after it was built was still the safest highway for motor travel in the United States.

The good roads movement became a rather neglected cause once Colonel Pope had become a multi-millionaire and the bicycle was no longer a national fad. After 1899 the League of American Wheelmen, which had brought about some slight road improvements, slowly expired. That left good roads strictly in the lap of the automobile manufacturers and the A.A.A.

The industry wanted good roads and talked good roads but most of its driving personalities were too busy turning out automobiles to do anything constructive. The most Detroit did for a long while was to lay the first mile of concrete highway in the United States. It was constructed on Woodward Avenue just north of Detroit's city limits. Motorists came from miles around to ride on that piece of concrete. That was in 1908. That was in the 20th century!

What the good roads movement needed was someone to build a fire under all the super-salesmen, super-planners and super-producers of the industry. It needed to have men like John Willys and Flanders and Chapin and Durant get on the ball.

The man who finally built the fire under them was Carl Fisher, a super-visionary, who got the cockeyed notion in 1912 of building a road from New York to San Francisco, which he proposed to call the "Ocean-to-Ocean Rock Highway."

Carl Fisher was a man who thought only in millions. Any

figure less than a million was just a piddlin' little backwoods amount. Fisher kept that kind of money in the petty-cash drawer of his thinking equipment. When he visualized his Ocean-to-Ocean Highway, he didn't consider the cost important; all he wanted was action. He said, "Let's build it before we're too old to enjoy it."

Fisher's Prest-O-Lite Company and his Indianapolis Speedway were both a very important part of the industry, so he was able to approach everybody in the automobile business on a personal basis. He proposed on Sept. 6, 1912, that the industry tax itself one-third of one per cent for three years and thus raise $10,000,000. But no part of this tax was to be payable until the $10,000,000 was pledged.

Furthermore, Fisher wanted the money now! He told the industry that there was no time to fool around. He expected everybody to sign up by January 1, 1913, so that the road could be finished on May 1, 1915, in time for the San Francisco Exposition. That was the sort of action Mr. Fisher liked, but he was doomed to disappointment, even though, for a while, he had the boys going along with his dream.

The first important pledge came from Frank A. Seiberling, president of Goodyear Tire and Rubber Company, who promised $300,000. This started the ball rolling and Fisher sent wires to all important companies pressing them for quick action. The pledges began to come in then, from one automobile manufacturer after another. It looked as though Fisher was going to have his Ocean-to-Ocean Rock Highway in jig time. Auditors estimated that the pledges had reached $4,000,000. Mr. Fisher began to expand his plans. He could envision $20,000,000 from the automobile and allied industries. Then there would be private donations, additional grants from each state, material donations, etc., etc. Mr. Fisher had built, in his imagination, a highway worth $100,-000,000 before the bubble burst.

The fellow who burst it was Henry Ford. Fisher had to have Ford's pledge for he controlled seventy-five per cent of the automobile business, but as usual, if the rest of the industry was *for* something Henry was *against* it. He still had his terrible mad on. He wouldn't give one-third of one per cent of his gross business for three years and that was that. He wouldn't give a lead nickel!

The grandiose plans for a quick and easy road from ocean to ocean went out the window. It was obvious that if the road was to be built it would take a lot of cajoling, a lot of exhortation and a lot of downright hard work.

At about this point somebody suggested that there was no glamour in a road that was called the "Ocean-to-Ocean Rock Highway." Congressman William Borland, who was trying to interest his Washington colleagues in good roads, suggested that what Fisher's road needed was a name that would stir the emotions, a patriotic name. Fisher's friend Elbert Hubbard suggested "The American Road," which was as dull as Mr. Hubbard's writings. No one seems to know, for certain, who suggested the magic word "Lincoln," but at a meeting attended by Henry B. Joy, as spokesman for the Detroit manufacturers, the name of the proposed road was changed to the "Lincoln Memorial Highway."

It was an inspiration. A man who wouldn't support something named after Lincoln would beat his own mother. So in April, 1913, The Lincoln Highway Association was incorporated and Henry B. Joy was chosen as its first president.

Joy was a much more practical man than Fisher. As president of the Packard Motor Car Company he was one of the ablest men in the industry. He visualized the Lincoln Highway as a public relations project, rather than a job to be accomplished by the industry single-handed. There was more to putting a road across the continent than raising the money to help build it. The people of the United States had to want it and approve of it. The states through which it was to pass had to give assistance. Every newspaper and every magazine would need to be sold on the idea and for that matter it would be a good idea to sell every schoolchild.

The Lincoln Memorial Highway forthwith developed into one of the most gigantic publicity campaigns the country had ever seen. It became the real spearhead of the good roads movement. It was the holy cause which only infidels could resist. It was an example of a very high-class public relations job.

The first sustained publicity barrage came from a tour sponsored by the Indiana Automobile Manufacturers Association and the Hoosier Motor Club. Although there was as yet no Lincoln Highway route to follow, the tour was made through those states where it was believed the road would pass. The intention was to arouse interest among western states for the Lincoln Highway project.

This it did beyond anyone's expectations, but it also caused considerable anguish in those states through which the tour passed but which were later left off the Lincoln Highway route.

Every automobile manufacturer in Indiana sent at least one car on the long trek from Indianapolis to San Francisco; seventeen cars and two trucks transported a personnel of seventy men. The caravan included two doctors, with equipment, its own official photographer, an official speechmaker, representatives from the Postal and Western Union telegraph companies, an observer from the Royal Automobile Club of Great Britain, representatives from the A.A.A. and the American Highway Association, a correspondent for all Hearst newspapers, reporters from two Indianapolis dailies, as well as the Chicago *Tribune,* and a press representative of The Lincoln Highway Association.

Elwood Haynes, Indiana's pioneer auto maker, was one of the most prominent men on the tour, and Carl Fisher was also along as the official spokesman for The Lincoln Highway Association.

One of the nineteen expert drivers was Ray Harroun, winner of the first Indianapolis Memorial Day Race. The official map maker for the Blue Book Corporation was also on hand, to lay out a cross-continent route for the *Official A.A.A. Blue Books.*

Of the various makes of motor cars and trucks that made that historic tour not one is manufactured today. They were a Marmon, two Marions, a Pilot "60," two Hayneses, two Americans, a McFarland, two Appersons, two Hendersons, an Empire, a Pathfinder "40," two Premiers, a Brown truck and a Premier truck. The latter carried a supply of tires provided by the G. and J. Tire Company. The other truck carried camping equipment, repair parts and food supplies.

The tour started on July 1, 1913. Advance publicity had brought many requests from various cities across the country, to be included in the caravan's itinerary. More than one hundred communities offered special inducement in the form of newly improved roads.

Civic pride induced every city along the entire route to see that within its own township or county the road was scraped, dragged and graded for the well-publicized tourists that were heading their way. In one small town the whole masculine population turned out to prepare a road for the motorists. One state spent $25,000 to improve the road over which they would pass.

Governors and mayors greeted the caravan in every state and sometimes traveled with it across their own states. Each city in which the tourists stopped for the night entertained them with banquets and speech-making; and each night a flood of publicity poured over the telegraph wires to all the country, promoting the cause of good roads.

After thirty-four days, as they neared San Francisco, a welcoming committee of 1,200 cars came out from Oakland to greet them; it was the opening ceremony in what was to be the biggest celebration of the trip. As usual California outdid itself.

That same year the Lincoln Highway Association sent

Henry B. Joy, its president, along with Carl Fisher to the Governors' annual meeting in Colorado Springs to secure their cooperation for the proposed route of the Lincoln Highway. This route had been laid out with the avowed purpose of creating the most direct and practical road from New York to San Francisco.

Unfortunately the most direct road by-passed Colorado. The governor of the Rocky Mountain state, who was host to Joy and Fisher, made such a moving plea for an alternate route through Denver, that he finally won their consent to a compromise that was to cause no end of trouble. This compromise was called the Denver loop and before long communities in most every state across the nation were asking for an alternate route just like Denver's.

On his way back from the Governors' meeting Joy wrote out a document proclaiming the route of the Lincoln Highway. It was as corny and pretentious as a nominating speech, but Joy was a first-rate publicist and knew that public opinion was best nurtured by a generous helping of hot air.

The route, proclaimed on September 10, 1913, was as follows: New York, Jersey City, Trenton, Philadelphia, Gettysburg, Pittsburgh, Canton, Marion, Lima, Fort Wayne, South Bend, Chicago Heights, Joliet, DeKalb, Clinton, Cedar Rapids, Ames, Council Bluffs, Omaha, Kearney, North Platte, Julesburg, Fort Morgan, Denver, Fort Collins, Cheyenne, Laramie, Granger, Salt Lake City, Ely, Reno, Truckee, Placerville, Sacramento, Oakland, San Francisco.

Back in Detroit, Joy had his proclamation printed up on heavy paper, using an impressive type face. Then it was sent to every newspaper in the country with a news story that impressed wire editors almost as much as though the proclamation had come from President Lincoln himself. The story hit the front pages.

October 31, 1913, was then designated as the day on which all cities, towns and villages along the new route would dedicate their portion of the Lincoln Memorial Highway. And so, from coast to coast, editors carried stories about the opening of the new highway. Actually there was no highway at all—but merely a red line on a map, showing where the dirt roads and a few gravel roads might someday become macadam from ocean to ocean. And, it was hoped, that in some states sections of the road might even be made of concrete.

This was only the beginning. For the next fourteen years millions of words would flow from the Association headquarters in Detroit before the Lincoln Highway would be a reality. National magazines were dunned for free space to appeal for funds; a list of 3,000 millionaires was circularized for cash donations. Every person who owned an automobile was solicited for five dollar membership certificates in the Lincoln Highway Association. Even the school kids were asked for penny contributions to the fund.

Important writers were inveigled into writing articles about the highway. The top magazines printed stories. President Wilson was persuaded not only to buy a five dollar certificate but also to make a speech for the cause. The Association attempted for years to furnish speakers at any gathering where the audience was willing to listen to a plea for good roads in general, and the Lincoln Highway in particular.

In 1915 a motion picture was made, showing the sights to be observed in traveling from New York to San Francisco along the Lincoln Highway. It still had only a few scattered miles of hard surface in its whole length, but the public was anxious to see what the highway looked like, so the picture became a popular release in the nation's movie theaters and eventually returned a profit to the Association.

Following World War I, Frank A. Seiberling, the new president of the Association, assisted by various members of the board, did some adroit selling and persuaded the army to undertake a completely motorized transcontinental expedition from Washington, D.C., to San Francisco over the Lincoln Highway. The trip was made by 79 vehicles, 260 enlisted men and 35 officers. The road was not too well marked, even at this time, but an official car of the Lincoln Highway Association led the way. A press representative rode in the official car just to see that the Lincoln Highway got proper billing during the sixty-two-day trek across the country.

Thus the highway not only picked up another million or so words of free publicity, but a good many bridges along the route were strengthened or repaired by army engineers, so that the heavy, motorized equipment could get through.

As the fame of the Lincoln Highway grew it benefited from front-page news stories which developed without the aid of the Association's press representatives. Most of these stories resulted from various coast-to-coast races against time; the Lincoln Highway was used for these record-breaking runs because it was definitely the shortest and easiest way to get from San Francisco to New York. In 1916 the Hudson Super-Six became the automobile of the year when it flashed across the continent via the Lincoln Highway in 5 days and 15 hours, a record that was to stand until 1920.

One of the finest schemes conceived to promote good roads was originated by Henry Joy, assisted by the Portland Cement Association, which had been interested in the Lincoln Highway idea from its inception. The cement manufacturers offered to give enough cement to build one mile of road in any county that would follow the specifications of the cement association. In other words, the cement industry was willing to donate material to prove to the public that concrete highways were the best.

Toward the end of 1914 the first of these one-mile highways was built near Malta, Illinois. Joy named it a "seedling mile," expressing the hope that from it more miles of good road would grow.

These seedling miles were laid down almost entirely in

the Middle West, where the farmer resisted hard roads because he thought they would benefit only the city folk. But once he had driven over a seedling mile during the rainy season, while all the surrounding roads were hub deep in mud, he began to change his mind. Seedling miles began to be scattered from Illinois to Wyoming, and everywhere they were constructed the sentiment for more hard roads grew.

But it is said that it took a football game and a cloudburst to bring hard roads to Iowa. The game was an annual affair played on Thanksgiving Day between Iowa and Iowa State and was traditionally the most important football event in Iowa. Half the farmers in the state always turned out to see that game. But one fatal Thanksgiving Day there was a torrential rainstorm. Roads that were ordinarily frozen hard on Thanksgiving were turned into quagmires. As a result it was a week before some of the farmers shoveled their way out. That same year the state legislature put through a gasoline tax to build hard roads throughout the state.

Had the automobile industry been less determined in its efforts to see the highway completed, the whole idea might have expired in its early stages. Such men as Joy, Chapin, Willys, Durant, Fisher, Seiberling and in later years Edsel Ford financed the overhead expenses of the Association out of their own pockets, some of them contributing as much as $25,000.

However, it was not financial troubles but politicians, Chambers of Commerce and chiselers who gave the Association its biggest headaches. Trouble started the moment the route of the highway was announced. And the first mistake that was made was in conceding that alternate route to Denver.

Because the road was called the Lincoln Highway, efforts were made to have the route pass by Lincoln's birthplace and also through Springfield, Illinois, his later home.

Cleveland thought that it had been left off the route because of the rivalry between its auto makers and those of Detroit.

The Automobile Club of Southern California, of course, thought that the route should have ended at Los Angeles instead of San Francisco and put up a bitter fight to have it changed, or at least to have an alternate route.

Other California interests wanted the highway to go by way of Beckwith Pass and others favored a road through Yosemite.

The politicians of Iowa attempted to move the road farther south.

A local struggle between cities took place in Wyoming.

When the alternate Denver route was canceled Colorado papers condemned the whole project.

The Association even had to turn down President Woodrow Wilson, on his request to see the Lincoln Highway make a loop down below the Mason-Dixon line and through Washington, D.C. The sentimental arguments in favor of this change were hard to resist. The President argued that it would symbolize a united North and South. But the Association pointed out that it would also make the route 172 miles longer.

In Ohio, because of changing road conditions, the original route was shifted farther north. This brought Ohio's most prominent citizen into the fray. He was Senator Warren G. Harding. But the Association stood pat, and the Ohio committee finally accepted its decision.

It was in Utah that the Association met its toughest resistance and eventually went down in defeat. Utah had no sentimental qualms about opposing a project called the Lincoln Highway, for the Mormons had an old score to settle with President Lincoln. During the Civil War, when they had been suspected of sympathizing with the Confederacy, Lincoln had ordered troops into the territory to keep the Mormons in line. They hadn't cared much for Lincoln after that, so Utah could be hard-boiled as well as cynical about a road named for President Lincoln.

The argument started in 1915 over whether the Lincoln Highway would turn north out of Salt Lake City and then west toward Wendover, or go southwest toward Ely, Nevada. In the great expanses of the western states, where there were few or no county funds available for road improvement, the Lincoln Highway Association had been assisting with donations from the larger companies of the industry as well as some of its millionaire leaders.

The Association therefore offered to contribute $100,000 to build a road south and westward across the Great Salt Desert toward Ely. But the governor of the state, as well as his legislature were not interested in any westward road at all. However, if there was to be a road they wanted to see it cross the northern part of the desert into Wendover.

The Association stood pat; its engineers had reported the northern route to be impractical and uneconomical. So in 1918 the state finally agreed to build its section of the Lincoln Highway across the southerly portion of the desert. A contract was drawn up and $100,000 was deposited to the credit of the state. Utah then had the last laugh; it kept the money but refused to construct the highway.

The Association never got its money back and in 1923 the state finally got Federal funds to build the road to Wendover, where the governor and the legislature had wanted it in the first place. In their quarrel with President Lincoln the Mormons had finally won.

By 1916 there were 3,367,889 automobiles bouncing over America's inadequate roads and the industry's statisticians estimated that over a million and a half cars would be built that year. The pressure on Congress was too great to resist; something had to be done about roads. In that year the Federal Aid Road Act was passed, appropriating $75,000,000 for the purpose of assisting all states that desired to build rural post roads. The federal government would put up half the money if the states footed the rest of the bill and paid for the upkeep of the roads.

Although this was a step in the right direction the heavily populated eastern states benefited most from the Federal Aid Act, and more aid was needed for the western states so that roads could be built in sparsely settled areas connecting with the larger cities.

Eventually the Federal Highway Act of 1921 solved this problem and the final completion of Carl Fisher's Ocean-to-Ocean Rock Highway was in sight. But The Lincoln Highway Association continued until 1927, when it was voted to use what remained in the treasury to make certain that the Lincoln Highway would always be permanently marked. A Lincoln monument was designed which displayed the Lincoln Highway insignia and above it a bronze medallion bearing Lincoln's features in bas-relief. It was simple, tasteful and practical; three thousand of them were placed along the full length of the highway.

It is rather ironical that the Federal Highway Act, for which the Association fought and which helped complete the Lincoln Highway, was also the cause of its destruction. For it was this act that brought the numbering system to National Highways.

A good many other famous highways have gone the same way—the Dixie, the Midland, the Arrowhead Trail, the National Old Trail, the Rocky Mountain, the Sunshine and a score of others. But none was quite as famous as the Lincoln Highway, nor deserved to be.

Along the great length of that once-great road, it would probably be difficult today to find a single one of the three thousand "permanent" monuments erected to Lincoln in 1927. And it seems too bad that the highway which was once named for our greatest President, and which gave such impetus to the good roads movement, is now known as U. S. Routes 1, 30, 30N, 30S, 530, 40 and 50.

17

MR. FORD'S PARTNERS

1914
Production 548,139
Registration 1,664,003
The convertible coupé

THEY SHOULD HAVE been named Damon and Pythias instead of John and Horace, for there never was such a mutual admiration society as the brothers Dodge.

John was the older and the more domineering of the two, but when they argued, Horace could shout as loudly as John and they both had voices that could make the walls tremble. They were a couple of big, boisterous roughnecks who learned to operate a lathe in their father's machine shop at Port Huron, Michigan. Later they went to Windsor, Canada, and developed a ball-bearing bicycle, and sold out to the Canada Cycle and Motor Company for a profit of $7,500.

This money was invested in a machine shop in Detroit, under the name Dodge Brothers. A short time later R. E. Olds put the brothers in the automobile business by handing them a contract to furnish transmissions for his Merry Oldsmobile—two thousand at a crack. Twenty-five years later the Dodge brothers' widows sold the business for $166,000,000.

The Dodges were among Detroit's first super-producers.

They would work for fifteen and twenty hours at a stretch. It is said that in the early days they sometimes kept going until two in the morning, then went to sleep on benches in their machine shop, in order to be on the job at six in the morning.

At times they could be as gentle and sentimental as a couple of grandmothers and again as tough and uncompromising as a pair of gang leaders. Two elderly colored waiters, in the brothers' favorite bar, died suddenly during a flu epidemic. When the Dodges learned that they had left their widows penniless they supported the two women for years.

In contrast, John was having difficulty, one night, cranking his car; a stranger stopped to watch and remarked with a chuckle, "What's wrong? Can't you start 'er?"

The chuckle infuriated John. He walked over to the inquisitive stranger, knocked him cold and then returned to his cranking.

Despite their fanatical devotion to each other the brothers occasionally had epic quarrels. These usually took place in barrooms and over seemingly trivial matters. One night at the Pontchartrain or Churchill's, or one of the other bars along Woodward Avenue that the motor makers patronized, they had a historic quarrel as to where they would go for a vacation aboard the palatial $300,000 yacht which they owned jointly.

The story has been told a number of different ways but the general idea was that John wanted to sail to Georgian Bay and then on to Lake Superior, while Horace preferred to go the other direction ending up at the Thousand Islands.

"Goddamn it!" shouted John. "There's only one way to settle this. I'll match you for the boat!"

John tossed a coin and Horace won the yacht.

"Hell!" John remarked. "Now I'll have to go along with you to the Thousand Islands."

"Oh no!" Horace replied. "You'll be my guest so of course I'll have to take you to Georgian Bay."

Despite a lack of formal education and manners that were sometimes frowned on by Detroit's social set, the Dodges were said to have had a great devotion to fine music. They contributed large sums to the support of the Detroit Symphony Orchestra and to the building of Orchestra Hall. When Horace Dodge's daughter was married, the orchestra volunteered its services to play for the wedding and the reception afterwards.

In 1903 the Dodge brothers took a contract to build engines and chassis for the car designed by Henry Ford and C. H. Wills. It meant giving up the Oldsmobile business, but the Dodges were willing to gamble. They foresaw that the automobile business was going to be big. They had made a lot of money already but not nearly as much as they could make if the Ford car panned out. How much no one could possibly foresee.

The Dodges were too smart, however, to go out on a limb for Henry Ford, who had twice failed in the automobile business. To be on the safe side they insisted that Alex Malcolmson, the big money man of the Ford Motor Company, guarantee their bills; and in addition, if the Ford Motor Company failed to pay for delivered merchandise, the Dodges had the right to take over any unsold cars and market them.

As an added bonus the Dodges were given one hundred shares of Ford Motor Company stock. It seems incredible that in the next sixteen years those one hundred shares would bring them over $4,000,000 in dividends!

There is no doubt that the Dodges were greatly instrumental in Ford's success, even though he had built up an important name with his racing cars. For the Dodge brothers supplied Henry with the production knowledge that he lacked. They delivered to him a complete car, except for wheels and body. Ford and Wills had merely to do a simple assembly job in order to start shipping cars.

Even though the Ford Motor Company started making

money almost the moment its first car was delivered the Dodge brothers were never too happy in their arrangement with Ford. Nobody could work with Ford, or for that matter with the ex-bookkeeper James Couzens, who was the company's general manager. You didn't work *with* Ford and Couzens; you worked *for* them. And the Dodge brothers were not of a disposition to work for anybody. For ten years they fought and argued with Ford and Couzens. Meanwhile, their contract with Ford was making millions for them in addition to the dividends on their Ford stock.

But even though they were millionaires the Dodges were not happy. They felt that while they were actually making the Ford car, Ford was getting the biggest slice of the pie. Furthermore they had a suspicion that Ford might decide some day to cut them loose. Their contract could be canceled by either party giving a year's notice. In July, 1913, the Dodge brothers gave notice that they would not deliver merchandise to Ford after July, 1914.

A short time later advertisements and news stories appeared in the newspapers announcing that there was soon to be a new car in the automotive world and that dealer franchises were open from coast to coast. The Dodge brothers stated that their car would not compete with the Ford, but would be priced three or four hundred dollars higher.

John Dodge incurred Ford's wrath by adding to this statement, "Think of all the Ford owners who would like to own an automobile!"

Although the name of the Dodge brothers was unknown to most of the public, automobile dealers were well aware that the Ford car was largely the product of the Dodge plant. More than 22,000 applications for dealer contracts poured into the offices of Dodge Brothers.

Before a car had even been designed the advertising campaign started—one of the most effective that any automobile company ever staged. The public had been surfeited with exaggerated, misleading and dishonest advertising. The Dodge campaign was a model of simple dignity, without hokum or razzle-dazzle. On billboards from coast to coast appeared the Dodge Brothers name, in distinctive white letters on a blue background. Above the name appeared one word—sometimes two. They were such words as "Dependable," "Reliable," "Honest Value," "Sturdy," "Sound." There was no talk of holding all the world's records, or of being the world's finest motor car, or of unparalleled leadership, or breathtaking beauty. None of that usual tripe, so the public knew instinctively that the Dodge brothers must be down-to-earth guys, that there was integrity behind their advertising campaign. When the Dodge brothers' car (it was always a Dodge Brothers in the ads—never plain Dodge) appeared on the market, public acceptance was immediate and overwhelming.

But meantime Ford had been busy with a new idea of his own—a scheme that was to knock the breath out of every motor maker in Detroit and to make most of the industrial world think that Henry had gone crazy.

On January 5, 1914, the Detroit newspapers were notified that the Ford Motor Company was about to release an important news story. The reporters gathered at ten o'clock in the office of James Couzens, general manager. They were ushered into the presence of Mr. Couzens and Mr. Ford and, while the latter twisted impatiently in his chair, Couzens read a prepared statement:

"The Ford Motor Company, the greatest and most successful automobile manufacturing company in the world, will on January 12, inaugurate the greatest revolution in the matter of rewards for its workers ever known to the industrial world.

"At one stroke it will reduce the hours of labor from nine

to eight, and add to every man's pay a share of the profits of the house. The smallest amount to be received by any man twenty-two years old, and upward, will be five dollars a day. The minimum wage is now two dollars and thirty-four cents per day. . . ."

The statement went on to explain that Mr. Ford and Mr. Couzens had worked out this method of dividing their profits with their employees, by estimating what the profits would be for the coming year. The statement ended with these pious paragraphs:

"This will apply to every man of twenty-two years or upward without regard to the nature of his employment. In order that the young man, from eighteen to twenty-two years of age, may be entitled to a share in the profits he must show himself sober, saving, steady, industrious and must satisfy the superintendent and staff that his money will not be wasted in riotous living.

"Young men who are supporting families, widowed mothers, younger brothers and sisters, will be treated like those over twenty-two.

"It is estimated that over ten millions of dollars will thus be distributed over and above the regular wages of the men."

That last sentence sounds a bit like the fine print in the contract. For although nothing was said in the statement about the wage hike being an experiment, it was undoubtedly just that, and the reference to the "regular wages of the men" was an escape hatch in case Ford and Couzens were wrong in their guess that the $5-a-day wage would work.

They doubtless had the interests of their workmen at heart because every man has a conscience and nobody likes to see another human being go hungry. But there is a great deal of difference between the personal interest a man has in his employees if they number fifteen or if they number fifteen thousand. Couzens has been characterized by friends as a misanthrope. Ford, in his ultimate attitude toward his employees, was certainly less than philanthropic. So it is impossible to believe that they were more interested in the men than they were in the car.

It is almost invariably so with those who have created something out of nothing; whether it is a steel mill, a painting, a symphony or a patent gadget makes no difference; they will love that thing more than they love even their family, their friends or life itself. That was how Ford and Couzens felt about their four-wheeled god. It came first, and any largesse distributed to the men was because the god of tin and iron and rubber would benefit too, and probably more.

That Mr. Ford took advantage of the situation that day in January, 1914, to loop a halo over his brow was evidence of his instinctive talent for enticing free space from the newspapers. If his announcement to the press had told the complete truth it might also have contained the following paragraphs:

"The Ford Motor Company is aware that the I.W.W. is trying to organize our workers and there are rumors that a strike is impending as soon as we are in production on our new models.

"At the same time we realize our labor turnover is too high for top production figures. During peak months we employ 15,000 workers, and to maintain that level we must hire 53,000 men each year. By increasing our basic wage to five dollars per day we hope to nullify the efforts of the I.W.W. to unionize our plant, to decrease our labor turnover to a minimum, and to steal the best workmen in Detroit away from the other automobile factories.

"We are also quite aware that two shifts of nine hours each are less economical than three shifts of eight hours each. By making this change, which will allow us to operate our factories on a 24-hour schedule, we expect to increase plant efficiency considerably.

"High production is the religion of the Ford Motor Company. Today a Ford touring car costs $490. We hope that by doubling salaries we can triple production and in three years reduce the Ford touring car to $360—in ten years to $310.

"We also anticipate that this announcement will bring us publicity worth easily five million dollars."

It did. Every newspaper and every news agency in America, with one exception, carried the story. The editors of the Associated Press, an organization that looked with a jaundiced eye upon any statement released by a commercial enterprise, recognized a publicity stunt when they saw one, but failed to understand that, despite the free space Ford was grabbing, he had unleashed the biggest story that had ever come out of Detroit.

On the morning following the Ford announcement a mob gathered at the company's gates looking for work. Not only men in overalls, but clerks, bookkeepers and schoolteachers stampeded to the Highland Park plant seeking one of those five dollar jobs. A few days later some ten to twelve thousand men rioted outside the Ford factory. They were driven off with fire hoses. The company said that I.W.W.'s had started the trouble. The I.W.W. claimed that it was company police who struck the first blow.

The reaction of the conservative press to the five dollar wage was little short of hysterical. The New York *Times* saw only trouble ahead for the Ford Company and failure for its wage theories. It had this to say:

"The theory of the management of the Ford Company is distinctly Utopian and runs dead against all experience. The manufacturing industries of the country cannot follow an example which requires an eight-hour day and a standard of wages that from the scant outlines of the Ford Motor Company's plan seems to be approximately double the prevailing rate. . . ."

The *Wall Street Journal* held an even more cheerless view of what was ahead. In an editorial that should have been bordered in black the paper prophesied as follows:

"Had Henry Ford set aside a fund that would insure continuance of present wages paid to faithful employees or a pension of half their wages after years of faithful service, it would have been scientific, and according to the highest ethics and the true laws of giving.

"But to inject ten millions into a company's factory, and to double the minimum wage, without regard to length of service, is to apply Biblical or spiritual principles in the field where they do not belong. . . .

"If the newspapers of the day are correctly reporting the latest invention and advertisement of Henry Ford, he has in his social endeavor committed economic blunders, if not crimes. They may return to plague him and the industry he represents, as well as organized society."

The dire-predictions departments of the *Times* and the *Wall Street Journal* cannot be blamed for failing to realize that January 12, 1914, marked the beginning of a new economic era in the United States. It was not easy to guess that the automobile industry was soon to be the world's largest user of such materials as steel, malleable iron, plate glass, rubber, upholstery leather, mohair, and nickel.

And who could foresee that Detroit was to spawn 241,000 gasoline stations, 80,000 repair garages, 38,000 trucking companies and 24,000 taxi firms? Add to this hundreds of thousands of motels, tourist camps, parking lots, drive-in theaters, bus companies, car rental places, road-building firms, auto insurance and finance companies, and dozens of other types of businesses. The list is too long to enumerate.

Furthermore, who would have thought that some day more than six thousand villages and towns in the United States would be entirely dependent on buses and automobiles for transportation; that more than five million school children would use school buses; and that in one year more than forty million cars, buses and trucks would travel more than four hundred billion miles over two million miles of surfaced streets and rural highways in the United States?

The Dodge brothers, meanwhile, observed Mr. Ford's shenanigans with some alarm. It seemed to them that his desire to siphon off $10,000,000 of the Ford Company's profits into the pay envelopes of the workmen, was not so much an act of generosity toward his employees as one of revenge toward themselves. For the Dodges were entitled to ten per cent of all Ford profits. That was the amount of stock they held.

But, as they watched the operation of the $5-a-day plan, they had to admit that they had no reason to complain, since production increased in 1914, as did the company's dividends.

They were right about Ford's intentions, however. He was unhappy when the Dodges received dividends from the Ford Motor Company and then used them to expand the Dodge brothers' plant. Ford decided that would have to stop.

Late in 1916 Henry Ford and C. H. Wills, his chief engineer, dropped into the Dodge brothers' plant on an apparently friendly call, but it turned out to be a declaration of war. Ford announced that from then on Ford dividends would be held to a maximum of $1,200,000 per year. The rest of Ford's profits would go into plant expansion and improvements.

The Dodges had heard rumors of what was coming. It was said that Couzens had quarreled with Ford about his desire to plow twenty or thirty millions a year back into the business. They had fought over other matters, too. And finally Couzens, no more able to work for Ford than the Dodges, had resigned.

The other minority stockholders hesitated to oppose Ford's wishes, but the Dodge brothers brought suit against Henry to compel him to pay reasonable dividends and to prevent him from spending those dividends on expansion.

It took more than two years, a bitter court battle and a final ruling by Michigan's Supreme Court before Henry capitulated. The court ordered him to pay a special dividend of $19,000,000 plus five per cent interest for the period of litigation and to continue to pay reasonable dividends.

But Ford was not licked; he was still a contrary, stubborn character, who intended to run the Ford Motor Company the way he wanted to, regardless of courts and judges and those gadflies, the Dodge brothers.

Even before the Michigan Supreme Court decision he had planned his tactics. On December 30, 1918, he resigned as president of the Ford Motor Company and placed Edsel Ford, twenty-five years old, in charge. Then he headed west for a vacation in California. When the decision of the courts was announced, Ford broke a story in the Los Angeles *Times* that he was starting a new company, to manufacture a new car priced at around $250.

At once Ford sales started to slip and the minority stockholders began to worry, for if Henry was serious in his threat what would happen to the Ford Motor Company? Meanwhile Ford sent agents out to buy up every share of stock in the company. They had instructions to buy all or none. He wanted no more suits by minority groups. The final payoff by Ford was as follows:

> James Couzens, who originally purchased 24 shares, but later acquired additional shares $29,308,858
> Rosetta Couzens, 1 share 260,000

John Anderson, 50 shares	12,500,000
John Gray, 105 shares	26,250,000
Horace Rackham, 50 shares	12,500,000
John Dodge, 50 shares	12,500,000
Horace Dodge, 50 shares	12,500,000

Alex Malcolmson, who had organized the company, put up most of the money and secured the services of the Dodge brothers, had once owned 255 shares of the stock. He had sold out in 1906 to Ford and Couzens for $175,000. If he had held on to his shares he could have sold them at this time for $66,300,000.

18

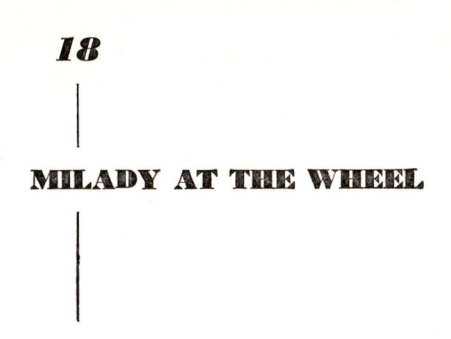

MILADY AT THE WHEEL

1915
Production 895,930
Registration 2,332,426
The V-8 engine

THE LADIES OF Parisian society were the first females to drive automobiles. The cars were powered by electricity and even the very earliest ones moved with quiet dignity and were as simple to manipulate as a rocking chair.

The first member of the weaker sex who viewed an electric automobile must have sensed that this machine was to emancipate womankind. She knew she could never be adept at harnessing a horse and hitching it to a carriage, but the electric automobile was a different animal; it would obviously respond to a woman's hand as quickly as to any man's. You simply got in, gripped the steering tiller, pulled a lever and away you went.

The first electric automobile in the United States was said to have been built by William Morris, of Des Moines, in 1891. He brought his contraption to Chicago in 1892.

"Ever since its arrival," said the *Western Electrician*, "it has attracted the greatest attention. The sight of a well-loaded carriage moving along the streets at a spanking pace, with no horse in front, and apparently with nothing on board to give it motion, is one that has been too much even for the wide-awake Chicagoan. In passing through the business section, way had to be cleared by the police for the passage of the carriage."

For a brief span of years from about 1898 to 1904 it looked as though the average family would find the electric automobile to be the most satisfactory substitute for the horse. It was rapidly replacing public hansom cabs and broughams, and it had the backing of several large and wealthy manufacturers of storage batteries, electric motors and carriages. *Outing* magazine estimated in 1900 that New York, Chicago and Boston could boast a total of 2,370 cars, which were divided as follows: 1,170 steam, 800 electric and 400 gasoline.

Although this figure does not agree with today's estimate by the Automobile Manufacturers Association, the proportions are probably correct. In Chicago, at that time, the electric automobile predominated over both steam and gasoline. This may have been due to the fact that the Woods Motor Vehicle Company, of Chicago, was the first in the country to manufacture electric automobiles commercially.

Other popular electric cars in those early days were the Waverly, the Studebaker, the Rauch and Lang, the Ohio, the Columbus, the National, the Baker and the Columbia.

The last was manufactured by the Electric Vehicle Company, which had been formed by Colonel Albert A. Pope and a group of wealthy men who owned large eastern traction interests.

Columbia Electrics were available in numerous body types including runabouts, surreys, tonneaus, cabriolets, broughams, delivery wagons, ambulances and police patrols. The owners of the company were so sure that the electric car would dominate the automobile business that instead of recognizing its weaknesses they visualized a huge chain of electric charging stations dotting the countryside. Needless to say they also expected to own the charging stations.

In every large city from New York to Chicago they set up subsidiary companies to operate electric cab and car rental services. In 1899 a reporter for *McClure's Magazine* got an interview, at the New York headquarters of the Electric Vehicle Company, that clearly reflected just how the big shots of the company were thinking. A part of the article follows:

"The New York cab company expects soon to have ten charging-stations in operation in various parts of the city, so that a cab will never have far to go for a new charge of electricity. Indeed, all the manufacturers of electrical vehicles speak with confidence of the day when the whole of the United States will be as thoroughly sprinkled with electric charging-stations as it is today with bicycle road-houses. One manufacturer has already issued lists of hundreds of central stations throughout New England, New York, and other Eastern States where automobiles may be provided with power.

"It is not hard to imagine what a country touring-station will be like on a sunny summer afternoon some five or ten years hence. Long rows of vehicles will stand backed up comfortably to the charging bars, each with its electric plug filling the battery with power. The owners will be lolling at the tables on the verandas of the nearby road-house. Men with repair kits will bustle about, tightening up a nut here, oiling this bearing, and regulating that gear. From a long rubber tube compressed air will be hissing into pneumatic tires. There will also be many gasoline carts and road-wagons and tricycles, and they, too, will need repairs and pumping, and their owners will employ themselves busily in filling their little tin cans with gasoline, recharging their tanks, refilling the water-jackets, and looking to the workings of their sparking devices. And then there will be boys selling peanuts, arnica, and court-plasters, and undoubtedly a cynical old farmer or two with a pair of ambling mares to carry home such of these new-fangled vehicles as may become hopelessly indisposed. Add to this bustling assembly of amateur 'self-propellers' a host of bicycle riders—for there will doubtless be as many bicycles in those days as ever—and it will be a sight to awaken every serious-minded horse to an uneasy consideration of his future.

"The new electric cabs are unquestionably immensely popular as fashionable conveyances. A number of the wealthy people of New York, including Mr. Frank Gould, Mr. Cornelius Vanderbilt, Mr. O. H. P. Belmont, and Mr. Richard McCurdy, have a cab or brougham and driver constantly on call at the home station of the company, for which they pay at the rate of $180 a month. Several prominent physicians are similarly provided, motor vehicles being especially adapted to the varied necessities of a physician's practice."

One of the great faults of the electric car was that by nature it was ladylike. It belonged to the carriage maker, the upholsterer and the glazier. These were all crafts that smacked of the gentle touch. Gasoline automobiles, on the other hand, were vehicles of the blacksmith, the engineer and the grease ball mechanic.

The electric car had a maximum speed of twenty miles an hour, unless designed for racing, and it rolled along the avenue as smug and silent as a fat cat stalking a birdbath. The only time it ever got out of order was when it ran out of juice. For mid-Victorian ladies, whose social activities were confined to a radius of five miles, the electric phaeton or coupé was quite satisfactory.

But a man wanted something a little more exciting. He wanted to exceed the speed limit and he liked the sound of an occasional backfire while on the boulevard. It made people turn around and stare, made him feel like a bit of a hellion. And, of course, the tinkering instinct in every red-blooded American male drew him inevitably toward the gasoline car.

So almost from the very beginning the electric automobile became the approved vehicle for females. Consequently they grew more and more feminine. The electric coupé took on a dainty, interior-decorated look. It developed curved, plate-glass windows, fawn- or burgundy-colored broadcloth upholstery, ruffled silk curtains, vanity compartments and bud vases. Soon the average man would rather have walked down the street without his pants than drive an electric coupé.

In the opening years of the twentieth century, most women were perfectly content with the new freedom that their electrics gave them. They wanted nothing speedier or more powerful. But there were a good many men who thought it was rather disgraceful to see a woman scooting about at the tiller of an automobile. It was, in fact, damn dangerous! In *Outing* magazine for 1904 an article appeared under the title "Why Women Are, Or Are Not, Good Chauffeuses." The author very wisely did not sign his name. He said, in part: "The only thing about a car which a woman does not have to teach herself with patience and skill is how to dress for it. From the first, the long, graceful motor coats, like the old dust-coats reborn into a world of perfect cut, have appealed to women who go a-motoring. . . . Far from being unbecoming, the rather bewildering fashions in motor chapeaux, with the long veils tightly tied under the chin, frame a pretty face enchantingly."

This sweet talk was not to be forgiven by his female readers, however, for the writer went on to point out that women were not physically equipped for the strain and stress of driving a motor car. They were simply a bundle of nerves and might easily go to pieces in the midst of a motoring crisis. Nor were they mentally equipped to make the instant decisions that were necessary when traveling at speeds of twenty to twenty-five miles per hour. Women would never be able to learn how to handle an automobile, this writer had decided; however, he had also observed that, despite their lack of skill with motor cars, women managed somehow to "get around them, just as she always managed to get around the male sex."

But the women driver had many defenders, too. Mostly other women, it must be admitted. One Mary Mullett, also writing in *Outing* magazine, had quite an opposite view from the anonymous male critic. She said:

"In Newport last summer, fifteen or twenty women might have been seen any pleasant day, driving their own cars. In Washington—well, my private opinion is that in Washington half those women who are forever skimming around in little electrics, could run them in their sleep—and with one finger at that.

"Even in New York there are women sufficiently plucky and expert to take a machine into and through that wonderful tangle of traffic which makes Fifth Avenue one of the show thoroughfares of the world.

"To drive an auto on Fifth Avenue at five o'clock in the afternoon is a trick which is calculated to make even the coolest man suspect that he has a few nerves concealed about him. Yet I know of a woman who does that trick whenever she feels like it!"

Even in the early days there were a few feminists who insisted on trying their hand at driving powerful gasoline cars. One of these was Joan Newton Cuneo, who drove her own car in the first Glidden Tour. Then she was invited to Atlantic City to compete in speed trials and races with men drivers. There she drove a mile in 1 minute 18 2/5 seconds. Almost 46 miles per hour!

After that Miss Cuneo was a confirmed speed demon. She bought a racing car, raced at numerous county fairs and broke the track record at the Rockland County Fair, at Orangeburg, New York.

Finally in 1909 she entered a three-day racing meet at

New Orleans and came second to Ralph De Palma in a fifty-mile race.

Miss Cuneo wrote an account of her racing activities in the November, 1910, issue of *Country Life* magazine, and challenged any amateur male driver to show a better record than hers, which included everything from a perfect score in the 1908 Glidden Tour to several track records and a hatful of medals.

Although there were not many women as anxious for high speeds as Miss Cuneo, the great majority of them soon wanted something with a little more zip than an electric coupé could offer.

I recall that my mother refused absolutely to let father buy her an electric. She learned to drive the Marmon and used to frighten everybody in the block when she backed that juggernaut out of our garage. But the only thing that ever worried mother was cranking the Marmon. She would set the crank in place for a down-stroke, then with the aid of a chair climb up and stand on the crank handle; next she held onto the Boyce MotoMeter and bounced until the weight of her body turned the engine over. One day she forgot to retard the spark. The engine backfired, of course, and tossed mother into the air. When she came down she hit her cheek against the MotoMeter. In no time at all her eye was closed and then it took on a beautiful purplish-blue-green hue. Mother stayed home for two weeks, missing any number of bridge parties and lectures at the Twentieth Century Club. But she didn't stop driving or cranking the car.

By 1910 the electric automobile seemed to have settled into a groove from which it could never be dislodged. It served two classes of customers. First it was the approved car for well-to-do society matrons with numerous chins. Second, it was commonly used as a delivery wagon by B. Altman & Company, Marshall Field & Company and other retail houses which felt no confidence in the ability of a $15-a-week employee to learn how to crank and shift gears.

The companies that manufactured electrics seemed to feel secure with this business, certain that there would always be society matrons, and that underpaid employees could never solve the intricacies of the gasoline car.

But they were in for a rude awakening. Down in Dayton, Ohio, an engineer named Charles F. Kettering was even then perspiring over one of the most important inventions of the gasoline age and one that was to lay the electric automobile low. It was the self-starter.

Kettering may be the only legitimate genius ever produced by the automobile business. As head of the General Motors Research Laboratories he has received more billing than any other inventor of his day—Edison and Don Ameche excepted. Unfortunately General Motors' public relations staff has hopped up his accomplishments with a lot of stultifying mumbo-jumbo and miracle-man stuff, as well as crediting the master with some of the most asinine platitudes of the age. Consequently it is difficult, at this time, to evaluate or get a clear picture of the real Kettering. But it would seem that there must be at least a touch of genius behind the multitude of improvements for the automobile that have come from General Motors Research Laboratories—such wonders as Ethyl gasoline, Synchro-mesh transmission, Duco finish and Hydra-matic transmission, all of which were brought to perfection under Kettering's guidance.

Kettering's early inventions were perfected while he was head of the Inventions Department of the National Cash Register Company. Among these were the first electrically operated cash register.

A few years later he started a consulting engineering laboratory to serve companies that were too small to have their own laboratories. There, influenced by the work he had done on the electric cash register, he began to develop an electric self-starter.

After a number of failures typical of all invention, he finally succeeded in building an electric starter as well as a complete battery ignition and lighting system for automobiles.

In 1911 Kettering convinced Henry Leland, of Cadillac, that his starter was practical. It was tried out on a few cars as optional equipment. Then in 1912 it was adopted as standard equipment on the Cadillac. A few years later Kettering and his Dayton Engineering Laboratories became the General Motors Research Laboratories.

The year before Leland tried Kettering's self-starter, the seven, strong, silent Fisher brothers, who had arrived in Detroit, one by one from Norwalk, Ohio, and who had started their own body-building business in 1907, persuaded Leland to try another radical idea on the Cadillac.

It was a revolutionary new body design. The industry was already familiar with such closed cars as the limousine, the town car, the coupé and the taxicab. But what the Fishers had designed was today's sedan. It was a strange-looking, two-door job with the doors placed amidships, but for the first time all who rode in a four passenger car were completely protected from wind and rain. No longer was it necessary to wear special motoring wardrobes in an automobile.

These two improvements—the electric starter and the enclosed body were to create a revolution in the motoring habits of the nation. It took a number of years before the full effect of the sedan body was felt. That was because the manufacturers kept it priced sky-high so as not to hurt their expensive limousine business. But Hudson finally split the closed-car market wide open by bringing out a sedan priced only $300 above its open car. After that the lid was off and the country went sedan happy.

But the electric self-starter had already placed women on practically equal terms with their husbands. When it no longer took muscle to start a car the ladies quickly commandeered the family bus and the era of the accordion fender and the baffled traffic cop was at hand.

For the most part they were content for a year or two to drive within the confines of the city limits. But one morning in the summer of 1915 the nation awoke to read that a lovely cinema favorite was about to attempt the most daring motor trip that a lone and unprotected female had yet undertaken.

The lady's name was Anita King, more commonly called "The Paramount Girl," for at that time all movie stars had trick soubriquets of that kind. It seemed that Miss King, a daring stunt girl in her day, had been grieving over the death of her younger sister and had decided to get away from the tinsel of Hollywood for a while. She wanted to be alone to think out life's problems. So she had decided to take a solitary motor trip from Los Angeles to New York, via the Lincoln Highway.

The Kissel Motor Car Company, of Hartford, Wisconsin, kindly offered to lend her a Kisselkar for her lonely jaunt to New York, and the mayors of San Francisco and Los Angeles, both anxious to send messages to the mayor of New York, asked Miss King to deliver same for them. This information was all painted on the side of Miss King's Kisselkar so that she would not have to stop along the way and answer questions.

As she left Los Angeles Miss King wore a suede motoring coat, a suede racing helmet, goggles and a dazzling smile. Paramount's press agents followed Miss King at a respectful distance, and also preceded her, through the unadvertised courtesy of the Kissel Motor Car Company.

There was not a day of Miss King's famous crossing of the continent that was not fraught with danger or excitement. It was positively as thrilling as a movie script.

In a lonely mountain pass she stopped to pick up a strange man on foot. He tried to molest her and steal her car. She quickly covered him with a small pearl-handled revolver and could easily have shot him between the eyes. But woman's intuition told her that this poor unfortunate man was a victim of circumstances. Instead of shooting him she gave him a lecture, drove him on to the next town and turned him loose without saying a word to the authorities.

Then came the Great Salt Desert. Halfway across she found herself lost on its salt-encrusted expanse. With all the water boiled out of her radiator and her last drop of drinking water gone, it looked as though Miss King was a goner. She stumbled out onto the hot desert sands and fell fainting beside her faithful Kisselkar.

She knew not how long she lay thus in the broiling sun, but when she came to she was in the shade of a Joshua tree, strong arms were holding her, and cool water was trickling down her throat. She had been rescued by three desert prospectors. They filled her radiator and sent her on her way, followed closely by her press representative and two photographers, who had been recording this thrilling life drama from behind a near-by giant cactus plant.

But according to Miss King her "real big lasting thrill of the trip came on a lonely rain-swept hill in Wyoming." Miss King had been driving all day and was passing a farm when she saw a young girl waving to her to stop. But let the reporter for *Sunset* magazine describe what took place, egged on by the Paramount publicity department:

"A girl of about sixteen came running through the gate and up to the car, breathless, wide-eyed, pale.

" 'Oh,' she gasped, 'I thought you wasn't going to stop!'

" 'I wasn't,' answered Miss King unamiably.

" 'But I've been waiting for two days,' protested the little girl. 'They said you'd come by, two days ago, and I've been watching all the time. And I haven't slept a wink for fear you might go by in the night.'

"The child's distraught appearance confirmed the statement.

" 'But why have you been so foolish?' said Miss King.

" 'No,' said the girl. 'It isn't foolish. It's life and death. I can't stand it any longer. I have to go.' She clung to the car, and looked up appealingly into the puzzled eyes of the Paramount Girl. 'Oh, please take me with you!'

" 'Why, child,' cried Miss King. 'What in the world do you mean?'

"Then followed, in the drizzle of that darkening afternoon, the impassioned recital of a little drama which is being enacted in countless homes all over the country, though Anita King had never understood it until then. The story of the screen-struck little girl to whom the humdrum routine of home had become unbearable under the spur of a newborn ambition to be a motion picture star. Impatience of the home which had become a prison, a naive assurance that 'the pictures' meant life's real opportunity, despair at the dull parental wits that could not understand. Anita King listened to the flood of eager words from the white-faced youngster on the running board. And as she listened, her soul awoke to a responsibility. . . ."

So Miss King told the girl that Hollywood was no place for her; stay home, marry and have kiddies, she advised, then she got back in her Kisselkar and was off again in the rain and mud.

There wasn't much subtlety to Hollywood publicity in those days and probably there didn't need to be, for millions of women from coast to coast waited and watched for Anita King, with her Mary Pickford curls and her girlish figure, to come barreling down the road or the boulevard in her big Kisselkar.

Some saw her with their own eyes and some had to read about her in the newspapers, but surely there was not a woman in the country but envied Miss King her derring-do and her ability to drive a six-cylinder 60-horsepower Kisselkar across the country without the help of a man.

When The Paramount Girl finally reached New York and drove down Broadway, the throngs along the curb cheered for her long and loud, and very soon the women of America had their husband's cars by the steering wheel and were plotting a course straight down emancipation road. The following year the automobile industry doubled its output.

19

BEAUTY vs. THE BEAST

1916
Production 1,525,578
Registration 3,367,889
Windshield wipers

THE LITTLE MAN with the lust for power who was known as Billy Durant was not ordinarily of a vindictive nature. But he couldn't quite forgive the way in which he had been ousted from the presidency of General Motors by a group of bankers who loved money like a pirate crew loves loot.

That was in the fall of 1910 and Durant was to cherish his resentment for three years before he evolved a plan for revenge. Meanwhile he went back to Flint, where he had first entered the automobile business, and started a new company. It was called the Little Motor Car Company and its product was the Little car. Taking a page from Ford's book of success, Durant at first built only one model—a roadster priced to compete with Ford at $650.

Durant managed to swing this deal on an outlay of $26,500 cash by taking over the Flint Wagon Works and reorganizing it. In the first year he disposed of some 3,500 Littles as well as several thousand buggies.

But one car was not enough for Durant; he soon formed

the Chevrolet Motor Company of Michigan, combining it with the Little Company, and in 1913 introduced the Chevrolet car.

Louis Chevrolet had been a member of the famous Buick racing team headed by Bob Burman. But he was more than a race driver; he was also a designer and self-taught engineer. Durant, while still in power at General Motors, had personally financed Chevrolet in his experiments with a small car, which was a fine break for Super-Promoter Durant.

Chevrolet had two cars ready for Durant just when he needed them; they were the Baby Grand touring car and the Royal Mail roadster. The Chevrolet name gave them immediate buyer interest, but aside from that the new cars were designed to please the eye; they were low-priced cars dressed up to look like more expensive merchandise.

The time was ripe for a low-priced, "pretty" car, for some of the public were getting a little tired of looking at all those Fords on the road. Granted that there was nothing to beat a Ford, nevertheless, they were something like a man's wife—durable and practical, but not nearly as streamlined and cute as the little grass widow next door. So a lot of people went for Chevrolets like Ben Turpin chasing a bathing beauty in a Mack Sennett comedy.

Those first Chevrolets weren't so hot mechanically. They were held together with stove bolts and cotter pins but they sure looked good compared to Fords, which had all their beauty concealed beneath their unesthetic exteriors. In 1913 and 1914 Durant sold sixteen thousand Chevvies. That was nothing compared to Ford's output but it was a good start and the company piled up a profit of $1,300,000. Maybe the public didn't know anything about art, but it knew what it liked.

The success of the Chevrolet car set tongues wagging in Detroit and Flint and Pontiac and everywhere that automobile men gathered. Billy Durant had done it again. You couldn't stop the Little Giant. Chevrolet was the biggest little car on wheels. It was going to be bigger than Ford. Get on the bandwagon! Grab some of that Chevrolet stock!

At the same time General Motors had recovered in such magnificent style from its 1910 financial ailments that nobody believed it had ever been very sick. From 1913 to 1916 it earned $58,000,000, but the bankers who controlled it paid out not one penny of dividends on the common stock.

Meanwhile, Durant had developed a fascinating contact in the person of John J. Raskob, treasurer of the E. I. du Pont de Nemours Company. Here was a growing industrial empire controlled by a family with as much imagination and daring as Billy Durant himself, as well as a practical realization of their responsibility to stockholders and the public.

The du Ponts dealt in basic products. They had supplied the gunpowder for all our wars since 1812 and had branched out into peacetime chemicals. When Durant had expanded General Motors he had taken over his sources of supply in order to be sure of having parts and materials. The du Pont theory of expansion was just the opposite. They preferred to control their markets. When their laboratories created a new product they wanted to be sure they had customers for it.

The automobile industry was just the sort of expanding market that the du Ponts wished to have a finger in. So when shrewd, brilliant, tough-minded John Raskob and Durant, the super-promoter, came to them with a scheme for grabbing control of General Motors, the du Ponts listened, acquiesced in the idea and agreed to supply the money to help accomplish the coup.

Durant then formed a new holding company very much like General Motors. It was called Chevrolet Motors Company of Delaware and was first incorporated for $20,000,000 and later the capitalization was increased to $80,000,000.

However, the incorporation papers were not filed for fear of tipping off the enemy to what was brewing.

The Chevrolet Motor Company of Michigan was then absorbed by Chevrolet of Delaware. After that Durant went quietly to all of his friends who owned large blocks of General Motors stock. There were a good many friends and a good many shares that he had handed out in exchange for various companies while he had been president of General Motors. Durant offered to trade them five shares of new Chevrolet for one share of General Motors. There were plenty of takers, for most of Durant's old friends were willing to ride along with him. After all, wasn't he the greatest crapshooter in the business? When Billy was in a winning streak all you had to do was ride with him. General Motors stock poured into the Chevrolet treasury in huge blocks.

At the same time Durant, his family, his friends and the du Ponts were buying General Motors stock on the open market as fast as it was offered for sale. The price of the stock rose in 1915 from 82 to 558, driven up by the demand that Durant had created.

That rising market made every owner of General Motors stock keep his eye on the ticker. The common stock had never paid a dividend, so there were plenty of investors who had never gained a dime from their investment. This was their chance to clean up. They sold and Durant bought.

Rumors swept through Wall Street that the Little Giant was up to something. He had the dice again and he was throwing naturals. The bankers who controlled General Motors heard, too, of course. But it was hard for them to believe that enough shares would be dumped into the market for him to buy a controlling interest. Or that Durant could borrow enough cash to capture those shares if they were dumped. After all, where would he get it? Surely no bank wanted to get involved with a fellow like Willie Durant, who liked to gamble that he could make Big Dick the hard way.

Not until it was too late did those who had tossed Durant out of General Motors discover who was backing him and how many of his old friends had exchanged their General Motors stock for Chevrolet of Delaware, a company they had never heard of before.

The men of Wall Street knew, when they went to the directors' meeting on September 16, 1915, that the dapper little man from Flint had licked them at their own game. So they sat and waited for their dismissal, waited for Durant to come in and hand them their walking papers. And when he did come he was possibly a little embarrassed over his triumph; it was so complete and humiliating to his enemies; but still, revenge was sweet. He strode into the meeting followed by secretaries carrying baskets filled with securities and proxies which had been counted and totaled only a few hours earlier by Durant himself. When the contents of the baskets had been dumped on the table, Durant, with a touch of the ham, but still underplaying it, said quietly, "Gentlemen, I control this company."

And then Durant declared a dividend on the common stock. It was the first the company had ever paid and it was a humdinger—fifty dollars a share! Thus the new management justified the price that General Motors common was selling for. After that the bankers who had once held complete control of the company resigned and their loan was paid off; then Pierre S. du Pont became chairman of the board of General Motors, four du Pont men became directors, and Billy Durant once more was elected president of General Motors. It was quite a victory for the little fellow with the lust for power.

Unfortunately Durant was not a man who loved automobiles; he only loved power and bigness. After he had stepped in again as president there was only the legal problem of getting Chevrolet to disgorge General Motors so that Durant's child could become one of the big, happy family it had swallowed. That was accomplished by means of a masterful operation performed by a whole battalion of corporation lawyers; then Durant forgot about Chevrolet and went off on another buying spree.

In the flush of wartime and post-war prosperity the Durant expansion program went almost unnoticed, though occasionally the du Ponts may have wondered about deals like the purchase of the Scripps-Booth car, and the same with the Sheridan. But by 1919 earnings had reached $60,000,000 and the company declared a dividend of $22,000,000. Who could complain about a president who showed that kind of profit, even though he did buy a couple of turkeys in the meantime?

But when Billy set out to take over the tractor and farm-implement business he bit off a lot more than he could chew. First he bought a dog in California called the Sampson Tractor Company along with a few smaller outfits; then he combined them with the Janesville Machine Company at Janesville, Wisconsin. Out of the plant at Janesville were supposed to come tractors and farm gadgets that would make International Harvester holler "Uncle!" What came out of it was a headache that cost General Motors $42,000,000. The du Ponts realized then that if they didn't look out that mild, soft-spoken little man, with the $150 suits and the aplomb of a movie actor, would break them.

In the spring of 1920 the post-war deflation began. By fall General Motors was in trouble again. And Durant was in even more serious difficulties. The market had been dropping for months and he had been trying to support the price of General Motors stock. But this time he was rolling snake eyes instead of naturals. As the market receded point by point Billy kept buying, buying, sure that it would reverse its trend. Finally he was in up to his neck. He had bought $35,000,000-worth of General Motors stock and he didn't have enough cash to cover his margins.

When Durant's brokers threatened to sell him out the du Ponts realized that a forced sale of that magnitude might crack the market wide open, damage the credit of General Motors, and possibly start a financial panic. With the help of J. P. Morgan and Company they got Billy Durant out of hock. He still had a couple of millions left when it was all over but he was washed up for good at General Motors.

The post-war depression caught Henry Ford out on a limb, too. In order to buy out Couzens, the Dodge brothers and the other minority stockholders he had borrowed $75,000,000 from eastern bankers.

Henry had expected to pay off that loan from one year's profits and a cash reserve of $20,000,000. But then the bottom dropped out of the market and Ford sales skidded by 50 per cent. It looked as though there might not be any profit for 1921. Just the opposite.

On top of that Ford had a large inventory at inflated prices. Everybody said he had gotten rid of the minority stockholders only to fall into the hands of the bankers. Out of the frying pan into the fire. For Henry, who had a farmer's antipathy to Wall Street and its bankers, this was a fate worse than death.

Ford had no talent for finance but he knew where the money came from; it came from his dealers who paid spot cash for his cars when they were delivered. Obviously, then, the thing to do was deliver cars to them and make them pay for them. If a dealer refused, cancel his franchise. He had made them rich, now it was up to them to help him meet that $75,000,000 loan.

While the rest of Detroit was cutting production to meet the decreased dealer demand Henry kept his assembly lines moving at top speed. His dealers got Fords till their showrooms and warehouses were crammed. They got them and paid for them. If they didn't have the cash they went to their local banks and borrowed it. And for the first time they had to be salesmen. Instead of sitting in their showrooms and taking orders they went out and hustled them. It broke a few of them and alienated the majority of them, but Henry pulled himself out of trouble, paid off the bankers and then thumbed his nose at them.

There was, all this while, a man working for Henry Ford whose name was William Knudsen. He had been acquired by Ford in the purchase of a Buffalo steel mill, where he had been superintendent. Ford brought him to Highland Park and in the course of company expansion Knudsen set up fourteen assembly plants for Ford.

Over the years, as the organization grew, it lost something that had originally made it function better than any other. A certain *esprit de corps* among the top executives and camaraderie with the boss were gradually diluted by the very bigness of the company, until there was nothing to be gained by working for Ford but a salary. The great affection they once had for the homely Model T grew into a cynical distaste; except for Ford himself there was no one left who admired his little beast of burden. That was when the executives who had helped make Ford, the man, and Ford, the car, began to resign or get fired.

One of these was Knudsen. And when he quit, Ford lost a man who was to make a lot of trouble for him. For Bill Knudsen went to Chevrolet. It was 1921 and Durant was out of General Motors; he was starting all over again with the Durant and the Star.

So Bill Knudsen took over Chevrolet and did for it what Durant had never done for any car. He made it his hobby; he gave it loving attention; he turned it into the most popular car in America.

Ford was unprepared for the awful truth. He couldn't believe that he was wrong. He had been right for almost twenty years, but now, day by day, his sales decreased and Chevrolet's sales curve went up. In 1926 production on the Model T fell off by 335,000 units, while Chevrolet's output increased.

That was when Henry decreed a new car. He announced

that he would stop when he had built his fifteen millionth Model T. Then he would start all over again with a car to be known as the Model A. Bill Knudsen's little beauty had finally won out over Ford's beast of burden.

20

THE BOY FROM POTTAWATOMIE

1925
Production *3,735,171*
Registration *17,439,701*
Duco finish and chromium plating

IN 1921 THERE were eighty-eight firms in the United States manufacturing automobiles. But strangely enough, as production figures mounted the number of automobile companies decreased. Where once there had not been enough cars to go around, the industry was now able to turn out more than could be sold.

In this competitive market, firms which already had volume production were best able to cut prices for still larger volume. They could produce cheaper, advertise more extensively, hire the best engineers and executives, and attract the best dealers. The others were in a fix. That's why, from 1921 to 1928, a great many excellent cars were muscled out of existence. Here is a list of old-time automobiles that once could be seen on the streets of any big American city, and the year of their demise:

| Jackson | 1921 | Halladay | 1921 |
| Metz | 1921 | Briscoe | 1921 |

Regal	1922	Mercer	1925
Pan-American	1922	Wills-St. Claire	1925
King	1922	Haynes	1925
Mitchell	1922	American	1925
Saxon	1922	Cole	1925
Chalmers	1923	Cleveland	1926
Winton	1924	Apperson	1926
National	1924	Premier	1927
Elgin	1924	Jewett	1927
Crane-Simplex	1924	Paige-Detroit	1927
Crawford	1924	Case	1927
Westcott	1925	Davis	1928
Stanley Steamer	1925	Diana	1928

During this shakeout period, when weaker sisters were losing their grip almost monthly, the greatest super-producer the industry ever knew, found the tough going just to his liking. His name was Walter Percy Chrysler.

Chrysler was another Horatio Alger character. Born in Pottawatomie County, Kansas, he quit school the year the Duryeas started building their first automobile and found a job in a Union Pacific roundhouse wiping engines. When he had saved enough money he took a course in mechanical engineering from the International Correspondence School. Chrysler needed more schooling as much as he needed a clubfoot. He was a big, tough, two-fisted guy determined to make a million and headed sure as hell for success. There was no nonsense about Chrysler; he saw he couldn't get any place in Pottawatomie County, so he got out of there. By the time he was thirty-three he was superintendent of motive power for the Chicago and Great Western. Then he became manager of the American Locomotive Works at Pittsburgh.

There is a story that has been told and retold to the effect that Chrysler saw a Locomobile at the Chicago Automobile

Show in 1905 and fell in love with it. He is said to have taken his life savings of $700 and borrowed an additional $4,300 in order to purchase the Locomobile, a gleaming white monster with red leather upholstery. Then he is supposed to have shipped the car home, put it in the barn and there disassembled it nut by bolt just to learn how an automobile was built.

This is a press agent yarn which defeats itself. No banker in his right mind would have loaned $4,300 on a $5,000 car in 1905. Besides, the story makes Chrysler sound like a damn fool when obviously he was a man of sound and practical intelligence. If he had wanted to tear a car apart he could have bought a second-hand Locomobile for $1,000. Or he could have bought a new Ford for $850. Surely a man who would later have bankers begging him to cure their $50,000,000 headaches did not go in debt $4,300 merely to learn how a Locomobile was built.

Chrysler may, at some time, have taken a car apart and put it back together again but if so it probably needed it. And there was no loan against it—not in 1905.

But it is quite probable that he never bothered a great deal about the guts of an automobile. Chrysler was a production man, not an automotive engineer. Getting things produced, economically and efficiently, was his special talent. The fact that he was a good mechanic and a fairly good monkey-wrench engineer may have been a factor in his success but they were incidental compared with his skill as a production man.

The story is also told of Chrysler that he quit a job with the American Locomotive Works which paid him $12,000 a year to take one at Buick for $6,000. The press agents and writers of articles for popular magazines insist upon making him sound like a half-wit. They leave out the fact that in addition to his salary at Buick he had a bonus arrangement which eventually made him a millionaire.

The president of Buick at that time was Charles W. Nash,

who went to work for Billy Durant, in 1899, polishing lamps in the Durant-Dort Carriage Company. He rose to be general superintendent, and, in 1910, Durant, even though he had just been dumped from the presidency of General Motors, persuaded its directors to place his man, Nash, in charge of Buick. Nash looked around for a works manager to help him pull Buick out of its difficulties and found Chrysler.

The two men understood each other and worked well together. Even though Nash had come from a carriage factory and Chrysler from a locomotive plant they had what it took to get Buick rolling. In 1912 Nash, the lamp polisher, became president of General Motors, and Chrysler, the engine wiper, took over the presidency of Buick.

When Durant came riding back into power as the biggest stockholder in General Motors he found that Buick was the strongest unit in the company and was anxious to see both Nash and Chrysler remain where they were. But Nash knew that with Shoot-a-Million Durant in power he would be a mere figurehead president, and that in all probability Durant would kick the props out from under the solid financial structure that he, Nash, had built up. So in 1916 he resigned and, with the backing of Wall Street, bought the Thomas B. Jeffery Company at Kenosha, where the Rambler car had once been made and then the Jeffery. A new firm was formed called the Nash Motors Company.

Nash urged Chrysler to join him at Kenosha, but Chrysler turned him down. He was sitting pretty where he was, with stock bonuses coming up and Buick going like a box factory on fire. So Nash wished him luck but warned him to be on the lookout for the moment when Durant started to overexpand.

It was four years before Chrysler decided it was time to run for the storm cellar. He is said to have sold his General Motors holdings for several millions. Some say he was just lucky and some say that he knew what he was doing, but at least he was no longer with General Motors when Durant took his second tumble from power.

Chrysler was forty-five years old the year he resigned from Buick. It was his intention to loaf for the rest of his life. He got on a ship and went to Europe to relax.

Then somebody jerked a rug from under the automobile business. A lot of companies took a tumble and needed help to get back on their feet. General Motors tried to get Chrysler back; Nash still wanted him; Packard made an offer; and Wall Street had two or three jobs for him. He could no more relax than an old fire-engine horse when somebody sounds a gong. He had forgotten how to loaf, if he had ever known.

One company in serious trouble was Willys-Overland. It owed something like $46,000,000. The bankers offered Chrysler a salary of $750,000 a year to take charge of this super-headache. That was the sort of trouble Chrysler liked. He took the job on and before the year was out had reduced the company's indebtedness to $18,000,000.

The bankers were so pleased by this major operation that they asked him to take on the prize headache of the industry. It was the Maxwell Motor Company.

The history of Maxwell is as complicated as restaurant hash. John Maxwell was a mechanic working for the Apperson brothers at the time they built Elwood Haynes' first automobile. Later he went to Detroit and landed a job with the Olds Motor Works. There he and Roy Chapin worked together testing the early Oldsmobiles. His experience with these early cars made a competent automotive engineer out of Maxwell and in 1903 he designed a car of his own.

These designs were shown to Benjamin Briscoe who owned a sheet metal plant in Detroit that had been doing considerable work for Olds. Briscoe had already been mixed up in an unfortunate venture. Just a short time before he had disposed of the controlling interest in Buick to a group of men in Flint, taking a small loss. But Briscoe knew there was big money to be made in automobiles so he decided to back Maxwell. The result was the Maxwell-Briscoe Motor Company.

The Maxwell car was a quick success, but it had been launched on a shoestring. To expand the business Briscoe went to Wall Street and secured additional capital. As has been mentioned in an earlier chapter, he and Billy Durant tried to form a big merger with Ford and Reo; then later they tried to form a holding company with the help of J. P. Morgan. These plans fell through, but Briscoe, assisted by those eastern capitalists who were interested in the Electric Vehicle Company, formed a holding company in competition with Durant's General Motors called the United States Motor Company. Briscoe's company eventually controlled some 150 firms including the companies that manufactured Columbia, Brush, Stoddard-Dayton, Briscoe and Maxwell. But in 1912 the weak members of the corporation became too big a load for Maxwell to carry and the United States Motor Company went into receivership. By 1920 the Maxwell Motor Company was still saddled with a brutal indebtedness. At this time the Chalmers Motor Company was also in the hands of the bankers. It was made a subsidiary of Maxwell and the two companies were dropped into Chrysler's lap with the blessings of the banking group that controlled them.

Chrysler was still struggling to get Willys-Overland out of trouble but he took on the additional load with the enthusiasm of a Frank Merriwell charging into the big game with the score 21 to 0 against dear old Rutgers.

The banks had already sunk over $18,000,000 in the Maxwell setup and the company owed its creditors $35,000,000! Chrysler decreed that it would take another $15,000,000 to save the home team. The bankers groaned but agreed to the additional financing and gave Chrysler a free hand to rescue Maxwell if he could.

There were some 26,000 Maxwells sitting in warehouses

over the country waiting to be sold. There was no market for them; the dealers had lost their morale; the public was keeping its money in the banks.

Chrysler knew that the first thing he must do was to get the company's money out of those Maxwells. He did it by slashing the price to the bone. The company made only $5 on each car but it got its cash out of those Maxwells. Then Chrysler put out a new Maxwell and a new advertising slogan. It was very simple. The car was no longer called the Maxwell. It became The Good Maxwell.

For some reason people believed those ads and in 1922 Maxwell sales shot up to 48,850 and the company earned $2,000,000. But its subsidiary, Chalmers, wasn't able to get over the hump. The company lost a million dollars. Ruthlessly Chrysler eliminated Chalmers and concentrated on the Maxwell. By 1923 The Good Maxwell was going along in good shape. Another few years and that big debt to the bankers would be paid off. But Chrysler wasn't entirely satisfied. For two years, at least, he had wanted to make a deal with Fred Zeder who had designed the famous EMF car. With the purchase of EMF by Studebaker, Zeder had gone to work for the old wagon-making firm, then later had organized the Zeder, Skelton, Breer Engineering Company. This trio had designed a new car with such innovations as four-wheel hydraulic brakes, an all-steel body, and a high-compression, high-speed engine. They hoped to sell the car to one of the big companies.

Chrysler had first wanted to make their machine at the Willys-Overland plant, but that deal had fallen through. Then he had toyed with the new car when he shifted to Maxwell. But finally he had been forced to turn down his friend Zeder.

So Billy Durant, who was now on his own, became interested in Zeder's car, as did the Whites, in Cleveland, and the Studebaker crowd. But they were timid about bringing out anything quite as revolutionary as this new car.

For a while Zeder almost had backing from Wall Street to put out a car under his own name. But finally Chrysler got things in shape at Maxwell and was able to negotiate with Zeder. He turned the Chalmers plant over to the engineering firm and by 1924 a car called the Chrysler was coming off the production line.

Although Chrysler was one of the best known figures in the automotive world, the general public was none too familiar with him. So a national advertising campaign shouted his greatness to the public and informed them that his name was pronounced Cry-sler. And the public relations men were turned loose with instructions to make him as well known as Ford.

In the year that the Chrysler car was born, 32,000 were sold against 50,000 Maxwells. The following year the Chrysler Corporation was formed, Maxwell Motor Company was absorbed by it and the Maxwell name was dropped.

By 1928 Zeder, Skelton and Breer had engineered two more cars for Chrysler. They were called the DeSoto and the Plymouth. The Chrysler, which had once sold for $750, was moved up into a high-price bracket and DeSoto and Plymouth went into competition with Ford and the low-priced cars of General Motors.

Meanwhile, the banking firm of Dillon, Read & Company, which had purchased Dodge Brothers from the two Dodge widows, had been watching Chrysler turn the Maxwell lemon into a plum. They were anxious to get out of the automobile business and suggested a merger with Chrysler. Chrysler needed the plant facilities of Dodge, so he was willing, and the merger was finally effected with the transfer of $170,000,000-worth of Chrysler stock.

The Chrysler Corporation with four different cars under its banner was now a full-fledged competitor of General Motors and Ford. Less than fifteen years after Walter Chrysler took over the all-but-defunct Maxwell Motor Company, the Chrysler Corporation had cornered, for its share, twenty-seven per cent of all motor car sales in America.

Thus out of a colossal failure, the boy from Pottawatomie County built a phenomenal success.

21

FOUR WHEELS—NO BRAKES

1930
Production 2,784,745
Registration 22,972,745
Free-wheeling

IN 1904 *Outing* magazine ran an article entitled "The Value of Last Year's Automobile" and its author took a very gloomy view of the second-hand car business. From his attitude it seems likely that one of the second-hand car dealers of those days had sold him a lemon of considerable proportions. He advised that if you were going shopping in the second-hand car market (the term "used car" came later), you would do well to take an expert along, someone who could examine the car of your choice and advise you of its faults, otherwise you were very likely to be cheated by the sharpies who dealt in this sort of merchandise.

In the beginning, of course, dealers in new cars had nothing to do with second-hand cars. Few customers had old cars to get rid of and if they did it was their own problem. When you bought a new hat you didn't trade in your old one so why should an automobile dealer have to take your old car off your hands? You sold it yourself or you consigned it to a second-hand car broker who sold it for you on commission. There were, in most large cities, two or three of these fellows and they were regarded as decidedly unreliable merchants, which was usually true. It may be added that the attitude of the public toward used-car dealers hasn't changed much in forty years.

Back in 1913 only one automobile buyer out of every four already owned an automobile. But this ratio changed rather rapidly and by 1915 one buyer in every three had an old car to dispose of. Many a prospective buyer waited until his old car was sold before purchasing the new one. The smart dealers began taking in these old cars as part payment on a new one in order to make a quick sale. Thus the present system was established.

But the second-hand car of those days was hard to sell. Most people were prejudiced against them, especially since they could buy new Fords just as cheaply. Consequently old cars began to pile up across the nation, threatening a major panic in the automobile industry.

Two things prevented this. World War I helped considerably by slowing up auto production and by bringing wartime prosperity to the country. But the greatest impetus to the motor industry was caused by the introduction of instalment buying. Suddenly a lot of people who had no money found that they could buy a car by hocking their future salary. And that eventually helped to bring disaster. For during the period from 1920 to 1929 more than 31,000,000 passenger cars were sold in this country, most of them on the instalment plan. As a result the economy of the country began to revolve around those millions of cars.

The automobile became the biggest customer of the coal and iron mines, the steel mills, the plate-glass and the rubber factories and many others. When the motor companies borrowed money to expand in order to build more cars, all the companies that supplied them had to do the same. In addition we built roads and filling stations and suburbs at a terrific pace—all on the instalment plan—to take care of the growing auto industry. And the more people there were who had cars, the more there were who needed them, or thought they did. When, finally, almost everybody owed money to a bank or a finance company and almost every business was expanding on borrowed money or floating stock issues to meet the demands of this constantly expanding credit the actual cash money of the land was spread mighty thin. The place where it was spread the thinnest of all was in Wall Street. There, by putting up a hundred dollars in cash, you could buy a thousand dollars' worth of stock in one of the overexpanded companies of the nation, many of which could do business profitably only if some three million people continued to buy a new car each year on the instalment plan.

But by this time the used-car problem had reversed itself so that, instead of *one* out of four, there were *three* out of four buyers wanting to trade in an old car.

In 1927 General Motors noticed that used cars were collecting at an alarming rate on the lots of its dealers. So it decided to destroy some of these cars, an economic maneuver suggested by a dealer in Wyoming, which General Motors executives greeted with shouts of approval. When the government made the same experiment with pigs, a few years later, some of the same executives considered "plowing under" to be poor economy.

In any case, General Motors plowed under some 650,000 second-hand cars, by paying their dealers $25 for each car destroyed. Some of the other companies imitated this plan. For a while it seemed to help the situation. But it was not enough; they would have had to destroy several million cars to bolster up the false market that the automobile industry had created for itself.

In 1929 the sale of new automobiles reached the phenomenal total of 4,587,400. But near the close of that year something happened to the tightly stretched credit of the nation, something gave way, and in Wall Street there was a flood of selling orders that sent stock prices into a tail spin.

It may well be that the first unnoticed crack in America's economic dike occurred when some small-town automobile dealer realized that although he had sold twice as many new cars in 1929 as he had ever sold in any year before, he also had twice as many used cars parked in the lot next door which nobody seemed to want. On top of this he discovered that his working capital was tied up in those second-hand cars. So he did the obvious thing and cut the hell out of used-car prices. From then on it may have been a fast chain reaction, resulting finally in a great many ex-millionaires.

But whatever broke the bubble things were very soon in an awful mess. For the next three years automobile sales skidded until in 1932 production was at its lowest point in fifteen years—1,135,491.

On any used-car lot in America you could buy a car for fifty dollars. Jalopies were anywhere from ten to twenty dollars. That was when it seemed that every high school boy in America bought himself a Ford jalopy and covered it, from radiator cap to rear bumper, with numerous legends which reached a new high in unabashed impudence and a new low in native wit. Here are only a few of the typical inscriptions:

    Capacity 5 gals
    Chicken Here's Your Roost
    Open All Night
    Use No Hooks
    Exit Only [Painted on a door that wouldn't open]
    Use Can Opener [Ditto above]
    Standing Room Only
    Abandon All Hope Ye Who Enter Here
    4 Wheels—No Brakes
    The Mayflower—Many a Puritan Has Come Across In It

The Tin You Love To Touch
This Side Up
Fragile—Handle With Care

Usually these rolling wrecks were given pet names which were also painted on the side or rear. Leaping Lena, Galloping Gertrude, Jittery Jenny and Hot Hanna were typical. A sign painted near the radiator sometimes warned: Beware —Old Faithful Spouts Every 5 Minutes. Painted near the exhaust might be a sign: Please Don't Goose Me; I'm Too Old For Monkey Business.

When the proprietors of these jalopies left them at the curb unoccupied and unlocked, they often hung a sign on the door which said: Out To Lunch. The jalopy sometimes had accessories hung from its sides that more luxurious cars were never equipped with. Such things as a roll of toilet paper, a No Parking sign, a hot water bottle and a plumber's friend.

It seemed that one never saw a jalopy with a single occupant; they were always jammed to overflowing. Sometimes not only the running boards would have their full quota of passengers, but also the fenders. The nine passenger jalopy caused laws to be passed in many states limiting the number of passengers to a car and especially to the front seat and the driver's lap.

It was during the depression period from 1929 to 1938 that the jalopies flourished strongest, and during this period, also, some of our best automobiles found it too difficult to compete with General Motors, Ford and Chrysler. Here are the names that disappeared in those years:

Roosevelt	1929	(made by Marmon)
Locomobile	1929	
Jordan	1930	
Graham-Paige	1930	
Ruxton	1930	

Erskine	1930	(made by Studebaker)
Gardner	1931	
Willys-Knight	1932	
Peerless	1932	
Essex	1932	(made by Hudson)
Rockne	1933	(made by Studebaker)
Marmon	1933	
Willys-Overland	1933	
Franklin	1934	
Duesenberg	1934	
Stutz	1935	
Austin Bantam	1935	
Reo	1936	
Auburn	1936	
Cord	1937	
Brewster	1937	
Pierce-Arrow	1938	(made by Studebaker)

By 1939 there were only twenty-one cars being manufactured in the United States. It will be noticed that three of the cars above were manufactured by Studebaker. Only by great good fortune did the oldest vehicle company in America remain in business. A man by the name of Albert R. Erskine, a former bookkeeper, who had risen to the vice presidency of the Underwood Typewriter Company, became president of Studebaker in 1915, just at the moment when the stronger companies were to have their most rapid growth. Erskine was a man of considerable personal charm but no great talent. He announced periodically, after 1929, that the depression was over and that Studebaker was planning a new program of expansion and increased production.

In 1930 he apparently thought he could pull the nation out of trouble by having Studebaker declare a dividend of close to $8,000,000, which was five times more than net profits. In addition he purchased the dying Pierce-Arrow company and then, even though Studebaker's Erskine car had flopped, he tooled up to make an automobile called the Rockne.

Automobile makers had named cars after everything from their baby daughter (Mercedes) to their favorite city (Sandusky) but this was the first time an auto maker had revealed the limit of his emotional fervor by naming a car after a football coach.

With Erskine at its helm Studebaker was in a sad way. When the Pierce-Arrow and the Rockne cars both did nose dives, his board of directors began to suspect, for the first time, that their president was not a financial wizard, but merely a good bookkeeper with a compelling ego. Which, of course, is a thumbnail sketch of too many business executives of the twenties. But just as Studebaker was about to go bankrupt, Mr. Erskine side-stepped the whole deal by shooting himself to death. Fortunately, the vice president in charge of sales was Paul G. Hoffman, who was able to rescue the company and thus retain for South Bend another industry besides the Notre Dame football team.

Just when the jalopy began to be passé among the younger motoring crowd is hard to trace. But today it is scorned by all hep teensters. A Ford with funny sayings painted on its sides is strictly for squares; it is as corny as "23 skiddoo." Today the proper conveyance among high school and college kids alike is either the conventional convertible coupé or the hot rod.

When Henry Ford decided, in 1932, to outdo Chevrolet and Plymouth by putting a V8 engine into the Ford car he inadvertently created that newest phenomenon of teen-age motoring—the hot rod. These little streamlined speedsters have become such an important industry in southern California that an annual Hot Rod Show is held each year in Los Angeles, which rivals in popularity the regular automobile show. It is sponsored by the Southern California

Timing Association, the parent organization of numerous neighborhood hot rod clubs. The S.C.T.A. was formed in 1938 and besides its other activities publishes the *Hot Rod* magazine, which has a circulation of 40,000.

While the teen-age lad who used to own a jalopy sometimes showed enough affection for his car to buy an imitation fox tail for its radiator cap, it was the fashion in those days to treat a jalopy with scorn and derision. It was left outdoors in rain and sun and snow. Its tires were smooth and often threadbare while its paint job was blistered and corroded by spots of rust. If a door wouldn't close it got kicked shut. If the engine missed or backfired no remedies were attempted except threats and maledictions. If a fender started to flop the owner tore it off and tossed it into the gutter with a gesture of contempt.

But today's youthful hot rod owner treats his car with admiration and true affection. He puts in many hours of loving care keeping its engine in top form and polishing its exterior. It has excellent tires and usually a glossy paint job. A good hot rod will often cost in the neighborhood of $2,000 or more, not counting the many hours of labor the owner has expended on it. For a hot rod is strictly a custom made car. Usually the owner has started with a Ford or a Mercury picked up on a used-car lot. He denudes it of all frou-frou such as fenders, lights and running boards. The body is lowered and if it is a coupé or a sedan the top is usually cut off or lowered.

Then comes the expensive job of rebuilding the motor. It is rebored, and a new crankshaft and connecting rods, new pistons, new valves, a new camshaft and new heads are installed. Also a magneto is always added. Two new carburetors and sometimes four are attached, as well as a new intake manifold. More than likely the car will get an electric fuel pump as well as a new rear end, and a special steering unit. A new instrument panel is often added with a speedometer that will register 150 miles per hour, a tachometer to show the engine's r.p.m. and a manifold pressure gauge.

Now comes some special bodywork to give the car better lines, then the windshield is rebuilt to half its former size and set at a rakish angle. The paint job may be either a sedate black or an extreme two-color combination, but it must be without a blemish. Next a good many parts of the car will be chrome-plated, but these will be mostly under the hood, for your average hot rodder believes that his engine should be a thing of polished beauty.

It is interesting to note that a hot rod seldom displays much chromium on the outside. In this its youthful designers show much better taste than the designers of Detroit.

Once the car has been painted it is ready to tune up and eventually will be taken to El Mirage Dry Lake for a speed trial. There the members of the Southern California Timing Association run their machines over a measured course under strict supervision. But before it is allowed to go to the starting line, the car is first inspected by a committee of experts to be sure that it is safe for high speeds.

Since the war a new type of hot rod has appeared on the West Coast. These use the wing tank from a P_38 for the body and the engine is placed behind the driver. These cigar-shaped little cars are the most streamlined that the hot rod experimenters have yet dreamed up and are much more functional in design than anything that has ever come out of Detroit's factories.

In 1948, Stuart Hilborn, of Los Angeles, drove his roadster-type hot rod over the El Mirage Dry Lake timing course at a speed of 150.5 miles per hour. It was the first time the 150-miles-per-hour mark had been broken in the S.C.T.A. But a year later, at the First Annual Bonneville National Speed Trials, at least half a dozen cars broke the 150 mile mark and one pair of hot rod enthusiasts had built a car that traveled in two directions at an average speed of 189.74 miles per hour.

This super hot rod was built by Alex Xydias and Dean Bachelor, using a 1948 Mercury engine on a chassis with an aluminum body that was designed by an aeronautical engineer. With special high-compression heads, three carburetors, special pistons and special intake manifold the engine turned up to 5,400 r.p.m. and delivered better than 225 horsepower. For fuel it used methyl alcohol instead of gasoline. By next year its two youthful owners expect to crack the 200-miles-per-hour mark.

Many new wrinkles are concocted by the hot-rodders each year and they are advancing so rapidly that the car builders in Detroit seem by comparison to travel at a snail's pace.

The *Hot Rod* magazine features a Hot Rod of the Month in every issue and some of these little beauties put to shame anything that can be seen in the showrooms of automobile row. It's no wonder that most of the designers and engineers of the Motor City are watching, slightly goggle-eyed, the activities of the hot rod builders.

22

JOHNNY-COME-LATELY

1946
Production *2,148,699*
Registration *28,100,188*
Hydra-matic transmission

THE NEWS SWEPT through Detroit with the speed of a grass fire and then across the nation. Detroit must stop making automobiles! They shook their heads along Woodward Avenue. It was almost as hard to believe as the bombs over Pearl Harbor. You might stop the moon and the sun and Niagara Falls, but how could you stop Detroit from making automobiles?

Nevertheless on January 30, 1942, the production lines ground slowly to a halt and 400,000 men washed up and joined the long queues at the pay windows. The number of automobiles assembled in those first thirty days of 1942 was 222,862; no more passenger cars came out of Detroit for almost four years. Instead, almost over night, the ingenious engineers and production men of Detroit began turning out tanks, shells, torpedoes, machine guns, airplanes and all the other instruments of war in quantities so fantastic that even the production figures of 1929 looked mild by comparison.

Three weeks after Pearl Harbor came the permanent

freeze on tires. You couldn't buy a new tire without breaking the law or getting a priority from the OPA. Almost everybody rushed out and bought a couple of used tires, just to be safe. Then they learned that the OPA wasn't going to allow them to keep these extra tires. Besides, you could get your old tires recapped as good as new. Meanwhile, Leon Henderson, of OPA, issued vague statements about the possibility of commandeering all private cars that were not a business necessity.

By this time everything was rationed. You applied to the ration board for gasoline stamps and you got only enough, supposedly, to take care of essential driving. On the eastern seaboard a shortage of gasoline cut the average car owner down to a bare minimum. It was hardly worth while for most motorists to keep their cars in operation. *Life* magazine in October, 1942, gave explicit instructions on how to service your car before putting it into dead storage.

Late in 1942 came the scrap drives. Uncle Sam needed rubber, nickel, scrap iron and aluminum, according to the newspapers. Depots were set up in public places to receive citizens' contributions. We denuded our cars of rubber floor mats and spare tires, and our kitchens of old pots and pans.

Westbrook Pegler suggested that the handsome chrome-plated bumpers on our automobiles were more or less replaceable with pieces of two-by-six and that the 28,000,000 cars in use could supply 150,000 tons of scrap steel for the blast furnaces. *Life* magazine at once suggested that it would like to take a picture of Pegler removing his bumpers for Uncle Sam. Pegler complied and soon it became fashionable to contribute your bumper to the scrap pile.

Fulton Lewis, Jr., the radio broadcaster, decided to lick the nickel shortage single-handed. Everybody had old door and ignition keys around the house and they were mostly made of nickel, he told his listeners. To help the cause of democracy just gather up those old door and ignition keys and ship them to Fulton Lewis, Jr., Washington, D.C. Keys descended on Lewis like locusts in Nebraska. Millions of them.

Early in 1943 the gasoline rationing in the East was tightened still more; six months later another cut was put into effect and the OPA sent investigators out to stop all cars and give summonses to those drivers who could not prove they were using their automobiles for business. But there was a shortage of investigators so the efforts of the OPA in this respect were pretty ineffective.

Nevertheless, New York City's boulevards, on a Sunday, were as empty as a football stadium in January. You could shoot a gun down Fifth Avenue without much risk of hitting anyone.

Gasoline rationing was not as extreme in most other parts of the country. The shortage was caused mostly by transportation difficulties. Those sections which had oil wells and refineries actually had plenty of gasoline. But they were rationed in order to save wear and tear on tires and cars.

But newly rich war workers were clamoring for automobiles, so the overstock of used cars that had piled up on the used-car lots in the Middle West and West during 1939 to 1941 were suddenly in demand.

Supposedly there was a ceiling price on all used cars, for OPA placed a price tag on everything from second-hand typewriters to a package of chewing gum. But to control the price of used cars would have taken a policeman for every used-car lot. Used-car dealers had always been horse traders by nature. This was their golden opportunity; it was a seller's market and they were shrewd operators. The price level of used cars advanced constantly higher until any car less than ten years old, in good condition, sold on the used-car lots for more than it had cost when new.

In places like Los Angeles, where used-car dealers had once led a cutthroat existence, they soon became men of wealth and fame. Mad Man Muntz, Honest John, and Wildman

Prichard, as well as the more dignified Les Kelley, "World's Largest Used Car Dealer," became the biggest buyers of radio time in Los Angeles. They also bought most of the classified advertising space in newspapers and most of the blue sky for skywriting purposes.

With the influx of war workers into Los Angeles, where distances were great and there were almost no transportation systems, the available supply of used cars soon dried up. The dealers then headed East, bought up cars at premium prices and shipped them back to Los Angeles by the carloads. The war of the used car-merchants then continued with new fury. Mad Man Muntz bought up every empty 24-sheet signboard he could find. Honest John covered a hundred square miles of sky with insistent messages proclaiming his trustworthiness. And Les Kelley of the Kelley Kar Company threatened to sue the next man who claimed to be a bigger used-car dealer than he.

But by 1945 the end of the war was in sight so the Society of Automotive Engineers decided to find out what the public really wanted in a post-war automobile. Chicago, New York, San Francisco and New Orleans were polled to get the low-down. Disregarding the varying tastes caused by climate, city dwellers voted for smaller, cheaper and more functional cars. They also wanted less chromium and a great many wanted the engine in the rear so that the hoods could be shorter, for better visibility.

The automobile industry didn't like the results of the poll so it disregarded them completely. Small cheap cars meant smaller grosses and smaller net earnings. Besides small cheap cars would be in competition with the cheap cars on the dealer's used-car lots, which was not to be tolerated. The industry also threw up its hands at the rear-engine idea. This would require a lot of engineering changes that no company was prepared to face. Besides, how did people know that was what they wanted? They'd never even seen such cars unless they had been to Europe.

So the post-war car that Americans had been waiting for with pent-up, mouth-watering desire turned out to be the biggest disappointment of the year. It was simply a 1942 car with slight body changes and more chromium. The only exception was the Studebaker Champion, a car that partially fulfilled the wants of many car buyers. It had good visibility, and was fairly compact and functional in design. However, it had the conventional front engine and it was much too expensive.

But the public was so hungry for cars that it forgot the small, well-engineered, well-designed post-war cars that it had been waiting for and signed up for any sort of car it could get.

The only car makers who talked about cars of advanced design were newcomers, who had little or no chance of ever actually manufacturing on a quantity basis, and one old-timer who had been making a famous vehicle for the army. This was the Willys Jeep.

The jeep, as manufactured for the army, was actually a substitute for the cavalry horse. It had a four-wheel drive and could function over fields and ditches as well as highways, could turn on a dime and practically climb trees. Converted to peacetime use it remained functional but grew too wide and too long and certainly twice as expensive as it should have been.

Just before the war Powel Crosley, Jr., manufacturer of cheap radios and refrigerators had begun making a small cycle-car type of automobile, a midget intended to sell for peanuts and to fill the vacancy left in the automotive field ever since the demise of Ford's Model T.

After the war Crosley sold his other interests and concentrated on his midget car. It filled many of the requirements of the average American. It was cheap and easy to park. But it was not cheap enough and it was too small for a comfortable motor vacation. It seemed to be almost but not quite the answer to what the average city driver needed.

Of the post-war newcomers the two that cut the widest swathes were Henry Kaiser and Preston Tucker. Both obtained ex-war plants from the government and both launched stock-selling campaigns to finance their operations.

Tucker promised that he was going to manufacture a rear-engine car of sleek and modern design that looked like some of the $30,000 beauties that were to be seen at the Paris Automobile show.

Kaiser had risen to prominence during the war by turning out Liberty ships on a production line. He took over the Willow Run bomber plant in Detroit and teamed up with Joseph Frazer, president of the Graham-Paige Motors Corporation, and an old hand at the automobile game. They announced that they would make a front-driver car with all the advantages of the old Cord front-drive, along with a lot of new improvements.

Detroit observed the two newcomers with cynical amusement. How did these Johnny-come-lateleys think they were going to get material to build cars? Steel, for instance? The steel plants couldn't supply their old customers let alone any new ones. Or take nuts and bolts. Did they think the nut people would dump old customers in favor of neophytes in the auto game?

Detroit was right about Tucker. He couldn't cut it. He turned out to be a better promoter than manufacturer and in 1949 was indicted by the Federal government for mail fraud, violation of the Securities Act and conspiracy—all in pursuance of a scheme to defraud the public. In January, 1950, however, he was acquitted on all counts.

Henry Kaiser and Joe Frazer were of sterner and more experienced stuff. Although the industry's pessimists had prophesied that they would never make a hundred cars, Kaiser-Frazer announced on October 1, 1947, that the company had turned out 100,000 cars and was the "fourth largest producer of automobiles" in the United States. Which was probably true at that moment.

Kaiser and Frazer had solved their manufacturing difficulties by purchasing their own steel mill and by paying premium prices to get the parts they needed. The cars they turned out were not the front-drive jobs they had promised, but they had sleek lines with a minimum of chrome and they sold well, even though overpriced. For you could sell any new car in 1947, and by December, 1948, the company claimed to have sold 325,000 cars.

In 1946, beset by strikes and material shortages, Detroit's automobile factories turned out 2,148,699 cars. The factory list price of those cars was fantastically high but many of them sold for from twenty to thirty per cent higher than list price.

There may have been honest new-car dealers who did not scrounge their auto-starved customers but they seemed to be a small minority. The methods by which dealers took an extra cut above the list price were numerous. Some of them took money under the table. Others made their extra profit by giving a new-car purchaser an average of fifty per cent below book value for his old car.

Some buyers were so anxious for new cars that they offered to give the dealer their old car if they could get a new one at once. They became preferred customers and got quick delivery.

Sometimes a new-car dealer would have an arrangement with a used-car lot whereby cars would be transferred to the used-car man through dummy buyers. The used-car dealer, of course, could sell the new car for any price he wished. since he was not hampered by factory list prices. A $2,000 automobile on the used-car lot was usually priced at about $2,700 or $3,000.

Some new-car dealers refused to sell a new car unless they could take an old car in trade. That old car traded in at too low a figure was where their extra take came from.

Many dealers considered themselves to be models of virtue because they sold new cars without insisting on a trade-in.

But these merchants usually loaded the car with extra equipment such as fog lights, a heater, a radio, seat covers and any other extra gadgets that could be piled onto it, thus running up their profit as much as two or three hundred dollars.

This sort of thing continued far into 1948. By that time the automobile factories had begun to make something a little better than the 1942 models with a different curve to the fenders. But beneath the new slick lines and the smell of new paint and leather, there was also the odor of unscrupulous and grasping dealers who took advantage of the shortage of new cars to bilk their neighbors.

The American motorist will remember 1946, 1947 and 1948 for several long years and look with skepticism on the bright and beautiful words that come from automobile advertising agencies and press bureaus in the future.

23

THOSE DREAM BOATS

1950
Production 6,750,000 (estimated)
Registration 41,000,000 (estimated)
Jet propulsion

IN FIFTY YEARS the automobile has come a long way. There were some eight thousand cars in the United States back in 1900. In 1950 there are many sections of the country that average one car for every family. The overall average is five cars to every seven families.

But necessary as the motor car is, it contributes buffets as well as blessings to our way of life. In January, 1900, the first serious automobile accident was recorded in the New York papers. It happened when an electric hansom cab skidded in Union Square, struck the curb and caused the driver to be thrown from his high perch into the street. The driverless cab then ran over the driver, after which it headed for the equestrian statue of George Washington. But the granite pedestal on which the statue rested stopped the cab and thus prevented further damage. It was not recorded whether the driver of the cab recovered, but the New York *Herald* suggested that the Electric Vehicle Company had better do something to prevent similar accidents in the future. The paper felt that automobiles should not become a menace to human life.

Today our motor cars kill more than thirty-two thousand people each year and injure a million.

In 1902, New York newspapers reported that one Joseph Hughes had been awarded damages of $12,000 in his suit against Mr. Felix Warburg for injuries sustained when his horses were frightened by Mr. Warburg's automobile at Seabright, New Jersey. One of the horses was killed and Mr. Hughes was permanently injured. This was the first important judgment ever awarded a plaintiff in an automobile case.

Today, automobile accidents cause a yearly property damage of $1,100,000,000. The annual cost in wage losses, medical expense and insurance is $1,700,000,000.

The total value of all passenger cars, trucks and buses produced last year was $6,711,612,000, so possibly statisticians can prove that we achieve a net gain, provided we charge off lost lives and crippled bodies at some nominal fee.

The automobile also is to blame for many small nuisances. For instance, it annoys us with traffic jams and the problem of where to park. It also is the greatest single reason why half the nation is living on the instalment plan. And it has certainly given sex its biggest boost since Little Egypt.

Sex in the automobile is evident everywhere these days in an amusing but nonetheless dangerous manifestation called one-armed driving. The automobile has also done much to promote a courting device known as the necking party. At the risk of upsetting moralists I will point out that if one out of every thirty-five automobiles is being used tonight by a boy and a girl that's over a million potential necking parties. Some of those cars will doubtless be a well-known make, with seats that convert into beds. If mothers used to worry about their daughters out in a surrey with the fringe on top, think of today's mother worrying about a sedan with a built-in Ostermoor. And then there are the motels. Thousands of them. How they do crowd up on Saturday night!

And the automobile is responsible for those 24-sheet billboards that despoil our countryside; also, more directly, it is to blame for cluttering up our newspapers with advertising that insults the average intelligence. Modern copywriters seem to think in moronic grooves. To illustrate, there is the oh-goody school of ad writers who can't do without the word "thrill." Then there is the advertising in which a "miracle" is revealed. Another favorite with the boys in the advertising agencies is the "beauty" theme.

Crude though they were, I prefer the advertisements of the early days. At least they usually showed some imagination, and the ad writers weren't looking over each other's shoulders. Take this ad for the Ohio Motor Car Company in 1911. The headline said, "Only Two Cars a Day but Tested on Hills and Straight-Away." That made some sense —told a dramatic story. You could visualize the painstaking care with which those two cars were assembled and the strenuous test run that followed.

Then there was "Buy a Bates and Keep Your Dates." Seven words told the whole story. Drama and romance! You've got a date with a beautiful blonde. If you don't get there first your rival may show up in a Maxwell. You don't dare take a chance on a car that might break down. No, sir. You'll win that lovely bit of feminine pulchritude only if you buy a Bates!

Another slogan with class was "Ride in a Glide *Then* Decide." This combined the beauty of rhyme with practicality. You felt that here was a car manufactured by gentlemen of culture. It was a friendly invitation to sample the luxurious Glide. No high pressure; no rush act. And if, by any chance, you chose another car, no hard feelings.

One of my favorites was the slogan that advertised the Reliance car. "No Noise About It But the Horn." The copywriter of those early days could give his imagination free rein. There were no precedents; nothing was hackneyed. He could be witty, gutty, gay—or merely dull, like the men who were to follow him. For instance, in 1915:

Paige—"The Most Beautiful Car in America"
Partin-Palmer—"The Big Buy of the Year"

What a familiar ring they have. Thirty-five years they sounded just as phoney as they do today, rephrased to read "The Most Beautiful Thing On Wheels" and "Today's Best Buy."

It doesn't seem possible that copywriters are being paid to rework these tired slogans, but they are. For today the automobile dollars are spread far and wide and generously. Even the farmer, the lumberjack, the miner, the cowhand and the sheep herder will get a few automobile dollars for their labors.

Fifty years ago between two and three thousand people made their living from the automobile business. Today more than one job out of seven would not exist were it not for the automobile. Even in Nevada, where the major industries are gambling and divorces and there are fewer wage earners than in any other state, 14,000 workers owe allegiance to the automobile. In Missouri, which once tried to keep motorists out by charging a two-dollar license fee for every county, more than 230,000 people get a weekly pay check directly from the automobile or allied industries. In Iowa, where farmers once fought to keep their mud roads, 5,000 men are now employed merely to keep the state's 62,000 miles of hard-surfaced highways in good shape for the 900,000 passenger cars and trucks owned by the Iowans of today.

There are some 52,000,000 people licensed to drive an automobile in 1950. Five and a half million children will ride to school every weekday in buses. Over six thousand cities will depend entirely on buses and private cars for their transportation.

These are just a few of the thousands of statistics put out by the Automobile Manufacturers Association, which is supported by the nine automobile companies (not including Ford) and fourteen truck manufacturers that make all the automobiles, trucks and buses in this country.

Today four monkey-wrench engineers are left who created automobiles in the pioneer days; they are Frank Duryea, Edgar Apperson, Ransom E. Olds and Charles King. But the super-salesmen and the super-producers burned themselves out more quickly than the engineers. Gone is bull-necked, hard-living Walter Flanders, who helped Ford produce the first Model T's; and so is soft-spoken William Knudsen, who put Chevrolet production ahead of Ford and then turned Detroit from automobiles to tanks and torpedoes; and John Willys, who turned a sporting goods store into a giant corporation topped only by Ford and General Motors; and Roy Chapin who helped create Oldsmobile and Hudson; and Henry Joy who made Packard great; and Chrysler, the engine wiper, who built himself a motor empire after he was forty-five; and the Dodge brothers, who were enriched by Henry's Model T and who helped make Henry rich.

There were a few tough old birds like Billy Durant and Charles Nash and Henry Ford who lived to a ripe old age despite the nerve-grinding strain of producing and selling in an industry that barred no holds and showed no mercy. But most of the others died too soon, though willingly no doubt, dazzled and bewitched by the Goddess Machina and her lavish rewards of power and wealth and glory.

Strangely enough the cars those men created twenty-five and fifty years ago have a new vogue. The patina of age has given them a new glamor and even increased their value above their original cost. For there are now thousands of owners of old and ancient automobiles who have banded themselves together into such organizations as the Veteran Motor Car Club, the Antique Automobile Club and the Horseless Carriage Club for the purpose of holding tours, exhibitions and contests, but also to preserve old-time automobiles, their accessories and their romantic lore.

The Horseless Carriage Club, founded in Los Angeles, issues a quarterly magazine with news of automotive antiquarians from coast to coast.

The latest club devoted to antique motor vehicles is the National Association of Fire Engine Collectors, which held its first meet on Long Island in 1949. The fire engine fans are said to be the most rabid of all.

The antiquarians have also revived the Glidden Tour. Each summer the ancient car owners gather from all parts of the country to emulate the old-time reliability tours, except that now they travel on concrete highways instead of the mud roads of 1905. Today there are specialists in repairing and restoring old cars. They find ancient autos in barns and scrap heaps, rusted and moldering away, so badly decayed that it would seem impossible for anyone to do anything with them. But the expert knows the exact shape that a missing tonneau should be and just the type of wheels and tires that the ancient wreck should have. When he has rebuilt the car by hand and has it once more in running condition he can sell it at a good price to some fan.

Your real automobile antiquarian is more rabid than a searcher after antique furniture. He is not satisfied with one car nor with fifty, if he can afford more. There are several collectors who own more than a hundred antique cars. James Melton, the Metropolitan opera star, has one of the most famous and valuable collections. It has one car dating from 1897 when the first factory production was set up at the Pope Manufacturing Company's plant in Hartford, Connecticut. Every car has been restored to its original condition insofar as it is possible. Melton's antique cars are kept in a museum on Route 7 near Norwalk, Connecticut, and may be viewed by the public for a small admission fee.

Some of the old-car fans specialize in racers. And the Horseless Carriage Club even holds speed events for these enthusiasts.

Today's racing cars are of another breed entirely, of course, than those old timers. The twenty-eight foot monster in which Britisher John Cobb traveled 394.196 miles per hour in 1947 makes a record-buster like the Stanley brothers' steamer of 1906 look as fragile and inefficient as a canoe on wheels, while its record time of two miles a minute is merely a slow waltz. On the other hand today's four-cylinder Indianapolis racers seem like toys compared with Barney Oldfield's famous Blitzen Benz of 1910.

In Los Angeles, which has become the racing car and hot rod center of the United States, the Meyer and Drake Engineering Corporation turns out practically all the racing engines used at Indianapolis and in the popular midget cars, while Kurtis-Kraft, Inc., builds most of the chassis and bodies for the midget racers. Fanning out from the Meyer and Drake plant are half a dozen builders of Indianapolis racers, the most important being Lou Moore's shop which has fallen into an enviable rut by winning the Indianapolis race for three years running.

Los Angeles has more custom body shops and specialists in hot rods than any other city in the country. The latter include manufacturers of high compression heads, racing manifolds, magnetos, crankshafts and cams, special gear boxes, mufflers, carburetors and dealers in souped-up cars.

Today, in fact, Los Angeles seems to be the only place in the United States where the automobile manufacturer is building a car to suit the particular needs of its consumers. By this I mean that Detroit is now strictly a producer of dream boats.

There is nothing wrong with a dream boat, of course, except that it is a car designed by salesmen and not by engineers. It is big and fat with rounded corners and white side wall tires and forty-pound bumpers covered with chromium. Inside it is wider and longer, and outside it is wider and longer, too, despite those ads.

And strangely enough the American buyer has been buffaloed and pushed around for so many years by the auto makers that along with today's outrageous prices he accepts the discomforts of an overly long, overly wide, overly powerful car fifty weeks out of the year just so that he can have large-car comfort on a two weeks' vacation tour.

The car purchaser today is stuck with the Detroit formula of making the new car an expensive car, so that the man who wants cheap transportation will have to purchase one of the used cars that the dealer has for sale.

In the days of the Model T a man with only $400 or $500 or $750 to spend on a car could buy a new Ford. I remember when my father used to order a new Ford the same way he ordered a ton of coal. He'd call Len Small, the Ford dealer, on the telephone.

"Len, send me out a Ford coop. . . . This afternoon is okay. . . . What about my old car? . . . A hundred dollars? Fine. . . . So long, Len."

Detroit could build a car for $495 if it wished to, but it won't as long as it is selling six million cars a year for $1,500 or more.

The only American cars today that are suitable for city driving are the Crosley and the Willys Jeep. Unfortunately the latter isn't up to advance expectations and both are too high priced.

There is nothing else that a city driver has to choose from except the foreign cars. The British Austin and Anglia, as well as some of the other low-priced foreign cars, are excellent, but the import duty and transportation makes them a little high, even though they are about $500 cheaper than a Ford.

The Detroit manufacturers like to call their cars "full-size cars" a phrase originated by one of the industry's press agents to try to combat the demonstrable fact that even Ford and Chevrolet are not full-size cars, but oversize monsters. A standard garage that was built twenty years ago is too short for them. Many apartment buildings have garages for their tenants that are now too narrow to hold the average American car. You can drive in all right, but you can't get out of the car once you are in.

Parking today's car takes a driver of better than average skill. Many women are helpless when confronted by the necessity of parking parallel to the curb in a short parking space. And a person who is a poor judge of distance soon has a complete set of dented fenders.

Grooved thinking has been a serious handicap to the advancement of automobile design in this country. As Charles Kettering has pointed out, when we first started building automobiles we had a horse fixation. Anything that varied too far from a buggy or a carriage was too radical for the early salesman—and the public, too.

Gradually automobiles got away from that carriage look. By 1905 practically all automobiles had the engine in front. And it's stayed there ever since. The salesmen and the super-salesmen are afraid to move it back where it belongs, above the rear axle. Many engineers would like to change it, but most salesmen are afraid they'll have a car that won't look like an automobile.

So we must have an expensive drive shaft running from the engine to the rear wheels. This gives all cars a hump in the floor. We also have radiator cap ornaments on practically all cars, despite the fact that there hasn't been an exposed radiator cap in at least fifteen years. We also have six or eight cylinders to drive our cars. Four are enough for Indianapolis racing cars that will do 180 miles an hour, but for the long-suffering American public, Detroit furnishes from two to four extra cylinders.

Ever since 1903 when American manufacturers began to copy the lines of the Renault, the De Dion-Bouton and the Panhard the designers have taken most of their ideas from Europe. Unfortunately in recent years they have bedizened American cars with too much chromium and added a few lines and curves of their own. It is as though a hack artist were to make a copy of Mona Lisa and add to the lady's charms a flashing Pepsodent smile, red hair and a rhinestone tiara.

It is time the American designers and engineers began to copy some of the smaller European cars, with their economical engines, located in the rear, their functional body designs, their complete lack of unnecessary folderol, such as radios, overdrive, oversize tires and many other refinements that add cost to the new car.

Some cars seem to be eight months' pregnant, with power plants capable of hauling ten-ton trucks. Some are low racy jobs that do well on the open highway, but just let them try a road deep in snow or a country road with a high crown and they're stuck. This is true of most of today's cars.

General Motors has a policy of making all of its cars conform in design. The sameness of the General Motors product is so extreme that radio comedians make jokes about it. Sample: "I'm gonna punch four holes in the fender of my Chevrolet so everybody will think I own a Buick."

The General Motors policy is founded on the theory that Cadillac can't be wrong. Therefore the design for Cadillac is first decided by G.M. policy makers, then the other divisions copy it with minor changes. The Cadillac is one of America's small gods, so its lines are always admired, not because they are beautiful but because they are Cadillac. Ergo: any car that looks like a Cadillac is beautiful.

This theory of design has worked wonderfully for General

Motors and will probably go on working, but it is creating an awful lot of automobiles unsuitable for city driving.

There was a time when a man bought a car and had a special tonneau fitted to it, one that suited his fancy to a T—painted maroon with gold striping. Then he installed one of several types of windshields, with brass trim, and bought a fancy top, made to order, of white canvas with tan leather trimming. He bought a four-tone bulb-type French horn that played a six-note bugle call, and added a Moto-Meter and a $125 speedometer. As a final touch, he might add a set of fore-doors to keep the breezes out of the front seat.

In those days no man climbed in the wrong car by mistake and tried to drive it off, simply because he couldn't tell his own automobile from his neighbors at the curb. No indeed! But today on a Sunday, the bumper-to-bumper line-up of cars on any highway looks like so many sausages emerging from a machine.

A recent advertisement of General Motors endeavored to prove how much more for your money you get in today's car than you did in yesterday's. They made the following comparison between a Buick of 1928 and a Chevrolet of 1948.

The Buick (1928)		The Chevrolet (1948)	
List Price	$1,320	List Price	$1,280
Horsepower	74	Horsepower	90
Maximum speed	64.75	Maximum speed	81.8
Curb weight	3,764 lbs.	Curb Weight	3,225 lbs.
Cylinders	6	Cylinders	6
Wheelbase	115.75	Wheelbase	116

The only trouble with this comparison is that they picked the wrong car to compare with the modern Chevrolet. Let's examine a Pontiac of 1933. Here's what the advertisement says:

Pontiac, the Economy Straight 8; 115-Inch Wheelbase; 3,265 Pounds of Weight; 78 Actual Miles Per Hour; 77 Horsepower.
Price—$585 F.O.B. Pontiac.

Aside from the fact that you don't get as much for your money today, no matter what the advertisemens say, there are certain values that they forgot to tote up in any of these ads. You can't balance them off with a dollar sign or a Hydra-matic clutch or electric windows or radios or an overdrive. Here are some of the values we got way back in the days of the Marmon and the Winton Six and the Model T Ford:

We drove through a countryside uncluttered by motels, hotdog stands and billboards. When we hit a thirty-mile-an-hour clip that was just about the car's limit, but it was just fast enough and we had time to enjoy the view, without risk to life and limb. We sometimes had a lot of trouble with the motor and with blowouts, but when we stopped by the roadside a brother motorist was sure to pull up alongside and ask if we needed any help. That old 1909 Marmon might look funny today, but the Marmon brothers who designed its vitals didn't have to make any concessions to some industrial designer who wanted to lower the running board or lengthen the wheelbase. And what was stylish in 1909 didn't look silly in 1912. And best of all it was all yours— *you* owned it, not the finance company.

INDEX

Abbott-Detroit, 114
Adams, 57, 59, 167
Adams, Frederick Upham, 52, 53, 54, 55, 56
Aermore horn, 171
Alco, 210
American, 105, 114, 204, 217, 260
American Automobile Association, 144, 145, 202, 203, 209, 210, 213, 216
American Automobile Club, 62
American Bicycle Company, 16, 92, 164
American Bicycler, The, 135, 136, quoted, 136-137; 145
American Highway Association, 216
American Locomotive Works, 260, 261
Anderson, John, 236
Anglia, 293
Antique Automobile Club, 291
Apperson, 17, 49, 62, 114, 121, 199, 217, 260
Apperson, Edgar and Elmer, 41, 42, 71, 163, 263, 290
Arnold, Schwinn and Company, 164, 165
Around-the-World Race, 205, 208
Arrow, 48
Association of Licensed Automobile Manufacturers, 32, 102, 119-128, 130-133
Autocar, 62, 102, 121
Auto and Marine Power Company, 163
Automobile, The, quoted, 63-64, 125; 204
Automobile Club of America, 79
Automobile Club of France, 61
Automobile Fore Carriage Company, 32, 166
Automobile Handbook, The, quoted, 150-152, 156, 160, 161
Automobile Manufacturers Association, 47, 133, 228, 290

Automobile races,
 in America, 17, 37, 52, 107, 201, 210, 216, 276
 in England, 38
 in France, 29, 50
Automobile Show, 70, 75, 77, 83, 85, 91, 166, 260, 283
Auburn 273
Austin, 273, 293

Bachelor, Dean, 277
Baker, 238
Baker, Rauch and Lang Company, 168
Barney, Charles T., 127
Bates, 288
Benz, 33, 41, 55, 56, 57, 58, 59, 200, 292
Berg Automobile Company, 121
Bishop, D. Wolfe, 61
Borland, William, 215
Boston *Herald,* 91
Bostwick, A. C., 61
Boyce MotoMeter, 243
Brady, Anthony M., 31, 32
Brayton, George B., 25, 26, 129, 132
Brewster, 273
Briscoe, 259, 264
Briscoe, Benjamin, 190, 263, 264
Brookes, L. Elliott, 150-154, 156-158, 160, 161
Brown, 217
Brush, 114, 264
Buffalo Gasoline Motor Company, 32, 121, 122
Buggyaut, 39, 40
Buick, 49, 121, 189, 190, 191, 197, 202, 251, 261-263, 295, 290
Buick, David, 189

Cadillac, 22, 49, 114, 115, 121, 183, 191, 192, 197, 199, 245, 295
Cadillac Automobile Company, 120, 121, 123, 192, 194
Cadillac Motor Corporation, 245

299

INDEX

Cameron, William, 47
Canada Cycle and Motor Company, 225
Cannon Ball, 96
Cartercar, 167, 168, 196
Case, 163, 260
Cave, Henry, 128
Chalmers, 181, 260, 264-266
Chalmers, Hugh, 182, 183
Chapin, Ray D., 71-73, 181-183, 213, 221, 263, 290
Chevrolet, 149, 251-255, 257, 274, 290, 293, 295, 296
Chevrolet, Louis, 251
Chicago *Inter-Ocean*, 76, quoted, 77, 78
Chicago *Times Herald*, 52, 53, 54, 55, 59, 68
Chicago *Tribune*, 53, 54, 55, 57, 59
Chrysler, 16, 181, 266
Chrysler, Walter Percy, 260-267, 290
Clark, Louis S., 102
Clement, Bayard, 209
Cleveland, 76, 260
Coffin, Howard E., 181, 182, 183
Cohn, David L., 47
Cole, 105, 260
Columbia, 30, 31, 49, 57, 76, 81, 121, 134, 163, 204, 238, 264
Columbus, 238
Columbus Buggy Company, 162
Commercial Motor Company, The, 121
Cooper, Tom, 48
Cord, 273, 283
Cosmopolitan, quoted, 51, 59, 60, quoted, 61; 93
Couzens, James, 115, 116, 123, 125, 195, 228-231, 234, 235, 256
Crane-Simplex, 260
Crawford, 260
Crestmobile, 121
Crosley, 293
Crosley, Powel, Jr., 282
Crowthers, Samuel, 45
Cuneo, Joan Newton, 242, 243

Daimler, 26, 33, 34, 50, 129
Daimler Mercedes, 127
Darracq, 210
Davis, 260
Dayton Engineering Laboratories, 245
De Dietrich, 209
De Dion, 80, 91, 177, 206, 207, 208
De Dion-Bouton, 64, 295
De Palma, Ralph, 210, 243
Depew, Chauncey, 60, 75

DeSoto, 266
Detroit, 177
Detroit Automobile Company, 48, 192
Detroit Auto Vehicle Company, 178
Detroit Electric Company, 48
Detroit *Free Press*, quoted, 44, 45
Diana, 260
Dixie Flyer, 162
Dodge, 181
Dodge, Horace and John, 115, 225-229, 234, 235, 236, 256, 266, 290
Duerr and Company, C. A., 124
Duesenberg, 105, 181, 273
du Pont, Pierre S., 254
du Pont de Nemours Company, E. I., 252, 253, 255
Durant, Billy, 188-198, 213, 250-258, 261-265, 290
Durant-Dort Carriage Company, 189, 261
Duryea, 37, 38, 39, 40, 41, 44, 55, 57, 58, 59, 61
Duryea, Charles and Frank, 28-30, 34-40, 42, 45, 52, 56, 57, 59, 61, 67, 68, 103, 290

Edwards, Gus, 75
Elco, 105
Electric Auto-Lite, 181
Electric Storage Battery Company, 168
Electric Vehicle Company, 31, 32, 81, 82, 86, 119-122, 124, 128, 129, 238, 264, 286
Electrobat, 56, 57, 58
Elgin, 260
Elgin Road Races, 209
Elkhart Carriage and Harness Manufacturing Company, 162
Elmore, 62, 103, 121, 169, 196
E. M. F., 181, 183, 184, 185, 186, 265
Empire, 105, 217
Enger Convertible Twelve, 168
Entz, Justice B., 168, 169
Erskine, 273, 274
Essex, 105, 273
Evans, Oliver, 88
Everitt, Bernard F., 183, 184, 185, 186
Ewing, 196

Fairbanks-Morse Company, 166
Federal Highway Act, 224
Fiat, 209, 210
Firestone, 162
Fisher Body, 22, 245
Fisher, Carl, 210, 213-215, 216, 218, 221, 224

INDEX

Flanders, 181, 205
Flanders, Walter E., 183, 184, 186, 187, 213, 290
Flint Wagon Works, 250
Ford, 17, 20, 21, 45, 47, 105, 114-118, 123-128, 131, 149, 150, 172, 183, 190, 250, 251, 261, 264, 269, 274, 282, 293, 294, 297
Ford, Edsel, 123, 221
Ford, Henry, 33, 34, 40, 44-49, 67, 75, 97, 102, 114-117, 119, 123-133, 150, 183, 184, 192, 195, 200, 201, 214, 215, 227-236, 256-258, 265, 274, 290
Ford Automobile Company, Henry, 48
Ford Motor Company, 49, 114, 115, 118, 123-125, 127, 131, 195, 227-236, 266
Fournier, 62
Franklin, 21, 49, 108, 109, 110, 121, 273
Frazer, Joseph, 283-285
Fredonia, 62
Fuller, 163

Gale, 163
Gardner, 273
Garford Company, 186
Gasoline Age, The, quoted, 31; 47
General Motors, 66, 108, 163, 169, 188, 190-193, 195-198, 250-258, 262-264, 266, 270, 272, 290, 295, 296
General Motors Research Laboratories, 244, 245
Glasscock, C. B., 31, 47
Glidden, Charles J., 202, 203
Glidden Tour, 202-204, 208, 209, 242, 243, 291
Glide, 288
Graham-Paige, 272, 283
Gray, John, 236
Grout, 95, 96
Gyroscope, 167

Halladay, 259
Harroun, Ray, 18, 210, 216
Haynes, 44, 49, 62, 71, 121, 163, 217, 260
Haynes-Apperson, 41, 42, 82, 91, 104, 121
Haynes, Elwood, 34, 40-42, 52, 56, 67, 82, 216, 263
HCS, 105
Henderson, 217
Heany Lamp Company, 196, 197
Heath, George, 209

Hilborn, Stuart, 276
Hoffman, Paul G., 274
Hollier, 163
Hoosier Motor Club, 216
Horseless Age, The, 38, quoted 105; 137, 202
Horseless Carriage Club, 291, 292
Horsey Horseless Carriage, 166
Hotchkiss Anti-Jolt Device, 171
Hot Rod, 275, 277
Hot Rod Show, 274
Hough, Charles M., 129, 130
Houpt-Rockwell, 114
Hubbard, Elbert, 215
Hudson, 16, 69, 183, 220, 245, 273, 290
Huff, E. S., 44
Hupmobile, 17, 114
Hupp, 181
Hydra-matic clutch, 168

Indiana Automobile Manufacturers Association, 216
Indianapolis races
  International Sweepstakes, 201
  Memorial Day race, 107, 216
  Speed classic, 17, 210
International, 121
I.W.W., 231, 232

Jackson, 259
Janesville Machine Company, 255
Jeantaud, 51
Jeffery, Thomas B., 107, 108, 122, 262
Jerico horn, 171
Jewett, 260
Jordan, 16, 272
Joy, Henry B., 11, 112, 113, 120, 215, 218, 220, 221, 290

Kaiser-Fraser, 283
Kaiser, Henry, 283-285
Keene, Foxhall, 63
Kentucky Wagon Manufacturing Company, 162
Kettering, Charles F., 244, 245, 294
King, 46, 58, 109, 181, 260
King, Anita, 246-249
King, Charles B., 46, 47, 52, 58, 59, 71, 101, 102, 290
Kirk, 121
Kisselkar, 113, 246, 247, 248, 249
Klaxon, 171
Knight, Charles, 181
Knox Waterless, 103, 110, 121, 200, 201
Knudsen, William, 257, 258, 290

INDEX

Kohlsaat, H. H., 52-59
Kurtis-Kraft Incorporated, 292

LaFayette, 105
LaFrance, 181
Lane, 95
Lansden Electric, 195
League of American Wheelmen, 104, 137
Leland, Henry, 120, 191, 192, 245
Leland, W. C., 192
Leland & Faulconer Manufacturing Company, 191, 192
Levassor, M., 34, 51
Lewis, Eugene W., 46
Lewis Spring and Axel Company, 163
Lincoln Highway Association, 215-217, 219, 222-224, 246
Lincoln Memorial Highway, 215-224, 246
Little, 250, 251
Locomobile, 49, 62, 81, 95, 121, 210, 260, 261, 272
Locomobile Company of America, 62, 80, 82, 94, 121, 210
Long Distance, 121
Long Island Motor Parkway, 213
Lozier, 18, 76, 103, 163, 200, 201, 210

Mabley Simplex, 209
Macfarlane, Peter Clark, 46, 47
Malcolmson, Alex, 227, 236
Mannheim, 33
Marion, 217
Marmon, 17, 18, 19, 20, 105, 106, 107, 159, 163, 200, 201, 210, 211, 217, 243, 272, 273, 297
Marriott, Fred, 97, 98, 200
Matheson, 103
Maxim, Hiram Percy, 30, 52, 56, 58, 168
Maxwell, 17, 181, 203, 204, 264, 265, 288
Maxwell-Briscoe Motor Company, 190, 195, 264
Maxwell, John D., 71, 190, 203, 204
Maxwell Motor Company, 263-266
McClure's Magazine, quoted, 239-240
McFarland, 217
Mercedes, 62, 63, 124, 200, 209, 210, 274
Mercer, 260
Mercury, 274, 277
Metz, 259
Metzger, William E., 183, 184, 185, 186
Metzger Automatic Windshield, 171

Meyer and Drake Engineering Corporation, 292
Miles, General Nelson A., 60
Mitchell, 103, 260
Mobile, 80, 81, 82, 94, 95, 149
Model Automobile Company, 166
Moline Plow Works, 163
Monroe, 105
Moore, Lou, 292
Morgan, J. P., 256, 264
Morris, 58
Morris, William, 237
Morrow Manufacturing Company, 181
Morse, 63
Moto-Bloc, 206
Motor-Drag, 56
Motor Memories, 46
Moto-Meter, 171, 296
Mueller, Oscar, 56, 58, 59
Mulford, Ralph, 18, 210

National, 105, 163, 200, 210, 238, 260
National Automobile Chamber of Commerce, 133
National Automobile Racing Association, 61
National Association of Fire Engine Collectors, 291
Nash, 108
Nash, Charles W., 108, 261, 262, 263, 290
Nash Motors Company, 262
New Process Gear, 181
New Era, 163
New York Economy Test, 204
New York *Herald,* 286
New York *Times,* quoted, 39; 206, 207, quoted, 232, 233
"999," 48
Nordyke, 107
Nordyke and Marmon, 163
Northern, 46, 58, 102, 121, 181
Northern Manufacturing Company, 102, 121

Oakland, 191
Oakland Motor Car Company, 191
Ocean-to-Ocean Rock Highway, 213, 214, 215, 224
Octoauto, 169
Official Automobile Blue Books, The, 144, 145, quoted, 146-147; 156, 217
Ohio, 238
Ohio Automobile Company, 111
Ohio Motor Company, 288

INDEX

Old Pacific, 112
Oldfield, Barney, 48, 49, 97, 104, 126, 164, 200, 292
Olds, Ransom E., 34, 40, 52, 66-75, 88, 120, 181, 190-192, 203, 225, 290
Olds Motor Vehicle Company, 68
Olds Motor Works, 68, 70, 121, 123, 181, 183, 190, 191, 263
Oldsmobile, 16, 17, 22, 49, 52, 62, 66, 69-75, 82, 115, 121, 149, 156, 170, 181, 183, 227, 263, 290
O.P.A., 279, 280
Orient, 76, 114, 121
Otto Engine, 25, 36, 45, 129, 132
Outing, quoted, 241, 242; 268
Overland, 105, 178
Overland Automobile Company, 178, 179, 180
Owen Magnetic, 168, 169
Owen, Ray M., 74, 75

Packard, 49, 62, 82, 110, 121, 200, 209, 263, 290
Packard, Colonel J. W., 110, 111, 112
Packard Electric Company, 111
Packard Motor Company, 111, 120
Packard Motor Car Company, 121, 123, 215
Paige, 289
Paige-Detroit, 260
Pan-American, 260
Panhard, 61, 80, 124, 209, 295
Panhard-Levassor, 34, 39, 50, 61
Partin-Palmer, 289
Parry, 105
Pathfinder, 217
Peerless, 49, 76, 102, 113, 121, 163, 201, 273
Peerless Motor Car Company, 121, 123
Peugeot, 210
Pierce, 76
Pierce, George N., 177, 182, 203
Pierce, Percy B., 203
Pierce-Arrow, 24, 49, 105, 110, 121, 155, 163, 177, 178, 203, 273
Pilot, 217
Plymouth, 121, 266, 274
Pontiac, 191, 297
Pope, 76
Pope, Colonel Albert A., 29-32, 52, 83, 100, 134, 135, 137, 145, 212, 213, 238
Pope-Hartford, 31, 49, 103, 134
Pope Manufacturing Company, 29, 31, 52, 57, 121, 134, 168, 291
Pope-Robinson, 121, 134

Pope-Robinson Company, 121
Pope-Toledo, 100, 101, 105, 121, 134, 156, 180, 209
Pope-Tribune, 134
Pope-Waverly, 105, 134
Pound, Arthur, 47
Portland Cement Association, 220
Pratt, 162
Premier, 105, 106, 110, 217, 260
Prest-O-Lite, 199, 210, 214
Prest-O-Starter, 199
Protos, 206, 207, 208
Prescott, 95

Rackham, Horace, 236
Rainier, 196
Rambler, 49, 62, 76, 107, 108, 122, 155, 163, 164, 177, 178, 204
Raskob, John J., 252
Rauch and Lang, 238
Red Flag Law, 38
Reeves, M. O., 169, 170
Regal, 250
Reliance, 288
Renault, 113, 209, 295
Reo, 17, 66, 103, 181, 190, 202, 203, 204, 264, 273
Resta, Dario, 210
Review of Reviews, quoted, 64
Richards, William C., 47
Ricker, A. L., 61, 62, 210
Riker Electric, 61, 91, 210
Riverside Machine Shop, 41
Rockne, 273, 274
Rogers, 56, 58, 59
Rogers, 113
Ross, 95, 97
Roosevelt, 105, 272
Royal, 17, 209
Royal Automobile Club of Great Britain, 216
Royal Automobile Club of London, 192
Ruxton, 272
Ryan, Thomas Fortune, 31, 32

Saginaw, 163
Sampson Tractor Company, 255
Sandusky, 121, 274
Saxon, 105, 260
Schwinn, Ignaz, 164, 165
Scientific American, quoted, 62, 65, 78-82, 122, quoted, 139-143
Scripps-Booth, 255
Searchmont, 121
Sears Motor Carriage, 113
Seiberling, Frank A., 214, 219, 221

INDEX

Selden, George Baldwin, 24-34, 45, 120, 122, 125-133, 169
Serpolet, M., 51
Sextoauto, 169
Sheridan, 255
Sizaire-Naudin, 206
Skene, 95
Smith, 209
Smith, S. L., 68
Smith, Urian, 166
Society of Automotive Engineers, 133
Spaulding and Company, A. G., 73, 74
Skinner, Kenneth A., 63, 64
Southern California Timing Association, 274, 276
Standard, 163
Standard Oil Company, 19
Standard Steel Car Company, 163
Standard Wheel Company, 178
Stanley, F. O., and F. E., 86, 88-98
Stanley Motor Carriage Company, 97, 99
Stanley Steamer, 17, 49, 87-99, 200, 260
Stanley Steamer Company, 17, 93
Star Safety Crank, 172
Stearns, 95, 121
Stearns, F. B., 102
Stearns Company, F. B., 102, 121
Stearns-Knight, 102
Stephens, 163
Stevens Arms and Tool Company, 39, 121
Stevens-Duryea, 17, 39, 49, 62, 103, 121
Stoddard-Dayton, 114, 264
Studebaker, 49, 121, 158, 181, 183, 185, 186, 205, 238, 265, 273, 282
Studebaker Automobile Company, 121, 273, 274
Studebaker Brothers Manufacturing Company, 186
Studebaker-Garford, 186
Sturges, 56, 57, 58, 59
Stutz, 16, 105, 201, 202, 273
Sunset, quoted, 247, 248
Sward, Keith, 47

Thomas-Detroit, 181, 182
Thomas Flyer, 15, 49, 113, 121, 182, 195, 206, 207, 208
Toledo, 33, 95
Tractobile, 95

Tribune, 163
Tucker, Preston, 283

United Motors Company, 195
U. S. Long Distance Automobile Company, 121
United States Motor Company, 264

Valley Boat and Engine Company, 163
Vanderbilt Cup Races, 209, 210
Vanderbilt, W. K., Jr., 62, 63, 209, 213
Velie, 114
Veteran Motor Car Club, 291

Walker, John B., 93, 94
Wall Street Journal, quoted, 233
Waltham, 95
Waltham Manufacturing Company, 121
Wanamaker, John, 113, 124
Waverly, 76, 105, 238
Welch, 196
Westcott, 260
Western Electrician, quoted, 237-238
Western Tool Works, 163
White, Arthur W., 58, 59, 265
White Steamer, 49, 62, 95, 168, 203
White, Walter C., 203
Whitney, 91, 92
Whitney, William C., 31, 32
Widener, P. A. B., 31, 32
Wills, C. H., 227, 234
Willys, John North, 177-181, 213, 221, 290
Willys-Jeep, 282, 293
Willys-Knight, 181, 273
Willys-Overland, 180, 197, 263, 264, 265, 273
Willys-St. Claire, 260
Winton, 17, 18, 40, 42, 48, 49, 62, 76, 104, 121, 177, 200, 201, 260, 297
Winton, Alexander, 34, 42, 43, 44, 45, 67, 79, 81, 82, 110, 111, 120, 126
Winton Motor Carriage Company, 32, 42, 81, 121, 123
Woods Motor Vehicle Company, 238

Xydias, Alex, 277

Zeder, Skelton, Breer Engineering Company, 265, 266
Zust, 206, 207, 208